The Science of Volleyball Practice Development and Drill Design

From Principles to Application

EDWARD SPOONER

iUniverse, Inc.
Bloomington

The Science of Volleyball Practice Development and Drill Design
From Principles to Application

iUniverse books may be ordered through booksellers or by contacting:

iUniverse
1663 Liberty Drive
Bloomington, IN 47403
www.iuniverse.com
1-800-Authors (1-800-288-4677)

ISBN: 978-1-4697-9159-3 (sc)
ISBN: 978-1-4697-9158-6 (e)

Library of Congress Control Number: 2012935071

Printed in the United States of America

iUniverse rev. date: 5/18/2012

Contents

PART 2:   THEORIES AND PRINCIPLES OF DRILL DESIGN   79

Preface: A Word from the Author

Comments are often made by coaches during practice and game situations, about the technical and tactical errors that occur and create ineffective skill execution and unsuccessful performance. When this occurs, the first question a coach has to ask themselves is was the error due to a physical inability to execute the skill effectively, secondly, was failure to execute the skill properly a result of a psychological lapse in concentration/attention focus and third, was the ability to execute accurately due to the coaches failure to provide and teach the skills and tactics needed to reduce errors in performance. As coach decided what to include in this book, he asked himself several questions: first, what would he want to know when faced with these problems and secondly what would the reader want to know in searching for answers that might solve failure in execution. The answered to both of these questions is that coaches and players who read this book should find information that either reinforces what they already know and do or will present answers that increases their knowledge on how to train-teach skill more efficiently. If the decision is made that they need to improve their knowledge and teaching ability, then this book will provide them with relevant new information that should help solve most performance problems. They will also find that the research and theories proposed in this book are based on scientific research that makes sense.

Coach believes that coaches/players who read this book want to learn something new in a simple and intellectual format without having to struggle to understand and remember difficult research theories. To achieve this, he has tried to make the book interesting, challenging and thought provoking. The information presented is targeted nor only for the new, inexperienced coach/player but may also provide experienced coaches with some new ideas and approaches to the way they coach and teach volleyball skills. Coach has written a stimulating and challenging book that provides both the basic and highly intellectual aspects of motor learning, biomechanics and a few of the psychological factors that affect athletic performance. The research and data represented in this work includes research theories from some of the most respected experts in their field of study. It is hoped that the book will inspire coaches to become better in the best job in the world—Coaching and Teaching young people to perform better and perhaps become a coach or teacher themselves one day.

In addition to the science of practice organization and motor learning a section regarding drill development (containing100 drills), is also included in this project. The information provided here is based on sound philosophies developed and time tested by many coaches and motor learning experts while being educationally sound and based on fundamental correctness. As a head and assistant coach at the club, high school, community college and Division I university levels, Coach has used this practice organization and drills to help develop successful programs that are sound both technically and tactically as well as being in agreement with the principles of sports psychology, anatomy, physiology and motor learning. Although the practice organization and drill format is for the most part his own concoction, a large portion of the ideas and drills have been adapted from the many camps, conferences, clinics, seminars, video tapes and books he has read during more than 60 years of playing and coaching.

The purpose of this thesis is to present information on efficient practice and drill organization that will fit every level of play. The objective of the drill section is to provide coaches with a wide variety of drills that can be adapted and modified to fit any skill level and an organizational process in which to display them. Coach urges you to take these drills and practice design and use your own creativity and imagination in adapting them to suit your needs and abilities as well as the performance level of your program. With the information provided here, as a foundation, you will be able to impart the proper technical-tactical training and the number of correct repetitions for skill mastery and success. This research has not been designed to teach the technique and tactics of the game but to provide coaches with a practice organization and drill format that is based on the principles of motor learning and sports psychology, which will enable them to successfully teach volleyball skills and tactics.

PART 1:
PRACTICE DESIGN
AND DEVELOPMENT

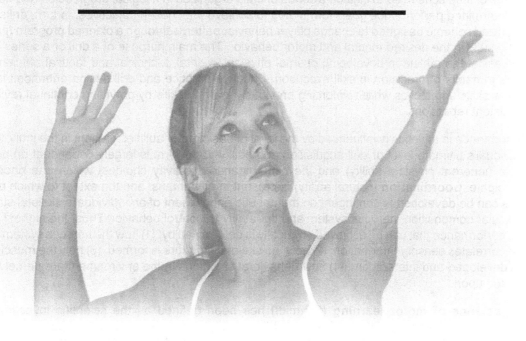

CHAPTER 1

How Players Learn and Acquire Motor Skills

"The average player moves until the breath in him is gone
But the champion has a will of iron that makes him carry on."

MOTOR LEARNING AND PERFORMANCE

Volleyball like tennis and a few other sports is a non-contact sport. Although size and strength are important, physical skill, fitness, mental strength, execution and training plays a big role in performance success. Unlike some sports, each volleyball player must be efficient in executing all the required skills of the game if team success is to occur. Being a game of many complexities both individually and as a team, volleyball is a difficult game to master. Although success is measured in wins and losses, success in volleyball should also include the ability to progress in the execution of the many diverse skills, phases and mental requirements of the game. Performance improvement and perfection is achieved by preparing each player for any situation that can occur during competition. This is best achieved through efficient practice organization, controlled drill procedures and routines that structure on the-court player movements while duplicating expected game behavior. Practice is a block of time scheduled to include a series of drills organized in a logical progression and based on predetermined performance goals formulated to achieve the chosen objectives. In turn, drills are an organized scheme designed to change player behavior patterns through a planned program (practice) that results in the desired mental and motor behavior. The main purpose of a drill or a series of drills is to assist the athlete in developing optimal physical, mental, technical and tactical efficiency that leads to habits of precision in skill execution. Effective practice and drill design enhances learning of new skills and tactics while reinforcing previously learned skills by providing continual review and consistent repetitions.

Performance in athletics is influenced by the level of basic motor abilities present in the individual. An individual's ultimate level of skill acquisition and ability to perform is largely dependent on personal talent (inherent physical ability) and the circumstances (activity choices) which one chooses to participate. **Coordination** (natural ability) is present in all humans, and the extent to which physical skills can be developed is contingent on the genetic endowment of an individual's skeletal structure, muscular composition, nervous system and the ability to control behavior. Thus, the highest level of skill performance that can be achieved physically is determined by: (1) how the nervous system senses and correlates sensory information; (2) how the skeletal structure is formed, (3) how the muscle fibers are developed and interact, and (4) how behavioral situations in the environment are perceived and reacted upon.

The **science of motor learning (Schmidt)** has been defined as the scientific investigation of performance associated with motor acts and the acquisition of motor skills, i.e., the study of finding the best ways for people to learn and perform physical skills. Motor learning is an invisible process or procedure through which an activity originates and behavior is changed irrespective of maturation, instinct or outside stimulants. Simply put, skill acquisition and performance are achieved through underlying biological and mechanical factors that result in observable changes in behavior thereby enabling muscles to move efficiently through a specific range of motion. Learned motor skills are a consequence of experience, education and training that interacts with the biological processes to achieve skill execution. In volleyball, as in all sports, learning motor skills consists of an interrelation of the internal neuromuscular process inherent in human motor responses **(motor control)** and the ability to efficiently reproduce motor movements **(skill execution).** To be most effective when instilling new skills or to change existing skills, motor learning requires a kinesthetic or muscle awareness, i.e., a sense of what the body is doing in relation to itself and in reaction to time and space. In additional to kinesthetic consideration, attention must also be given to the variables in learning: personality, cognitive ability, biological ability, and motivation, etc.

Motor programs are developed as a result of motor learning that occurs through the instruction and experiences that take place during training. Linking a nonexistent skill with an already existing skill, or several separate skills into additional combinations, results in a new motor program that can be stored in long term memory to be recalled for future use. Motor program development is the consequence of a complex interaction between physical, psychological and communication skills. In order for learning to transfer to physio-motor development, an intellectual comprehension, awareness and knowledge of incorrect and correct skill execution must take place.

Skill execution becomes more coordinated as the individual develops a kinesthetic sensitivity or feeling of how the body action relates to the skills to be performed. Passers, for example, develop a sense of feel about how the arms must be placed on ball contact to direct it to the target area. This results in less reliance on verbal and visual cues and a greater emphasis on muscle sense to control body movement. Repetition, concentration, and cueing also play an important role at this stage of development. However, motor learning and technical development will only take place when proper execution can be maintained over time. Thus, the old adage "perfect practice makes for perfect performance" must be changed to "practice makes perfect only if practice is perfected over time."

What is being considered here is the acquisition of motor skills through the development of motor programs which provide a player with the capability to respond accurately and efficiently to situations that arise in the environment. Skills seem to be acquired through a series of biological processes based on practice and experiences that leads to relatively permanent and lasting changes in behavior. Retention and retrieval of existing motor programs play a crucial role in effective skill execution. In order for motor learning to occur and skill to be retained, it is necessary for an athlete to understand the goal or objectives to be achieved (knowledge of performance) and the outcome of the required movement (knowledge of results). When this is accomplished a plan of action can be developed that will lead to accurate execution. If feedback is based on the actual way the movement skill was executed (knowledge of performance), skill execution will become increasingly effective and gradually change in response to repeated attempts and subsequent evaluation and modifications."

MOTOR ACT. — A motor act is the resulting action of perception, selective attention, interpretation and the decision making required to successfully execute a motor skill. The ability to receive serve can be used to briefly outline how information processing works when executing a motor skill (motor act). A player who is positioned to receive serve perceives (reads) the movement-body action of the server in anticipation of the type, direction and force of the serve. Once the ball is served, the receiver perceives the location of the serves and assumes a ready position in anticipation of receiving serve. The body receptors sense information as a result of serve execution, i.e., the speed, location and trajectory of the ball, while pre-conditioning the body and its extremities for assuming the passing position and initiating the passing action (motor program).

A proper body position takes place in relation to the passers court position with regard to the location, speed and movement of the ball. The eyes follow the service toss, ball contact, the ball's trajectory and projected flight path. The ears listen to ball contact and information communicated by teammates. The inner ear registers balance as the receiver position his/her body and limbs in a position to pass the ball. On contact with the ball, sensory organs relay information on muscle tension and joint positioning in readiness for execution. Information conveyed by body sensors is stored momentarily in **Short Term Sensory Storage (STSS)** before being replaced by new data. **Short Term Memory (STM)** selects information from **STSS** and quickly interprets and compares this data with information retrieved from **Long Term Memory (LTM).** This combining of data received enables the player to select the correct motor response (decision) and triggers a motor program. Simply put, based on the sensory information selected and placed in STM, a motor program is selected from LTM to be used in initiating and completing the passing action (Schmidt-Young).

The motor program selected from LTM is determined by past observations, experiences, and the knowledge accumulated during practice and past performance. Based on this motor program, a standard of correctness is determined and a plan-of-action chosen allowing the player to assume the proper court and body position. A pass is then executed and the ball directed to the target area. The accuracy of the pass (standard of correctness) is based on the ability to efficiently select environmental stimuli, interpret this data and make the correct decisions in response to that data. A new motor program is assembled or an existing program reaffirmed and returned to LTM after execution. Continued practice will reinforce this new motor program in LTM.

Sports science (Schmidt) indicates that what is learned in practice is actually a motor program or an image of motor control. Motor programs are responsible for sequencing or patterning movement to execute the desired skill. The parameters that affect the performance of a motor program are speed (time), space and muscle selection. Motor programs appear to be structured in advance and are not reflective, i.e., once an attacker starts his arm swing to ball contact, very little can be done to stop or alter the arm swing. In other words, the nervous system has very little influence in controlling muscle contraction or extension once it has begun.

When a beginner executes a simple skill, such as the serve in volleyball, several motor programs are necessary. He or she has a separate motor program for the toss; arm swing and ball contact, and follow through. Scientists refer to these as closed skills in which movement is structured in advance. However, in order for this skill to be executed effectively, in game situations, these simple motor programs must be combined into a single less complicated generalized motor program that is executed automatically without unconscious thought. This generalized process becomes increasingly important when executing open skills. Open skill execution requires the development of generalized motor programs that simplifies performance. In other words, a generalized ability is necessary to execute effectively in an open skilled environment that is never the same and ever changing.

In order for practice to be effective at the highest level coaches and players must understand and form concepts about how players learn and acquire motor skills. The following segment is a brief description of how motor skills are learned and retained. In developing motor performance skills, there are several performance standards that should be considered. These performance procedures must focus on decision making, the sensory aspects required in performance, how movement is formed, and the accuracy of movement. When teaching these principles individual differences must always be given considertion.

FACTORS THAT AFFECT LEARNING PERFORMANCE

Although genetic factors play a major role in athletic ability, many factors intertwine to affect performance success. There are several cognitive and physical processes that we can use in training that will enhance performance effectiveness. Knowledge, perception, selective attention, attention focus, memory, experience and decision making skills are informational and behavioral processing abilities that when maximized will improve motor learning and skill execution.

GENETICS. An individual's inherent physical skill (genetic disposition) is influenced by several underlying structural motor abilities whose excellence is genetically determined. The inherent/genetic motor abilities that have a major affect on performance are: (1) general coordination strength potential muscle type, (2) reaction time and speed capability, and (3) visual and auditory capacity. Recent research (Braden-Niednagel) indicates that there may be a fourth genetic factor, brain type, which may also significantly influence athletic ability. These genetic abilities are the encompassing factors in the ultimate level of motor ability and performance that can be achieved; they can be changed little by practice.

However, within the boundaries of an individual's inherent traits and characteristics, a motor performance act can be strengthened by improving motor skills through learned responses that perfect inherent physical ability. Ability to perform can also be enhanced by increasing physical proficiency through improved strength, flexibility and endurance. In other words, performance can be somewhat refined within given genetic capacities by improved muscular strength and endurance, without motor learning taking place. Although practice can produce improvement, the ability to execute at the highest level is a combination of genetics, fitness, activity choices, behavior and personality. The lack of innate ability to perform certain movements with control may explain why some athletes, who seem to have the required physical characteristics, never achieve high standards of performance. More importantly, perhaps they made the wrong activity choice. Because of a wrong activity choice many gifted athletes go unrecognized or fail to achieve to their potential.

THE COGNITIVE PROCESS. — Besides genetic physical characteristics, an athlete inherits an innate athletic IQ, i.e., (Schmidt-Braden) the ability to maximize and coordinate the mental process of performance with the physical process of skill execution will greatly affect performance outcome. In the execution of motor skills and performance in sports, there is a nonphysical or cognitive dimension consisting of perception, imagination, thought planning and decision making etc. This mental aspect of skill execution appears to be unidentifiable and observable only in its effects on performance. Hall of Fame basketball player Larry Bird is an example of an athlete who possesses an extremely high athletic IQ and uses it to maximize performance. Three time Olympic gold medalist Karch Kiraly, on the other hand, posses both tremendous inherent genetic physical abilities and an exceptional innate athletic IQ.

By understanding the role played by the mind, the non-physical dimension in athletic performance, an athlete can use his/her built-in learning system, acquired values and the knowledge obtained through previous experiences, to gain control over performance, that is, to optimize genetic ability. The significance of this psychological process becomes increasingly important when one considers the influence of tactical demands on performance success in sports. Tactics require an understanding of how to use a wide range of technical skills that function in conjunction with teammates, the opponent and the ball, while reacting strategically to all the possible situations confronted in competition. Highly specialized movement cannot occur without benefit of thought at the highest level. The more complex a movement task becomes the more complicated the cognitive process.

Cognitive learning and skill development is based on the understanding of three components: (1) the basic movement requirements, (2) goal establishment and (3) knowledge of the rules of execution. In the early stages of learning, information is processed slowly and execution is usually characterized by performance inconsistency that leads to gross errors in movement. Execution can be further hindered by the lack of consistent augmented feedback (e.g. what the instructor tells the player about skill execution) and is a crucial factor in skill learning. The following description is an attempt to simplify very complex research and make it understandable.

Research in motor learning indicates that as complicated motor programs (mental images) are combined into generalized motor programs a simpler motor program is to recreate. This simplicity can only occur when skills are perfected and practices so that little or no conscious thought process is required. Motor programs once generalized lead to generalized abilities that can operate regardless of the environmental circumstances. Automatic actions are especially important in executing advanced, highly sophisticated skills. Problems in the cognitive process occur when a different set of conditions are instituted under which a task is to be performed. Governed by these varying conditions, players for a short while are forced to consciously attend to the modified requirements of a task until a new cognitive map or image is formed and logged into long term memory. This can best be illustrated by the implementation of a combination, play action attack. Players moving in many different directions and loudly communicating many different verbal signals require conscious mental activity by the opponent thereby reducing the reaction time required by the defense to react.

KNOWLEDGE. — The physical ability to perform volleyball skills is indirectly related to the information and knowledge that are possessed by an athlete. In other words, doing what is known how to do it is the key successful skill execution. Although knowledge will not improve physical skill and performance beyond the inherent physical capability to perform (genetic limitations), it may allow for perfection of the inherent available natural abilities. Furthermore, increases in knowledge will reduce learning time and eventually produce a better performance. This is especially true with the elite or high-ability athlete.

Knowledge and learning can be improved through imitation, demonstrations, books, videos, and films. When a basic knowledge about the mechanical and physical aspects of the desired motor performance is made available (explanation and demonstration) to the athlete before execution, motor learning and skill improvement occur with increased efficiency and speed. Likewise, discussions, formal instruction and critical observation will accelerate the cognitive motor-learning process, reduce trial and error learning, and help to ensure correctness in execution. Increases in player knowledge should be in the area of learning skills and movement concepts associated with how the body should and can move.

This increased knowledge will assist in forming cognitive maps or motor programs by providing players with, an opportunity to develop motor skill through experimentation, explanation, guided discovery and problem solving. Skills are best taught through feedback that reinforces correct movement concepts. This consists of concepts regarding how the body should move, knowledge concepts of where and when the body should move, fitness concepts, and an idea of how the body functions during and after movement. For example, prior to executing the serve, performance would be improved if the server integrates information about the present situation with past experiences. In addition to previous game situations, instructions from the coach should include, who are the weak passers, the location of the serve and which serve he/she can execute most effectively. Knowledge provides the background for developing creative imagination and critical thinking skills. Inventiveness and originality are also critical thinking processes that require intellect to skillfully conceptualize, analyze and synthesize information. The knowledge generated by observation, experience, and reasoning can be used to guide communication and action so that motor learning and performance are maximized.

EXPERIENCE. — In addition to more information, athletes need better experiences. Previous positive and correct experiences provide the foundation for efficient and effective motor learning and performance. Research (Young-Kluka) indicates that the quality of past experiences (the knowledge accumulated in previous situations) helps to determine the amount of information that a player can process in a certain situation. Likewise, how an athlete feels about an activity and his/her performance is, in part, based on the kinds of experiences to which he/she has been exposed. Experiences provides the background for intuitive (unconscious) decisions that affects how a skill is acquired and determines the time interval essential for skill acquisition and motor learning to occur. The ability to instantly compare present experiences in (STM) with existing motor programs in (LTM) facilitates the learning process. This process enables a performer to quickly identify and correctly interpret the most relevant cues, while recognizing certain cues as irrelevant to successful performance (selective attention). Players often use feedback from past experience to teach themselves new skill acquisition and to improve performance (trial and error learning). Thus, better experiences will provide more useful information resulting in improved performance.

MEMORY. — Development of motor programs through motor learning requires that a mental image or map of the skill be embedded in the nervous system so that it can be recalled upon demand. Motor learning is the activity of storing relevant information about skill execution in memory so that it can be recalled immediately. In skill execution, memory can be considered the place where players store information about performance, i.e., what is perceived (perception), what decisions are made (interpretation) and what needs to be done (effecting). Information is retained in the mental process (long term memory) by practice, constant repetition and over-learning. However, before a skill can be transferred to long term (LTM) it must first become a part of short term (STM). In short, knowing the basic concepts and characteristics of short term memory will help the coach and player to quickly facilitate transmission of data from STM to LTM.

Information in STM consists of the sensory, perceptual and attention factors that a player is actually aware of at any given moment. Selective attention is the process that determines the relevant information that will be selected for storage in STM. When an athlete is subject to new sensory information and experiences, this information is extremely unstable in memory and can be forgotten very quickly unless acted upon. The maximum time limit (duration) for processing information into STM is thought to be as little as one second. In addition, the storage capacity of STM is limited to about six or eight (check your phone number) items which can be maintained efficiently in STM for approximately 20 to 30 seconds before information begins to deteriorate and is eventually lost. As a result, information in STM will probably be forgotten within 60 seconds of the presentation of this new material if not transferred into LTM or reinforced in STM.

Memory research (Schmidt-Sievens) indicates clearly that learners retain individual bits of data, facts and principles more completely when they are integrated into a coherent whole. Similarly, forgetting is reduced and long term retention more effective when skill acquisition consists of well-learned continuous motor tasks. The loss of data, however, can be reduced and motor learning improved by making the time between the presentation of instruction (demonstration) and the executions of a new skill practice as short as possible. Memory is also aided by reducing the number of points to remember, by grouping information that is closely related and by presenting a descriptive or mental picture of the information to be remembered prior to execution. Conversely, interference by other activities can also cause a loss of information in STM (forgetting). Therefore, when introducing a new skill, the coach should be sure that only the skill to be learned is practiced until it can be repeated successfully on succeeding trials before proceeding to another activity.

In addition, instruction on how to perform a skill is easier to remember if short descriptive phrases are used to explain skill execution rather than a lengthy dialogue. For instance, when teaching the serve, precise cue or key words such as step, toss, hit might be easier for beginners or unskilled players to remember than an elaborate explanation of how the skill should be executed.

The working memory (STM) provides the center for processing information to be transferred into long term memory. New motor programs are formed when the sensory information in STM is combined with relevant existing experience and transferred for storage in LTM. Consequently, new generalized motor programs are formed when information in STM is merged with existing motor programs in LTM. In addition to acting as a momentary storage space for new information, STM functions is a storage place for information retrieved from LTM when it is required for executing previously learned skills. For example, an attacker, by studying the defensive system of the opponent, puts information into short term memory that can be combined with previously learned information retrieved from LTM. Storage of this data in STM allows the player to choose the best type of attack in the least amount of time. That is, STM allows the information needed for effective skill execution to be retrieved quickly.

Once learned, motor skills are placed in LTM, which acts as a storage facility for relevant past experience, and a repository for motor new and existing motor programs. It is generally believed that the capacity of LTM is unlimited and information thought to have been forgotten is there, but for some reason there is difficulty in retrieval. If this concept is accurate, the problem of retrieving information is not retention but the ability to recall information upon demand. It has been generally concluded, that motor programs in LTM are available for recall for an indefinite period if they are practiced often enough to reinforce the original learning. More specifically, existing motor programs can be reinforced and retained in LTM if these previously learned skills are retrieved periodically for continual review and regular practice. For example, when teaching defensive movement, repeated practice of run-throughs can be used as a process for reinforcing and retaining run-through skills in LTM and as a lead-up activity in training parallel movement and pursuit skills.

INFORMATION PROCESSING IN MOTOR LEARNING AND PERFORMANCE

Understanding human performance requires knowledge of the types of sensory information that is detected and sent for processing and how quickly it can be processed to determine movement. In volleyball, as in other sports, efficient motor learning and skill performance are significantly influenced by the ability to process information efficiently and accurately. If a performer has little relevant experiences, restricted perceptual ability, limited knowledge and inefficient decision-making capability then information processing will be severely limited. Likewise, motor skill learning and performance improvement would be restricted, take longer or may not occur at all.

Motor learning, i.e. skill acquisition and execution, requires a complex mental process involving a series of perceptual, interpretive and evaluative procedures. These mental procedures require the reception of information from the environment and the selection of a plan-of-action; e.g., a server compiles sensory information about the receiving team (open area of the court-weak passers) and serves according to a plan-of-action drawn from this information. In other words, efficient perception (selection of sensory data) of a situation demands that we identify certain contingencies in the environment as important and instantaneously select a plan-of-action, such as, the decision not to play a ball hit close to the line, but out of bounds.

The important functions of information processing include: perception, selective attention, attention focus, interpretation, decision making, and effecting. Perception is the in-taking of information from the environment through the senses (visual, auditory, sensual). In particular, perception is the process of selecting and simplifying sensory data from the environment (awareness). Through selective attention, i.e. a blocker reads the direction, type and speed of a set in preparation for movement to the location of the attacker and point of attack. Decision making consists of identifying and interpreting certain contingencies in the environment and selecting an appropriate play action. For example, a blocker having selected the appropriate data decides the direction of the set and recalls a motor program from LTM based on that decision. Finally, effecting takes place as decisions are made in relation to perception, i.e., a blocker reads the set and attacker and interprets sensory information that allows movement to be initiated. Effecting is the outcome of what is perceived and the decisions made regarding the information received. It is this information that enables the athlete to react to the point of attack and execute an effective block. The motor program organized in this mental process lead to the activation of the correct muscles, in the proper sequence and with precise timing.

When learning and executing motor skills, players rely on the efficient operation of the central nervous system and the effective coordination of the decision making processes as information is received by the senses verbally, visually and kinesthetically. Remember that individuals have different information processing capabilities, that is, some are verbally-orientated while others process information better visually or kinesthetically. Although isolated here to expedite understanding, the factors involved in information processing are interrelated and do not stand alone in affecting motor learning and performance. Likewise, remember information processing of a skill/s varies to a great extent among individuals.

PERCEPTION. — Perception is the initial factor in affective skill execution. Perception in volleyball is the awareness, processing and reaction to the sensory information present in the environment. This includes sensory receptors in the body, position on the court, reactions of the opponent as well as the speed, location, and trajectory of the ball. Three separate functions occur in the process of perception 1. Data is received by various sensory organs including vision, audition and the body's proprioceptors 2.

Selection of the appropriate information is needed to initiate the desired body movements while ignoring irrelevant information, and 3. Information selected from the environment must be passed on to long term memory where it is compared to previous experiences in order to make distinctions between similar stimuli such as speed and space.

Successful athletic performance consists of a series of perceptual motor skills involving complex mental processes that culminate in a motor response. Perception is an unconscious awareness of the number, duration and intensity of conflicting stimuli present in a given performance environment. Generally, situations that take place on the volleyball court are as they are and cannot be changed. Only our perception, i.e., our mental comprehension of these situations, gained by means of our senses, our awareness and our understanding can be changed. Perceptual motor skills when developed provide the underlying sensory input for interpretation and decision making that precedes skill acquisition, execution and performance.

Perceptual proficiency requires effective stimulus-response compatibility in order to enhance attention selectivity. Stimulus-response compatibility is the degree to which a player perceives and identifies a particular event in a competitive environment as important, or related to, a specific plan-of-action. For example, before approaching the target zone, a setter must recognize and interpret the type of defense such as the position of block and floor defense (stimulus) and select the appropriate set and/or play action to be used (response) in relation to the strengths of the available attackers, the weakness in the defense being employed and the effectiveness of the pass. Perception in this condition requires a correct detection and selection of sensory data and a thorough recognition of the relevance of that data to the existing circumstances instantly.

Locating and recognizing important environmental cues can be enhanced by providing an athlete with a variety of volleyball related experiences and knowledge of game characteristics, concepts and phases. The ability to read (identify) the factors of speed, spin and direction that affect the flight of the ball requires a well defined spatial and temporal court awareness. The importance of perceptual efficiency in volleyball can be further explained by the following example. When preparing for an attack, a hitter must perceive the location, i.e. spatial awareness, and the speed, i.e. temporal awareness, of the pass in relation to the target zone and other players, in order to react accordingly. decisions are then made as to the most effective shot (plan-of-attack) based on the called play action. Once the ball is set and before the approach to attack has started, the height, speed and location of the set and the position of the defense must be re-identified. Upon starting the approach an attacker re-establishes (perceives) the position of the set (ball) in relation to the net, court, block and floor defense (spatial awareness).This perceptual ability is necessary in order to complete a plan-of-attack successfully, e.g. attacking the ball into the open court relative to the opponents court location and in relation to the speed and location of the incoming set. The problesm is that all this takes place in milli-seconds.

Coaches must design practice situations and skill execution based on these perceptual requirements. The major problem that a coach faces is that circumstances in the environment are perceived differently by each athlete due to differences in the way they processes information internally. Simply put each volleyball player perceives and processes sensory information received from the action taking place and the court. Therefore, a coach must take into account these differences when teaching technique and developing practice situations the result in the correct skill execution.

SELECTIVE ATTENTION. — In theory, our attention (or what we are actually aware of at any given moment) is based on the ability and readiness to receive and select information, for interpretation, from a variety of environmental sources (perception). Selective attention is a perceptual process of scanning sensory information for a particular stimulus and then searching memory for the appropriate response. To illustrate, during the performance of a skill, a multitude of sensory information is made available to the nervous system by body receptors. Because the ability to process information during performance is greatly limited in humans, irrelevant background information (environmental cues) must be repressed. Through the process of selective attention, focus can be directed to only those events which are most urgent and must be addressed first.

More specifically, selective attention provides an athlete with the mental process by which inappropriate information is ignored, so that immediate and relevant decisions can be made about important data such as the position played and the reactions demanded of a given competitive situation. Since only a limited amount of information can be processed effectively at any one time, complex situations must be simplified. It is extremely important when learning new skills, to reduce the number of environmental cues a player has to act upon and/or interpret. This is achieved by reducing the amount of information that must be processed. By presenting fewer events for selection during training, confusion is reduced and concentration improved, making motor learning, skill acquisition, and execution more efficient. Conversely, by offering a multitude of events that must be attended to by the offensive team can slow the selective attention process of the opponent thereby increasing the time needed by the defense to process attack information.

In order for learning to occur, a permanent change in performance (behavior) must take place that improves skill execution by reducing or eliminating distraction in the environment. The ability to use selective attention effectively depends on the quality of past experiences in conjunction with accessible knowledge. The ability to instantly identify (perceive) and process (interpret) information in terms of what is happening in a given volleyball setting reduces the reaction time needed between the appearance of an environmental situation and the initiation of the response movement. The ability to shorten reaction time is a direct result of the number of perceived alternatives that confront the athlete, the proficiency to isolate them and the competence to select the relevant cues. These factors, combined with talent and experience will enable a player to match the correct movement skill with the right cues thereby enhancing the ability to choose an appropriate course of action. Only through accurate selective attention, will performance at all levels be improved.

The importance of simplifying the environment through efficient selective attention can best be explained by referring to the unusual phenomena that occurs during high speed performance in sports. As the speed of play increases, players are instantly confronted with a multitude of sensory data that must be processed instantly. Although the inexperienced player receives the same data as experienced players, they lack the perceptual ability to accurately determine what is relevant. Since experienced players are able to perceive more information in a shorter period of time, action seems to slow down for them. For example, the jump serve, traveling in excess of 60 mph, is an excellent way to relate this occurrence to volleyball. When receiving a ball served at high speeds, the inexperienced player selects more irrelevant information and consequently; either reacts slower to the ball or makes the wrong decision. Thus, the inability to comprehend and quickly select the important sensory data available in the environment, i.e. speed, time and location, results in poor performance and ineffective execution.

Players can be taught to ignore non-relevant cues by directing attention only to relevant cues. Remember, that learners will direct attention to cues that are most meaningful or pertinent to him/her at the time. Players become more confident in an environment where meaningful cues enable them to reduce the amount of attention given to distractions occurring in the environment. Ample practice in focusing on relevant and meaningful cues will eliminate the effects of these distractions. Improvement in performance and learning can be achieved by instilling motivation as well as cues recognition, keeping points concerning how a skill should be executed to a minimum and by simplifying movement so that skills are performed efficiently in an uncomplicated environment. The problem that arises is that a serve travelling at 50-70 mile per hour reaches a passer in less than 3 seconds.

When a coach reminds a defensive player to read and anticipate the angle of attack, he/she is in a sense telling them to use their perceptive and selective skills to recognize the attack characteristics of the spiker. An efficient read, allows the defender to select the most relevant information, i.e., angle of approach, type of set, relationship of the set to the net and the body and arm position of the attacker in relation to the net and the block, at the moment of contact. Planning for selective attention reduces confusion by limiting the amount of information athletes have to think about. In conclusion, in order to attend to the most relevant environmental cues, the condition of execution should be simplified and reduced in number.

Greater concentration will occur when introducing a new skill to both a beginning or experienced player if only one or two items at a time are presented. In teaching an inexperienced player to hit the ball down the line he/she should, at first, only have to think about making contact with the ball. As a player progresses in the ability to execute the spike, the fundamentals of the approach, jump and arm movement that results in a down-the-line hit can be gradually introduced.

The Canadian Volleyball Association suggests that in planning for selective attention inexperienced players should execute skills in slow motion. Executing skill in this manner gives players more time to, select appropriate cues from the environment, receive adequate feedback and establish a better understanding of the requirements of performance. This study concluded that due to the large amount of information available in the environment, players with limited perceptual skill would be unable to attend to the multitude of accessible information. Therefore, instruction must be simplified to reduce sensory stimuli or slowed down so that more time is available for processing information. In summary, for selective attention to be most effective in skill acquisition and execution, a limitation must be placed on the number of environmental cues to attend to or a reduction of the speed at which the skill is performed. Slowing down the action will make more time available for processing available cues. However, for advanced players the most efficient learning takes place when skills are executed at game speed forcing the mind to effectively edit and interpret each situation quickly and accurately with little conscious awareness.

ATTENTION FOCUS. — The attention required to initiate skill execution may vary according to the skill or action being performed and the learning stage of the performer. When initiating instruction for beginning players, the demands of execution are often greater than their attention span ability. Therefore, when training a new skill the task to be performed it must be broken down into simplified parts so that the attention demand required is reduced. Similarly, when teaching a complex skill a coach must simplify the environment by breaking the skill to be learned into meaningful parts. The next step is to determine which part should be practiced first and then practice each part until execution becomes automatic. This training process reduces the attention demands required when executing open skills to the actual response required in playing a moving ball. Players can often execute the attack approach efficiently until a ball is introduced. This additional attention demand of the ball in conjunction with movement seems to make execution of the approach much more difficult thereby leading to errors in execution. Therefore, it may more effective to practice approach skill until perfected before proceeding to practicing the jump, arm swing skills and ball contact.

A player's ability to focus intently on selective sensory data and shift attention focus efficiently as needed between stimuli are characteristics of the elite and experienced athlete. During highly skilled performance that requires advanced motor development; many sensory inputs are confronted in selecting the appropriate motor program and establishing a plan of action. Consequently, a concentrated attention focus is needed to select relevant sensory responses and to execute a motor program effectively. More specifically, maintaining a focused attention requires an athlete to quickly survey the setting and narrow focus to the most important event. Narrowing and expanding attention focus allows a player to maximize relevant information derived from the situation. Thus, efficient attention focus improves performance by sustaining attention for the length of time required to develop a motor program or trigger a motor skill.

On the other hand, players who can shift attention focus quickly between sensory data, choose the relevant cues, and initiate the proper responses (skills) from the variety of motor programs available will maximize learning and performance. To illustrate, a defensive player must maintain concentration on the overall action-at-hand, while shifting attention focus from the pass to the set, and then the set to the attacker to determine the point of attack and contact point. For this reason, attention must be directed at quickly reading and interpreting the action taking place on the court while widening, narrowing, and shifting focus to the exact location of the ball. This interpretation takes place in relation to the court, the net and the other players. Accordingly, an athlete who is better able to maintain a focused and concentrated attention throughout practice and performance will learn faster and perform better, while committing fewer errors.

As we have seen, experience plays an important role in determining what environmental factors a volleyball player will or will not attend to, and how effectively he/she can anticipate and select the appropriate responses. An inexperienced player, confronted with large amounts of data to process and diagnose, will often attend to the wrong information or misinterpret what is actually happening. Moreover, due to the need to interpret large amounts of data in a short period of time, a player may either play poorly or fail to react. To further illustrate, when executing the attack, the objective is to pass the ball to the target area so that a multiple or play action attack can be initiated. A multiple attack provides a number of various stimuli for the defense to perceive and interpret. Several attackers moving simultaneously, in different directions, while shouting verbal commands, requires a tremendous amount of data to be processed and interpreted, e.g., player and ball movement, verbal cues, etc., in a severely limited amount of time available. This creates confusion by requiring cognitive thought, thereby causing hesitation on the part of an inexperienced defensive player.

THE DECISION-MAKING PROCESS. — The decision-making process is the final step in information processing. Decision making consists of stimulus identification through perception, a selection of the proper sensory information, an interpretation of the data received followed by the selection of a response program. This learning process requires a player to choose between important pieces of information, establish relationships between the information received and plan the execution of a motor program based on this information. Through the process of perception and selective attention, relevant information is received and instantly made available for interpretation and apt decision making. The decision-making process begins with the organization of information received and selected by the nervous system which then activates the proper muscles to achieve the desired movements.

Efficient decision-making requires an instant understanding (within milliseconds) of how the decisions made can be used to fulfill the skill objectives, the importance of these objectives to successful execution, and a realization of the possible alternative courses of action. However, temporal, event and spatial uncertainty lengthens the time needed to respond to factors that occur during performance. Thus,

the decision making process is responsible for determining the plan of action to be used in executing a skill and is a direct result of how each players perceives the environment. The decisions once made produces a motor program that translates information and organizes the limb, muscle and body movements required to execute a motor program selected from memory. If an error occurs when a novice player attempts to execute the motor program necessary for correct movement, it is most likely due to his/her failure to acquire and execute the correct set of environmental commands necessary for effective body movement.

Decisions, in volleyball, are based on data from a variety of environmental sources concerning the situations encountered during performance. The effects of the need for speed in decision-making can be illustrated by the action of the middle blocker in reacting to events taking place during a play action attack. Not only does the middle blocker have to read the velocity, location and type of attack, but he/she must automatically attend to a multitude of player movements, sounds, and other environmental cues in order to react instantly and correctly to the point of attack. Upon reaching the point of attack, the blocker, based on the information attended to, must then initiate the proper skill movement to complete the blocking action. If the correct motor program is selected and made available, successful execution will most likely occur.

Associative solutions accelerate the ability to initiate the proper action as the athlete quickly perceives and compares background information regarding the events taking place with previous experience. The ability to reach associative solution leads to independent productive thinking by analyzing a situation and transferring known solutions to new and similar problems as they arise. For example, players who are aware of the technical-tactical particularities of the opponent are better able to analyze situations quicker and accelerate the selection of responses that accurately fit the situation. To put it more precisely, experienced players, through the associative process, are able to quickly establish a mental connection between the perceived situation and the corresponding solution in order to reach tactical resolution at the appropriate moment.

Creative drill and practice situations that demand a player match his/her motor abilities with the correct decision-making process required during performance, will increase learning efficiency and performance. This can be achieved by increasing the quality of information received (perception) while decreasing the quantity of irrelevant information processed (selective attention). For example, a defensive player reads the environmental cues present in the action taking place on the court to select and process the appropriate data regarding the location of the pass, set and attacker in relation to the block. A plan-of-action is then chosen and a motor program selected in reaction to the player's perception of the situations as they occur. For instance, a motor act takes place by a defensive player, based on the perceived and selected information present allowing the defensive player to make a decision as to the appropriate motor program, moves to the point of contact and executes the correct defensive skill, i.e., digs the ball.

The actions and reactions (decisions) of a defensive player must be automatic, unconscious responses executed without thought, for efficient performance to occur reflectively in the decision-making function. To insure suitable decision making ability, practice must be a game-like process that requires the correct decision making procedures in choosing the appropriate motor program. An excellent illustration of the automatic responses required in the decision making process can be seen in the setter preparing, to execute a play action attack. He/she must automatically decide as to the type of set to be used in this situation based on the defensive alignment of the opponent, the offensive readiness of his/her teammates, and the game score.

The process of interpretation assists in the performance of the decision-making function but requires time. Reaction time is the time between the appearance of an event and the initiation of proper response. Well trained volleyball players usually require between two to three-tenth of a second to respond to stimuli present in a game/practice situation. Therefore, the player with the best response time has the best chance for success. Two factors, stress and anticipation play major roles in the ability to interpret and process information efficiently and quickly, by increasing or decreasing the time between the perceptions of a stimulus and executing a skill. Although stress will usually slow reaction time, anticipation will enable a player to react more quickly and will determine the results of execution. As a result, a defensive player who reads the location of the set and anticipates that a ball may be tipped over the block will reduce the reaction time needed to get to the point of contact.

Anticipation plays a major role in reaction, movement, and response time. Reaction time is time from when the flight of an incoming ball acts as a stimulus to movement until the time when a player initiates movement. Movement time is the time from when movement is initiated until the movement is completed Response time is the total time from the onset of stimulation to movement until action in completed. Several factor influence the speed at which an athlete is able to react: Auditory stimuli provide cues that alert an athlete to get ready for action. The fore period, is the time between receiving cues and the onset of a response. This period is in influenced by the intensity and number of stimuli available and the time between stimuli. In addition to these factors, concentration during the fore period, practice experiences, environmental conditions and the maturity of the athletes plays an important role in anticipation.

A novice player, who makes constant errors in execution, has not acquired the capacity to use the set of commands that control limb and body movements due to faulty perception and/or inadequate information processing and decision making. The execution process is determined by how information is perceived and the decisions made based those perceptions. Coordinated movement is achieved by selecting the correct motor program that makes the précised muscle contraction in conjunction with the correct sensory feedback. This is achieved by constant skill practice that moves the body and limbs in the desired sequence of movements. Decision-making is an area that requires involvement by the coach in order to develop a player capable of thinking about and solving performance problems. Realizing solutions to the tasks that occur in a system of play will require motor, perceptual and memory skills to achieve successful execution. By using different practice conditions such as controlled drills, situation drills and team play, events can be simulated that compel players to find the proper solutions to existing technical and tactical problems. Furthermore, decision-making ability can be improved by quizzing players as to their reason, either right or wrong, for making a particular decision.

Augmented feedback given correctly reinforces the appropriateness of these decisions and supplies alternate courses of action are also effective. Coaches must design practice situations and skill execution based on perceptual requirements present in the environment. The major problem that a coach faces in skill development is that circumstances in the environment are constantly changing and perceived differently by each athlete due to differences in the way they processes information internally. Simply put, each volleyball player does not perceive and process sensory information received from the action taking place on the court in the same way. Therefore, a coach must take into account these differences when teaching technique and developing practice situations that result in the correct skill execution.

Remember that science indicates that there is no such thing as muscle memory.

Chapter 2

The Stages in Motor Development

INTRODUCTION — Volleyball practice and drill design should be organized to comply with the following four stages of the motor learning process: introductory (verbal-cognitive), motor (perfection), autonomous (without conscious thought) and application (the ability to use motor programs in competitive situations). Research generally divides motor learning into three stages: verbal-cognitive, motor-perfection and autonomous/automatic. However, for the purpose of this project, I have included a competitive stage in which application (applying technique learned, perfected and automated into generalized motor programs) can be applied to tactical situations.

Experience indicates that the stages of motor learning are not distinct entities in themselves but overlap with the other stages. Thus, it figures that when developing specific volleyball skills, some athletes may still be in the cognitive stage while others have progressed to the perfection or autonomous phases. More specifically, a player may have developed perfection, automation and even tactical understanding of how to execute a particular skill while other skills are still in a lower stage of development. Training principles are somewhat different for each stage and depends on the experience, skill and the mental ability level of the players involved. The principles of motor learning indicate it is important for a player and coaches to realize that learning motor skills progress in stages that can be differentiated on the basis of the amount and nature of cognitive thought and the coordinated effort required in producing the desired results. Most recent research (Schmidt) purports that the earliest stage of motor learning is predominated by cognitive concerns about skill acquisition while learning in the later stages shifts focus more to training and perfecting automatic performance of generalized skills executed under the variable and random conditions found in competition.

In practice and drill improvement consideration must be given to the type of drills that will provide the most effective learning sequences. To be effective and efficient drill design must take into consideration the principles of motor learning, skill acquisition and readiness. Readiness plays an important role in determining at what stage a player should begin training and when to advance to the next level. Research (Spooner) indicates that readiness to perform can be estimated prior to skill execution by evaluating age, physical strength, experience and maturity. Studies (Young) in motor learning conclude that movement to a new stage of learning should not take place until skill acquisition is such that a player can perform the skills being learned with a reasonable degree of accuracy and control. The following data should help in developing a practice plan based on motor learning principles in relation to the stages of motor development. This information provides an attempt to simplify very complex research and make it understandable.

THE INTRODUCTORY/VERBAL-COGNITIVE STAGE OF SKILL LEARNING

The cognitive stage of learning and skill development is based on the understanding of 3 components: (1) the basic movement requirements, (2) goal establishment and (3) knowledge of the rules of execution. Learners in this stage processes information slowly and execution is usually characterized by performance inconsistency that leads to gross errors in movement. Execution is further hindered by the lack of consistent augmented feedback (e.g. what and how the instructor tells the player about skill execution) and is a crucial factor in skill learning.

When an athlete begins to acquire new skills, he/she is confronted with problems that are mostly cognitive in nature. That is, how is the basic skill executed? How do you win the game? When is the ball out of bounds? What is the best way to pass the ball, etc.? Performance at this stage is inconsistent, unstable and generally marked with a large number of gross motor errors. Although internal feedback tells the performer that something is wrong with performance, they are usually too inexperienced or knowledgeable to be aware of what to do on succeeding trials to achieve correct execution. Therefore, the objective of cognitive training is not to complicate matters by requiring a multiplicity of circumstances but to teach simple, effective motor skills.

The focus of the cognitive stage is concentrated on what the player should do, how to execute the skill efficiently and how performance success is achieved. To accomplish this, instruction should be simple, short verbal descriptions and execution based on cue words that produce visual pictures of the desired action. At this stage, lengthy verbal descriptions that do not conjure up visual images are very difficult to transfer into learned responses. When initiating new skills for a novice player or reviewing skill execution with an experienced player, instruction via demonstration, mirroring and modeling should be used to capitalize on the visual and observational learning capabilities of these players. As in all learning, motivation plays a key role in the cognitive stage. Therefore, learners must be given a good reason for extending the exhausting effort needed to learn motor skills. Modeling often provides this incentive. Short descriptions of the activity, with films, videotapes, pictures and demonstrations can be used to stimulate interest and the desire to learn.

Basic physical movement and conceptual skills are introduced and trained in the introductory phase of skill development. In this stage, physical training includes learning, improving, and consolidating basic volleyball-specific motor skills. Simple neuromuscular skills in which the muscles respond/ move in a reflexive manner through a specific range of motion are introduced. Research indicates that training during this introductory phase of motor learning is most effective when an athlete has a cognitive understanding of the objectives of performance and the movement patterns needed to achieve the assigned tasks. More specifically, each player should have a rudimentary comprehension of the order in which skills are to be executed in relation to the technical requirements imposed. In addition to comprehension, basic perceptual and selective responses must be developed that improve the ability to assess the trajectory, direction, timing and location of the incoming ball, i.e., basic spatial and temporal orientation. Concentration and verbal cueing also play an important role in this stage of motor development. Once cognitive ability is established in the introductory stage, technical training specific to volleyball can be instituted and perfected efficiently.

Learning seems to be most efficient in the verbal-cognitive stage of development when specific conditions are established that are constant, controlled and performed without tactical demands of competition. Identifying the type of skills to be trained and arranging them in a simple to complex order will assist in developing a cognitive understanding of each skill and improve practice planning. This process helps the novice in acquiring the ability to perform a rough approximation of the skill to be learned. In the introductory stage, simple discrete skills that involve a small number of joint movements and limb coordination should be the major points of emphasis. Training discrete skills in this phase can best be illustrated in learning the serve. Immature and inexperienced players often lack the strength and coordination to serve the ball overhand over the net from the base line. This lack of physical ability can lead to acquiring improper technique thereby hindering development. Moving these players closer to and/or lowering the net until proper technique in instilled and adequate strength and coordination established reduces learning time and the chance of learning poor serve techniques. However, if difficulty in coordinated execution continues, physical manipulation of a player through the desired range of motion, while verbally guiding the learner can be useful learning tool. The end result is the development of fundamental specialized motor programs that enable an athlete to combine correct body position and movement with proper-court-and-ball-location.

In an introductory drill, skill progression for teaching a sequence of attack skills begins with an introduction, explanation, demonstration and model of the skill to be learned. The introduction explains, to an athlete, what is to be learned and its importance to proper execution. An interesting introduction gets the players attention, creates interest and prepares him/her for the demonstration. Explanations are most effective if routines are maintained and players are organized in a position for optimal observation. Delivery should be with a firm, polite and fairly loud speaking voice that is conversational in tone. Explanations are most effective if they are enthusiastic, brief, simple and direct in presentation. Begin by telling them what you are going to tell them, and then tells them what you want them to know and conclude by telling them what you told them. The objective is to develop a cognitive comprehension (correct mental picture) of the skill to be executed.

To expedite the time between demonstration and skill execution it might be most efficient to explain and demonstrate how the drill to be used operates to lessen the loss of information in STM. Quickly following the model-demonstration the drill should be executed as closely representative of the model as physically possible. If problems occur in execution, the next step would be to divide the whole skill into separate segments. (e.g., the spike can be broken down into the approach, jump, arm swing, etc.)

If the part method is used, skill modeling is followed by teaching each attack skill separately. Three steps are needed to complete this phase of teaching attack skills. The first progression begins with an approach to the net from the 10 foot line. This allows players to practice approach and transition footwork in the direction of and off the net. The sequence would include proper foot movement and body position of the approach, the approach arm swing, followed by the pre jump and take off in relation to the court and net. The next sequence might be a wall hit drill. This progression provides an excellent opportunity to practice body and reverse shoulder and arm rotation into a hitting position, forward arm swing toward ball contact and concludes with a follow through after contact. The next sequence could be a self toss and hit from behind the 10 foot line to teach locating to the ball, jump, and ball contact timing. In addition to training location to the ball, this drill would combine the approach, arm swing, take-off, hitting motion, follow through and landing into a coordinated sequence of movement. Finally, the approach, jump, arm swing, follow-through and landing are combined and executed from a set at the net to complete the skill progression.

Each phase of skill execution continues until it can be executed with a reasonable degree of accuracy before progressing to the next skill. Once each segment of a skill has been learned through simple blocked repetitions and can be executed with reasonable efficiency, the segments are then re-linked together and practiced as a whole. Whole practice continues until a basic motor program is developed for the complete skill which can be executed with moderate competence (whole-part-whole learning). The end result is the acquisition of a new skill or the improvement of an already existing skill.

Training discrete skills in the introductory stage has a twofold objective: first, attention is focused on preplanning the desired activity to produce movement as a unit, and second, modification in technique from the intended execution is discouraged. Research (Braden) in tennis indicates that beginning players who thought about (planned) the movement response they wanted to make prior to execution were more likely to achieve successful skill execution. Since fatigue is not a problem in executing discrete skills, rest intervals can be minimized to increase the number of practice trials. However, in this stage, training a series of discrete skills (serial skill training) will require active rest intervals.

Regardless of whether the skill to be learned is open or closed, the goal of the introductory phase is to maximize the capability of making motor adjustments that approximate the skill being learned, i.e. to develop motor programs with basic movement patterns. The chance of success is greater if basic motor patterns are trained in a constant, uncomplicated environment where only one variant is performed. Blocked practice, i.e., repeating a skill in consecutive trials without interruption, appears to be a most effective means of training cognitive skills in the early stages of learning. On the other hand, practice, in which several elementary skills are arranged in small learning blocks, can also be productive if the sequences of trials are altered during practice.

The period for introducing new skills in the introductory stage, although very important, is often very short and based on the ability and experience of the players involved. Thus, if the skill level and ability to execute warrants, a coach can shorten or perhaps eliminate the time spent in the introductory phase thereby allowing more practice time in the advanced stages of motor learning. Notice, motor programs are not perfected or become automatic at this stage. Feedback after execution is an important characteristic of the verbal-cognitive stage of motor development. The goal of feedback is to correct large muscle errors in movement and should be about performance (knowledge of performance) rather than about outcome (knowledge of results). Thus, feedback/reinforcement is made prescriptive (as a guide to error correction) by indicating how to improve movement. Simple, encouragement and positive feedback that suggests only one change at a time provides the best results. In the introductory stage, feedback should be given at relatively high frequencies (after almost every trial).

However, faded feedback, the gradual reduction in the amount of feedback, should be instituted as skill level improves to reduce the possibility of a player developing dependency on and the need for constant feedback. Feedback should also be tailored to individual differences, proficiency level, and the rate of improvement of each performer. The ultimate goal of feedback at this level is to instill motivation and encourage players to begin developing the capability of self-evaluation in error correction. Motor learning experts (Schmidt-Young-Kluka) indicate that feedback is most efficient if the number of repetitions is limited to 1 feedback to about every 4 task attempts. Remember, the purpose in the introductory stage is for a player to be able to perform only a rudimentary but correct approximation of the skill being trained. Feedback and reinforcement will be discussed in great depth in Chapter 3.

The following outlines several of the most important components that affect learning motor skills in the Introductory/cognitive/verbal stage:

- The objective is to develop a cognitive comprehension (correct mental picture) of the skill being executed
- When introducing a new skill, explain what is to be learned and its importance to execution
- Basic movement that require establishing effective performance goals and a knowledge/ understandings of the basic rules of skill execution are key factors in learning fundamental cognitive motor programs
- Instruction should be in simple-short verbal descriptions or modeling that create visual descriptions
- Only a correct but rudimentary approximation of skill ability is require in cognitive learning
- Objective is to develop a basic understanding of spatial and temporal orientation
- Practice establishes conditions that are constant-controlled-preformed without tactical demands
- Practice consists mostly of blocked repetitions-part method-constant and progressive part practice
- Training consist of simple-closed-discrete skills
- The goal of feedback is to correct large muscle errors in movement (knowledge of performance)
- Skill correction should be based mainly on instantaneous-augmented-extrinsic-summary feedback
- Guidance techniques can be effective if players are having problems with skill execution
- Learning take place best when training is in a constant-uncomplicated environment

THE PERFECTION STAGE MOTOR

When a learner is able to structure general approximations of the skills initiated during the introductory/cognitive stage, he/she is ready for the motor stage of training (stage where motor programs are fully developed and performance becomes consistent). Since most of the basic fundamental mechanics of these skills has been learned in the cognitive stage, the objective is to establish long-term skill retention, increase the ability to recall motor programs and to develop execution perfection. In this stage of motor learning, the focus is on producing effective motor programs relative to environmental parameters, e.g. the capability of repeated, correct skill execution regardless of the situation. Once technical motor patterns become well-developed greater stress is placed on expanding the learning parameters, i.e., values such as speed/volume/spacing, etc. that affect movement. Practice at this stage consists of refining and fine tuning the desired skills until performance becomes smooth, fluid, highly coordinated and perfected.

The objective is to learn to execute these technical skills with precision and accuracy until perfected. Athletes must develop a relative mastery of basic volleyball motor programs, skills and movements introduced in the introductory stage, before perfection can be achieved. Therefore, In order for perfection to occur, an athlete must be able to repeat movements regularly and efficiently in the face of ever changing conditions found in game-like situations. A good example of a progressive drill series for perfecting attack skills might be to begin with a direct toss at the net for the attacker to hit. The next progression would be a toss to the setter who sets the attacker. As ability progresses, the toss could be made over the net to a receiver, who passes to the setter, who then sets the attacker. Eventually, a varied and random serve or toss could be executed to a formation of players, of which anyone of several players could initiate the pass, followed by a set and the attack.

Improvement in reaction speed, movement speed, body precision and motor accuracy characterizes this stage of development. Speed of perceptual response to ball movement is emphasized to quickly assess the trajectory, direction and location of the incoming ball. Although speed must often be sacrificed for accuracy when learning a new skill, it can gradually be increased as the athlete achieves a reasonable degree of movement (motor) skill, physical conditioning and success. As previously mentioned, there appears to be some disagreement among experts as to the speed at which skills should be executed when training inexperienced player movement. Recent research indicates that best results might be obtained with advanced players by practicing skill repetition at close to game speed.

However, executing at game speed may be difficult in the early stage of motor learning and lead to constant errors in execution. Most often body movements can be executed with a relatively high degree of accuracy, if ball speed is reduced to a point that a player can execute correctly and efficiently. Developing the ability to anticipate situations happening in the environment will increase reaction time thereby giving the athlete more time to respond. **The motor stage (perfection)** expands individual skills through constant correct repetition until each execution is stable and performance can be executed with a reasonable degree of accuracy and efficiency. Having said this, the optimal level of perfection is dependent on genetic ability, motivation and athletic experiences. Practice conditions in the motor stage are organized according to the types of skill, open/closed, discrete/serial and the level of a player's motor ability. Closed skills are practiced with a structure as close to game conditions as possible.

Opens skills are also executed under game-like conditions, but must be systematically varied with random movements to fit the changing condition that occur during competition. Thus, performing open skills in this stage requires the ability to adapt execution to the constantly changing conditions in the environment. Success in performing closed and open skills learned in the introductory/cognitive stage demands that skill be refined and perfected so that they can be reproduced instantaneously on demand. The goal is movement patterns that are correct, consistent and efficient from response to response. When execution becomes consistent and perfection attained, practice must be geared to both generalizing and automating motor programs.

In volleyball, random and variable changes in the order of task execution provide the best learning situations for training several skills intermittently or in sequence. In addition, this procedure produces the most effective long term retention and skill perfection, especially when exercising a series of discrete and serial skills. To illustrate this point, when learning to pass, set and hit, a player should routinely shift between skills after each repetition. The passer would, either, not pass from the same spot, pass the same type of serve, or pass twice in a row. Standing in the same spot to receive several serves in succession is not game specific and may be teaching bad habits. Generally, if the team is passing several balls in a row from the same court position during a game, it would indicate that the team is probably not siding out and the opponent is scoring. Similarly, a hitter would not make the same approach, hit the same angle or hit the same type of set twice in succession. Likewise, the setter will not approach the target from the same court position, set the same set or run the same play action consecutively. Once the ability to execute under varying conditions is established, practice organization can be highly diversified and motor programs practiced until performance is automatic.

In order to adapt skill execution to the demands of a variable and random environment, a large repertoire of motor patterns must be combined into generalized motor programs or images. Although blocked trials can be used to train and perfect specific motor skills, random skill execution should be the basis for training in this learning stage. Random and varied skill practice, in which a sequence of tasks/skills are experienced over consecutive trials, under game-like conditions, is the most effective form of organization and a powerful determinant in the quality of motor learning achieved. Regardless of the method of training, skills should be performed in as close to game conditions as possible while repetitions should be arranged that include the parameter of speed, distance, direction, and trajectory experienced individually or in various combinations.

Even though discrete and serial skills can be practiced in both a blocked and/or random fashion, serial skills that require a varied-random sequence of execution should make up most of this stage of training. That is, producing a generalized motor program for the spike requires an efficient coordination of the approach, jump, arm swing and ball contact while an effective attack requires a pass, set and hit. Both the spiking skills and the action of an attack can be performed in a varied and random fashion. For example, a spiker's approach can be made from varied angles to the net and the ball alternately attacked to randomly selected areas of the court. Likewise, the pass can be initiated from serves that are directed with varying speeds and trajectories to randomly selected court locations. It should be noted, that part practice (practicing a portion of the skill) has been shown to be beneficial in training discrete skills in the motor development stage. For example, to improve approach footwork and speed, it may be beneficial for a player to repeat just the approach at game speed until it can be executed efficiently.

Several forms of feedback (faded-summary and bandwidth) can be introduced at this stage of development. **Faded feedback** is most effective in reducing the need for feedback. It accomplishes permanent skill learning while reducing the dependency on external feedback, forcing the development of self-induced feedback. **Summary feedback,** feedback after skill execution, is also extremely important in this stage of learning in that it provides information regarding the accuracy of performance. This form of feedback is most effective if it is positive and given after correct execution. **Bandwidth feedback,** information is given only after an error occurs in movement, improves performance by indicating the amount and direction of an error in performance while reducing the amount of feedback presented. Remember, this extrinsic form of feedback is not given when execution is correct. Summary and bandwidth feedback are most effective when they are gradually reduced (faded feedback).

THE AUTONOMOUS STAGE (WITHOUT CONSCIOUS THOUGHT)

The next step in efficient skill learning and execution is automation. Coordination (effective performance movement) controls motor skill execution and operates best through unconscious (subliminal) thought. For this reason, a major objective of practice is to develop intuition (comprehension without effort or reasoning) that achieves efficient skill execution and occurs with very little thought process. If a player understands and reacts to a situation without thinking about it (unconscious thought), performance will be improved, reaction time reduced and the ability to execute efficiently increased. Since conscious trying often produces a negative outcome, skill execution without interference of thought during execution must occur if maximum performance is to result.

Once skill execution begins, too much information (thinking) slows reaction time and reduces the ability to perform efficiently; (e.g., movement to attack requires an unconscious thought process of reading the block in relation to the set and floor defense while executing the approach and spiking action). During this situation, a full awareness of thoughtful attention is not needed as the unconscious system controls the multiple and separate actions that occur during skill execution.

Unconscious thought enables an athlete to execute a skill automatically by minimizing the information derived from a competitive situation. When an athlete no longer needs to think about what he/she is doing, movements just seem to happen on their own (automation); the athlete just does it. For example, to be successful, a volleyball player who digs a ball hit at over 60 miles per hour must anticipate the speed of the ball, the reaction time available in relation to the incoming ball and the point of contact while executing the required motor program. This action takes place so quickly (less than a second) that conscious thought is virtually impossible and skill execution at this point in performance has now become virtually automatic. Cognitive thought at this point is unimaginable and a detriment to successful skill execution.

As technical skills become automatic, more attention can be directed to tactical efficiency and less to the selection and execution of technical motor programs. This is especially true for the experienced or elite athlete who is better able to limit environmental cues, focus on relevant sensory data and narrow his/her focus to a particular event. Some of the key phrases that have been used by sports psychologists to describe execution and performance that occurs without interference of thought are "mindlessness," "effortless effort" and "the quiet mind". Those players who can concentrate without trying to concentrate always seem to try hard, without trying hard, and achieve peak performance with seemingly very little effort. Although automatic execution requires very little thought, there is still an awareness of sight, sound and feel when playing the ball.

Research (Goppel-Loehr) associated with tennis studied the question of what do great players think about when they are performing at their best. i.e., what is going on in their mind during periods of peak performance? The athletes surveyed reported that they were not thinking about their actions as they performed but just reacting too situations as they occurred. It was concluded from this study, that thinking too much resulted in poor performance. However, not thinking at all can also cause trouble in performance. Thinking too much tends to cause a player to contemplate either past or future action; a leading cause of poor performance. Similarly, thoughts about poor past performance generally created anger and loss of confidence, while focusing on the future brought fear of failure. In fact, attention focus should be directed to opponent's action, ball movement and the desired result (the "now" time frame). Directing focus in this manner reduces the nervousness, anger and loss of concentration that often occurs during a match.

When a player finds he/she is thinking too much, they can reduce the thought process by focusing on breathing and by visualizing the skill they are about to execute. Since motor skills are best accomplished when they are spontaneous reactions, the object is to become so involved in performance that the skills are executed without conscious thought. The object must be for the player to coincide thoughts with performance so that the mechanics of execution flows freely. More specifically, if too much time is spent in the thought process, it becomes difficult to let actions occur spontaneously. Volleyball players who think too much are preventing the merging of execution into unconscious awareness.

Additional studies (Braden) of outstanding tennis players also indicate that during the inactive period between play very little time is spent contemplating their previous play, while inexperience players spent the entire free time replaying the point-match or not thinking at all. Visualization of correct skill execution or tactical performance during non-action periods, rather than replaying past performance or contemplating the next shot, is the best method for quieting the thought process. Creating pictures in the mind by seeing yourself executing the proper skill is most effective in keeping thoughts in the "now" mind frame. Once the desired picture has been created, the imagined can be copied during performance. There is however, a difference between practice and competition when processing information. During practice, time can be spent thinking about technical execution and tactical performance. Competition, on the other hand, is the time to suspend the thought process and become spontaneous, instinctive, creative and imaginative in execution.

Once perfected, individual technical-tactical skills are practiced until execution is reflexive - automatic and can be executed without conscious thought. Perfection of specific, individual skill executions (movement to attack, etc.) with stable and consistent technique is required so that attention can be exclusively directed to more complex tactical tasks required in competition. The tactical demands of competition require individual players to execute with correct technique according to the environmental situation encountered. Once individual and team technique has been mastered, the cognitive ability to resolve tactical problems under increasing and varying physical and psychological stress can be introduced. This demands the integration of preceptor-motor skills into a system of play that develops tactical intelligence. Once the ability to execute technically without conscious thought is established, the tactical stage of volleyball training can be instituted and trained.

Skill learning in the autonomous stage requires intensive training until perfected technical skills become automatic so that these skills can be easily applied to a complex competitive environment without conscious thought. When a player has achieved well-developed movement patterns, the next step in technical training is to produce automatic skill execution, i.e., sensory and movement analysis of skill execution that takes place without conscious thought. This advanced skill level is realized when the performer has a complete understanding of the skill and a generalized motor or mental image has been fully established. The athlete now pays little attention the basic physical aspects of task executions. As the attention demands given to physical execution are reduced, a player is able to perform cognitive activities on a higher ordered. Consequently, automatic-unconscious execution is now possible as the performer is able to efficiently filter out irrelevant information. Efficient selective attention is crucial to automatic executions in order to reduce distractions in the environment. Distraction reduction improves timing and anticipation while improving the accuracy of execution.

However, automatic reaction becomes much more difficult and almost impossible when two different responses are required by a given stimuli, i.e., the setter fakes a front set and sets a well-disguised back set. Reacting to multiple environmental stimuli slows response time because some conscious thought process is necessary before skill execution, thereby, reducing the reaction speed. Likewise, tactical decisions that require cognitive thought are difficult to automate. Although whole skill practice is effective for developing several skills in a series that can be executed automatically, a varied-random skill practice is essential if automatic training is to become generalized and game-specific.

In the autonomous stage, skilled performers must learn not only how to detect their own errors but also how to make the necessary adjustments to instantly correct them during performance. As skills become automatic and unconscious, self-feedback and self-talk during skill execution are virtually eliminated. In this instance, self-analysis may actually hinder performance in some instances. For the best results, skill feedback frequency should be intermittent and faded. Once play has stopped, evaluation and self-analysis can take place to reinforce strategic and tactical concepts. Automatic action coupled with improved self-confidence increases the ability to detect one's own errors. However, learning continues at a very slow rate in this stage of development.

APPLICATION/COMPETITIVE STAGE (TACTICS-TEAM PLAY) — Once technical skill can be executed with a reasonable degree of perfection and automation, sophisticated tactics that relate to game situations can be gradually introduced. As previously mentioned, if competitive training is to be game-specific and learning to transfer from practice to game situations, skill execution must be performed in a highly random and varied mode. That is, in this stage of skill learning, performance execution must be game-like in organization and structure. This type of practice calls for many kinds of activities, experiences and decision-making situations as they occur in competition and requires highly generalized motor programs.

The objective of this section is to give the reader examples of the progression from simple introductory skills to complex competitive skills. The process takes several simple motor programs and combines them into one generalized motor program that can be recalled from memory and executed automatically without conscious thought. For example, think about when you are driving down the road and the light turns red you do not say ooh! The lights red, I must pick up my foot and place it on the brake. Because that motor program has become automatic you simply without conscious thought pick up your foot and place it on the brake and hold it until the car comes to a halt.

Training, in the competitive stage, accounts for the actual characteristics of play by demanding automatic solutions to perceived tactical problems. In this stage of skill development, generalized individual techno-tactical skills are integrated into a specialized system of play. Once skills are automatic, the individual technical skills learned in the previous stages are merged with tactical concepts and integrated into competitive game-like executions, (e.g., adding a block and floor defense, to a pass, set and attack drill forces the player to make tactical decisions). In the competitive stage, isolated competitive situations can then be used to control play, to aid in decision making and to resolve tactical problems. Complete or partial phases of a game can be used to train the perceptual skills related to the discrimination, classification and interpretation of perceived data, i.e., the blockers attend to the pass, set and attacker in order to react to the perceived location of the point of attack. Tactical decisions are then made automatically as to where to set the block and the type of block to be used in relation to the attack possibilities of the opponent.

Competitive practice is not only a time for team play but also a time for learning to merge individual technical and tactical skills into a game-like-team sequence. Tactical intelligence is achieved by combining technical skills with tactical thought respective to the environmental conditions encountered. When developing tactical knowledge, emphasis is placed on a sequential order of skill execution and movement in relation to the correct on-the-court location and spatial-temporal orientation found in game situations. Practice at this stage consists of automating skills that have previously been perfected. As technical skills become automatic, a player is free to direct his/her attention and concentration to tactical execution (strategies) of the desired skill in a competitive situation. Automatic performance is quicker and more efficient under consistent mapping conditions, i.e., a given stimulus pattern always leads to the same response. Because skills executed automatically are much faster than controlled execution the performer is able to react very quickly and with better results. For example, when the ball is set to the left, the block automatically shifts to the right without conscious thought.

Although technical execution takes place under complex and stressful game-like conditions, performance conditions during practice are generally controlled. The ability to read and make instant decisions and reactions to the action occurring on the court is an excellent example of combining the various stages of learning. The competitive stage (team play-tactics) integrates perfected, automated technical skills to comply with the tactics of team play. For example, during competition a player execute the technical skills of a pass, set and hit etc. into a combination/play action series that can take place during many tactical situation that occur in game situations.

In a varied practice, i.e., one that has a wide range of experiences, emphasis is placed on arranging skill repetitions with different skill variants that are introduced and practiced randomly during each trial. Only, when proficiency in skill execution has been achieved and performance has become relatively automatic, can technical skills be applied efficiently to tactical execution. A varied-random form of training provides the best method for developing generalized motor programs, setting parameters for the skills to be learned and in meeting the new and ever-changing environmental demands of a volleyball match. That is, different dimensions and combinations of skill execution (speed, distance, direction, location and trajectory) are experienced on consecutive random repetitions. During this application phase, it is appropriate for the athlete to develop his/her own unique style or variation of skill execution. Imagination and creativity during performance is acceptable as long as accuracy and efficiency in execution can be maintained.

Much disagreement surrounds the use of feedback and reinforcement during the competitive stage of learning. There is, however, widespread agreement among most experts that when using reinforcement and feedback techniques during competition they should deal mainly with tactical execution. More specifically, attempting to offer advice about technique during game situations greatly reduces automatic responses, increases errors and in general will not improve but hinder technical and tactical execution. Mental practice can be used at this level of proficiency to gain control over emotional states, arousal levels and to attain confident and positive attitudes about performance. Visualization also offers an excellent avenue for rehearsing tactical execution and improving confidence under conditions of extreme stress.

Although external feedback can be an effective learning tool, the major function of skill evaluation in this stage is to develop intrinsic (internal) feedback techniques, i.e., the ability to self-detect errors, in order to recognize and correct skill execution. Intrinsic feedback allows a player to make effective self-evaluation that provides important performance guidelines; (e.g. one's evaluation of the accuracy of a pass to its intended target). Since the coach may not always be immediately present during skill practice, players must learn to correct their own performance problems. If a player is forced to learn how to detect errors and evaluate his/her skill performance, retention and recall will be improved. The capability of a player to detect his/her own errors will also reinforce existing learned responses more efficiently. A key to effective and efficient motor learning is how the coach determines when a person should progress through the various stages of motor development. Skilled coaches, by observing various changes taking place in individual behavior during practice and performance should be able to determine if acceptable learning has occurred and when progression to the next stage is appropriate. These changes may include: increases in skill knowledge, the ability to detect and correct errors, the process by which goals are achieved, improvement in coordination and movement, and the ability to control attention focus.

SUMMARY

Researchers have concluded that the goal of learning and performing a complex skill is best achieved by systematically improving the specific kinetic movement features required to execute the skill. Therefore, one of the objectives to be achieved in the stages of motor learning is for the athlete to develop the capability of identifying and correcting his/her own errors. However, it must be noted that error correction during performance can only be made when execution of a skill takes place at a very slow pace or at the conclusion of performance. When movement occurs at a rapid pace error correction is difficult or nearly impossible. There appears to be 3 types of learners: 1) the beginner who has no or very rudimentary motor programs and needs to achieve some: 2) The intermediate player who has developed motor programs which are ineffective and need extensive training to change them and 3) the experiences player who the correct motor programs but need to learn how to retrieve the right motor program at the right time. All three of these players need to change motor behavior. However the problem that arise in change a motor program takes at least 8 week of constantly executing the correct motor program in order to keep the old motor program from trying to creep back into performance (Braden/Schmidt).

It only seems obvious that experienced volleyball players will be able to execute in game situations better than novices. Besides difference in physical ability, the major distinction between advanced and beginning players is the amount and structure of knowledge and the extent of competitive experience. Advanced players possess the experiences that enable them to convert knowledge into concepts, while, novice players tend to structure their thoughts as independent facts and pieces of information. No doubt, the ability to perceive and select more relevant environmental cues is a characteristic that enables the experienced player to use the information available to determine how responses to specific situations should be performed. This advanced formation of strategic concepts make possible a problem-solving approach to resolving conditions as they appear in the environment. Beginners often direct their attention at inappropriate cues while skilled players are able to focus on the appropriate cues and thus experience greater success and less expenditure of energy. The ability of the novice to quickly attend to the appropriate cues as they appear in competitive situations will improve execution proficiency.

Skilled athletes seem to posses the capability to control limb and body movements so that the goal of execution is easier to attain. This ability to control performance enables these players to adapt execution to the new and novel demands of the varying situations in which performance takes place. For novice players, goal achievement is sporadic because movement is restricted by inflexibility, as the limbs seem to only work as single units. Talented performers, however, achieve their skill objectives by using only those muscles needed to achieve the task thereby diminishing caloric costs of performance while improving execution. As a player improves coordination through practice, movement control seems to be more specific, efficient and relaxed. Efficient movement means less expenditure of energy and effort thus making it seem as though skilled players perform with effortless ease. In addition, as a player becomes more efficient in skill execution, errors are to a great extent reduced. For, reducing errors is the goal of practice and the key to success.

CHAPTER 3

Evaluation/Error Correction and Motor Learning

INTRODUCTION

As mentioned earlier, coaches marvel at the ability of players to execute in practice but are bewildered by them when they cannot execute efficiently and accurately during competition. There are many psychological factors and mental practice techniques that can play an important role in skill retention and preparation for competition. Mental training such as task rehearsal, relaxation techniques, emotional control, confidence and positive attitude development will interact to improve skill execution. Therefore, mental practice should be part of every training session. However the mental techniques that will be covered in this manuscript are those factors that directly affect the execution and retention of motor skills and motor behavior. The teaching techniques of Feedback and Reinforcement are behavior procedures that have a tremendous effect on an athlete's ability to learn an execute sports skills. All coaches use these methods when coaching volleyball players with tremendous positive results. However, having said that, as I watch and listen to coaches as they conduct volleyball practice and coach during a game often do not use right type of feedback and reinforcement or use it to often and provide too much information. The following chapter on feedback and reinforcement is based on the research of Richard Schmidt, Donald Young and Darlene Kluka.

FEEDBACK

Players must learn what was done wrong and how to correct it and/or what was done right and how to improve it. **Feedback** is the information provided as a result of the movement created by muscle force and length, joint and body position, vision and audition. Probably the single most important factor in learning motor skills and improving volleyball performance is feedback. This mental and motivational process can be used to control on-going skill execution or be retained in memory to modify and control future behavior. A major role of a coach is to provide feedback about errors or correctness in execution, while giving directions as a means of modifying performance.

Effective feedback success is contingent on the quality and quantity of the information received and is based on the ability to accurately process of this data. Proper and accurate feedback will enable the performer to employ information about performance that alters subsequent skill execution. In fact, appropriate feedback reduces the internalization of errors and greatly affects the rate of learning. In reducing errors, there appears to be a comparison factor in determining what produces mistakes in performance. This factor consists of knowledge of how a particular movement felt in relation to how it should feel. Learning and performance are believed to be most effective when the learner can analyze and respond to feedback in an open environment, i.e. action that cannot be programmed in advance.

In general, feedback can be self-generated either via sensory perception during performance (internal) or supplied by supplemental feedback (external) following performance. External perceptual feedback is presented via sensory, visual or auditory stimuli, while internal movement feedback is obtained by muscle, tendon, and joint sensory input. External feedback is the only aspect of performance over which the coach has direct control and can be used as incentive to increase effort, to reinforce correct behavior, or to provide information for performance self-correction. Internal feedback, i.e., physical sensory information about performance, focuses on limb positioning, limb timing and body coordination. The ability to understand and use internal feedback increases and expands as players become more experienced and knowledgeable about how the body should feel during execution.

Three primary ways exist to convey technical/tactical information via feedback: verbally, visually, or kinesthetically. Telling players what to do is the most used and most common method of relaying feedback information. However, because verbal information does not transfer quickly or efficiently at the neuromuscular level, it is the least effective method of feedback learning.

Mental practice, visualization and imagery can be used effectively to enhance learning at this stage. Mental training is relevant for practicing the decision making process, reinforcing the conceptual elements of a skill and as a means of practicing technical and tactical skills when conditions are not favorable for physical training. Visualization of skilled performance will assist in perfecting skill execution by mentally rehearsing correct skill execution.

Visual feedback is slightly more effective than verbal feedback because transfer is more efficient; e.g., demonstration/modeling the technique to be learned. Studies (Schmidt-Young) in motor learning point out that the most efficient technique for conveying information is by kinesthetic feedback, which by passes the brain and provides a direct link for processing information at the neuromuscular level. That is, instead of telling or showing a player what to do, he/she is placed in the appropriate positions and physically or verbally manipulated through the desired movements. To illustrate, an attacker who is having trouble with shoulder rotation and arm extension when hitting the ball can be physically manipulated through the proper range of motion until a feeling of the correct execution is achieved.

For learning to take place, several forms of feedback must occur. In addition to correct practice, motor learning requires: (1) **a Knowledge of Performance (KP), i.e.,** what movement causes the ball to go in a certain direction, (2) **a Knowledge of Results (KR), i.e.,** where the ball went; and (3) **Reinforcement, i.e.,** the act of strengthening a desired behavior. Motor learning will be greatly hindered without an accurate KR or KP to provide motivation, increase interest and intensify the will to succeed. Accurate, positive and constructive feedback provides the best KR and KP and will produce the best results. More specifically, corrective feedback should not only tell the player what he/she is doing wrong, but more importantly, what he/she is doing right (**summary feedback**).

Skill acquisition demands that volleyball players develop a clear understanding of how they have performed. Knowledge of Performance (KP) provides this internal error-detection mechanism through external feedback; (e.g., when passing the ball, a performer knows the arms and/or body were out of position if the ball is not passed accurately to the target area). Thus, KP provides information about movement success in terms of meeting the performance goals, such as achieving the correct body position when passing the ball to the target area. If KP is to be effective, players must be given concrete instruction that shows how to achieve the desired skill execution. "Watch the ball" and "nice play" are expressions that give the athlete little useful information about performance (other than motivation) and will contribute little to performance improvement. "That was an excellent pass because the elbows were locked and the arms were away from the body at a forty-five degree angle," is an example of feedback that provides more efficient KP and increased learning. Better still, precise key (cue) words can be used: "thumbs together, elbows locked" etc. provide more effective feedback. Besides creating mental pictures, key words simplify information that keeps the brain from having to pick or choose the important parts of a lengthy statement or instruction.

Motor learning is difficult without both practice and error detection provided by a Knowledge of Results (KR). Knowledge of Results (feedback about the outcome of performance) in relation to the environmental goal/s provides a conscious or unconscious awareness regarding the results (outcome) of a sequence of movements in skill execution or physical performance, i.e., the accuracy of a pass to the target zone. Knowledge of Results plays an important role in supplying needed information and motivation for improving skill execution, especially in the early stages of volleyball training.

The more precise KR is given the more learning that occurs and the better the athlete is able to perform. The quality of KR feedback given is based on the precision used when describing the action. Quantitative information, such as "you missed the passing target by two feet" facilitate learning better than qualitative information, such as "you're off to the right," or "getting closer," etc. It is essential that feedback be specific. Telling an attacking player he/she is late contacting the ball does not provide adequate information to determine what late means. Moreover, telling a player to hit the ball earlier also does not supply enough information concerning how to accomplish this action. Informational feedback must convey <u>what</u> has to be done and <u>how</u> to do it.

Providing adequate feedback to a player who approaches early on the attack might be as follows: "To reduce your tendency to approach early (what), it is imperative that you delay your approach until the ball has reached its apex and is dropping (how)." It may be even more effective to state: "Being a little late on the approach is better than being early (what). This will force you to speed up your body movement and arm swing (how)." However, general feedback has its place and can play an important role in the training process by providing motivation; (e.g., "great effort," "good play, excellent approach" etc.). Research in motor learning infers that too detailed information regarding performance can also confuse a learner and deter learning. Information overload causes a player to lose focus and inhibits a player's ability to concentrate. Therefore, it is important when giving feedback, to limit the amount of information conveyed to the single most relevant piece of data that can be given at any one time. Additional information must not be provided until a player has demonstrated the ability to integrate, internalize and make use of prior information. So, tell them precisely what they need to know and why they need to know this information. Furthermore, there should be a short interval between a given KR and the next trial to allow players to absorb the data presented. It seems obvious the player instantly knows the result of performance (good or bad).

Players often recognize that their movement patterns are incorrect but fail to realize what should be done to bring about the right movement patterns. If a player cannot detect his/her own errors in performance (KP) through intrinsic feedback, no learning will occur. However, these individuals would be capable of changing behavior, if they knew what they were doing — either right or wrong. Thus, adequate KP is necessary for learning to occur and execution to improve. With extensive practice, a performer becomes less dependent on KR information and more subject to information stored in his/her own internal detection model of the correct performance (KP). If an athlete wants to improve, he/she should ask themselves what it was they did correctly and incorrectly. Although corrective comments are often considered as negative reinforcement, they play a role in learning by pointing out to a player what is not being done correctly. However, positive comments about correct skill execution and performance are often better than negative comments. Remember, practice will make perfect only if there is enough appropriate KP.

Self-detection of errors for correcting skill execution can be trained by constantly reminding players to evaluate their own performance in relation to their short term performance goals. This method of feedback can be further developed by asking players to evaluate their own performance immediately after execution and before Knowledge of Results (KR) and Knowledge of Performance (KP) is given by an outside source. In short, improvement in performance is enhanced by self evaluation, because errors can be corrected promptly after execution and without the aid of the coach. In addition, self-evaluation increases the number of trials that receive some form of feedback while reducing the amount of feedback required from outside sources, Training players in this manner directs the focus on response-produced intrinsic feedback that is highly sensitive to errors in movement patterning. As a result of self-detection, awareness of correct movement patterns can be efficiently established, intrinsic feedback improved and the opportunity for skill retention reinforced. Self-feedback is crucial during game situation due to the limits placed on substitutions, time-outs and the speed of the game.

If used correctly, external feedback improves performance and is crucial to efficient learning in the motor development stage. Extrinsic **feedback** comes to the player from an outside source; (e.g., verbalization from the coach-other players). To be effective, the coach should target and narrow feedback to one feature and by the use of simple cue words so that the player can readily process information on how to change skill execution and movement on the next attempt. Research indicates that giving feedback instantly after skill execution seems to hinder learning and interferes with the self-error detection process. This is especially important in random practice where several tasks are being executed alternately. In order for players to process information and make the needed self-correction, a minimum of five seconds is needed after feedback before extrinsic feedback is given.

REINFORCEMENT

Reinforcement is an extrinsic motivational feedback tool that can be used to increase the probability of a desired volleyball response (motor skill) occurring repeatedly. Reinforcement can be a positive or negative reward (tangible or intangible) used to critique performance. Sport psychologist (Schmidt-Young) agree that reinforcement is most efficient when presented in a positive manner that is brief and directly to the point. Positive reinforcement will motivate most athletes to practice longer and harder, thereby, improving skill execution through continued correct repetitions.

For efficient learning through reinforcement, a statement such as, "The location of the set about 3' high and inside the antenna was perfect, however, it may be best to reduce the speed of the set." This type of feedback will provide the best KR and KP for reinforcing the accuracy and execution of a shoot set. In addition to the type of reinforcement (positive, negative, etc.), the amount and timing of reinforcement is also critical to its effectiveness. Except in early learning, constant reinforcement given after every execution should be replaced by intermittent reinforcement. More specifically, **intermittent reinforcement** given only when the desired skill is demonstrated correctly is believed by some experts to be the most efficient form of reinforcement. Varied methods of reinforcement that provide intermittent information about skill performance, allows a player time to perceive a connection between proper execution and reinforcement.

Research (Schmidt-Goppel/Loehr) has concluded that constant reinforcement and feedback has two effects on a player's performance. First, reinforcing every play, despite the quality of feedback, not only creates information overload but limits the information that can be processed regarding proper skill execution. Secondly, positive recognition, given too frequently, hinders learning and may cause a player to forget learned material more quickly. Excessive positive reinforcement/feedback may create a motivated player, but it may also cause the player to perform only when reinforcement/feedback is present. Therefore, these factors are not necessary after every successful or unsuccessful attempt and should be spaced throughout practice. Perhaps, on every fourth or fifth attempt is adequate. A teaching technique more effective than over-reinforcement is a faded form of feedback that gradually decreases in the amount of information presented. Faded feedback forces the player to think and to analyze performance to determine if the skill was executed properly, rather than waiting for expected reinforcement from the coach. Faded feedback can be handled in two ways: first, by gradually diminishing the amount of feedback given and second, by reducing the intervals at which feedback is provided.

On the other hand, problems also arise when too little reinforcement is given. The lack of adequate positive reinforcement will produce low motivation and inhibit skill learning. To be most effective, reinforcement must be task-specific, directed at performance, and given fairly soon after performance takes place. Reinforcement given several minutes, hours or days after occurrence reduces effectiveness. In addition, reinforcement must also relate to the particular stage of motor learning. As an example, in the introductory stage of learning, emphasis is on reinforcing neuromuscular training, i.e., acquiring new motor (technical) skills. In this early learning period, reinforcement should be informative, motivational, and provide specific (KP) that is given after almost every attempt. Although proper execution must be continually stressed, concentrated focus should be directed to the outcome of performance in the advanced stages of motor learning (KR).

The objective of behavioral reinforcement is to increase the likelihood that a desired skill will be repeated and to instill a belief by a player that he/she can execute efficiently and successfully. Although undesirable behavior should be halted immediately, discipline as a means of reinforcement should be constructive. If possible, reprimands should be limited and avoided, especially, if it does not fit the misdeed. Consequently, performing a physical activity as punishment to reinforce a behavior, that has no purpose and no relationship to volleyball or the skill being learned, will provide little skill reinforcement or learning. When an error occurs or behavior is improper, repeating the skill being learned or a related skill several times in succession is an excellent means of positive reinforcement and may produce the best learning.

Furthermore, **punishment** if used as a reinforcement tool must be used very selectively and instituted only with careful consideration of a player's individual goals and personal needs. For punishment, i.e., **negative reinforcement**, to be effective, it must be demonstrated convincingly to the player that his/her best interests are being considered. This type of reinforcement will be effective only if a player believes that punishment is a motivational technique being used to achieve a common goal and that the coach has his/her best interest at heart. However, the best results are obtained by positively reinforcing the desired skills, behavior and attitudes. This action will enhance self-confidence, improve motivation and assist in skill development. An excellent example of using punishment in a positive manner would be to have a player who fails to extend the effort when playing defense to repeat the defensive sequence multi-times until maximum effort has been extended.

Reinforcement and feedback can have a cumulative effect on behavior. All activities connected to practice and the program contributes to an atmosphere that is either positive or negative. Since individual players and the team represent an accumulation of its experiences, the environment must produce a series of positive and productive experiences that will result in a quality program and superior learning experiences. If practice behavior is shoddy, inconsistent and undisciplined, an accumulation of negative experiences will arise resulting in the team's lack of pride, a poor self-image and lack-luster performance. On the other hand, if a coach requires high standards in behavior, an accumulation of good experiences should take place that create effectives/positive performance.

SUMMARY

Feedback is the information provided as a result of the movement created by muscle force and length, joint and body position, vision and audition. Probably the single most important factor in learning motor skills and improving volleyball performance is feedback. This mental and motivational process can be used to control on-going skill execution or be retained in memory to modify and control future behavior. A major role of a coach is to provide feedback about errors or correctness in execution, while giving directions as a means of modifying performance.

For learning to take place, several forms of feedback must occur. In addition to correct practice, motor learning requires: (1) **a Knowledge of Performance (KP), i.e.,** what movement causes the ball to go in a certain direction, (2) **a Knowledge of Results (KR), i.e.,** where the ball went; and (3) **Reinforcement, i.e.,** the act of strengthening a desired behavior. Motor learning will be greatly hindered if there is a lack of efficient feedback. Although extrinsic feedback (that is feedback from a coach, players and the environment etc.) plays an important role in learning, intrinsic feedback is the most important and effective means by which learning takes place. Self feedback from muscle movement and other internal sources is the most efficient process for learning how to analyze and respond to situations occurring in the environment. Leaning is a process based on practice and experiences that leads to a relative permanent change and the capability of responding to events that happen in the future is greatly influenced by some form of feedback.

CHAPTER 4

Practice Theory and Organization

INTRODUCTION

The success of any team in competition is determined by the quality and content of its practice time. An effective training philosophy is based on the concept that a team and individual players cannot perform skills or tactics in competitive situations that have not been anticipated and trained in practice. Therefore, training is not just the conducting of drills and team play but also the development of an overall team point of view. For performance to be maximized, expected behavior has to be outlined and programmed in progressive steps that result in the desired terminal behavior. It must be emphasized however that any practice plan is just a temporary guideline; it will need to be adjusted, revised and redefined as situations evolve requiring special attention.

Volleyball experts have concluded that there are three basic performance objectives to be achieved from volleyball training: first, to provide the experiences that will enable each player as well as the team to develop their maximum potential; second, to mold a group of individuals into a team; and third, to prepare a team for those situations that will occur during competition. Individual and team potential can be accomplished only if practice develops the behavior patterns and motor programs necessary for goal achievement while preparing players for every situation that could arise when competing. A major behavioral purpose of volleyball training is to develop the intense and concentrated conduct demanded for an optimal competitive effort. Preparing individual players and a team to achieve this purpose consists of three interrelated phases: **instruction**, **practice** and **training**.

Instruction is the cognitive phase of training in which knowledge and information are used to bring out the latent capacities of each individual. Instruction provides background data and informational experiences that can be applied to learning the fundamental physical and mental skills that develop basic motor programs.

Practice, is that part of training where skills are performed with systematic repetitions that produce learned motor responses. During this phase of training, new skills and/or existing skills are continually reproduced under varying degrees of intensity until proficiency (accuracy and perfection) have been obtained allowing acquisition and automatic reactions in performance are achieved. More specifically, the objective of practice is to produce trained movement patterns that develop into automatic responses to specific environmental cues. Since thinking doubles response time to a specific cue, practice must create athletes who can perform trained responses automatically, without conscious thought, thereby, reducing the time needed to react and execute specific skills. The closer the practice environment is to actual game experiences the higher the possibility that a skill learned in practice will be transfer to game situations. In addition the best learning takes place during a practice environment that contains repeated positive experiences.

A **training** program coordinates instruction and practice into an organized format that will achieve acquisition of advanced technical and tactical skills and concepts. Training is primarily geared to providing instructional and practice experiences that will enable the individual player and team to discover and achieve their optimal performance potential. A major concern of any training program is to instill new behavioral patterns and/or to improve or change existing behavior. Based on this assumption, the behavioral objectives of volleyball training are as follows: (1) to develop the appropriate behavioral patterns of cooperation, commitment and discipline, (2) to instill the competitive behaviors of intensity, concentration and mental toughness, and (3) to train the behavioral disciplines (mental/physical) needed to implant the technique, tactics and physical conditions required for maximum competitive effort and finally training must develop the physical strength, quickness and fitness necessary to compete and perform the require skills as close to perfection as possible.

PRACTICE DESIGN: THE INGREDIENTS FOR AN EFFECTIVE PRACTICE

PRACTICE PREPARATION — Practice is a block of time scheduled to include a series of drills organized in a logical progression and based on predetermined performance goals devise to achieve the chosen objectives. The procedures for teaching volleyball skills require an effective organization of individual and group activities. Performance improvement and excellence are a result of preparing each player-team for any situation that can occur during competition. This is achieved through controlled drill procedures and routines that structure on-the-court player movements while duplicating expected game behavior.

In the early part of the 20th century the auto industry and other big businesses introduced a process termed called "Scientific Team Management" as a basis for operating their rapidly expanding and increasingly complicated business operations. The basic premises by which these companies operated can be adapted to athletics to improve and solidify administrative procedures and policies. The major premise of Scientific Team Management as related to coaching and team management indicates that the outcome of practice and competition can be controlled by leaving nothing to chance. Control is achieved by preparing for all contingencies that might occur through careful planning, identification, and regulation of team activities.

Team success is to a large extent dependent on achievement of the objectives to which it strives. To achieve these objectives Scientific Team Management is divided into four basic steps: 1) the establishment of predetermined rules that organize and enforce effective administrative practices and policies: 2) efficient allocation of resources and personnel; 3) a means of evaluating the effectiveness of these procedures; and 4) performance based on personal motivation and responsibility.

An efficient and effective administrative process establishes predetermined explicit and comprehensive procedures, rules and routines that are fixed in advance in order to standardize the training process. Specialized operational rules that govern game and practice situations include: training rules, team personnel assignments and codification of performance descriptions. Procedures for promotion to a starting position and dismissal from team should also be developed. Systemized and standardized training procedures for participation must be established that control the training process, player identification and selection procedures. A systematic training program based on proven standardized training procedures that are specialization and simplified should also be developed.

Specialization by simplification provides for more extensive use of human resources while synchronizing individual tasks. The coordination of these tasks among team members allows for a high degree of efficiency through mastery of simple repetitive steps. In the process of simplification each skill to be learned must be reduced to its basic elements and then learned through a gradual progression from simple to complex tasks. Thus, the end results are that each skill becomes extremely simple and precise in execution. This requires a high volume of effort, a large number of repetitive tasks, clearly defined goals, and an in depth understanding of the principles of motor learning.

The next objective is to select, interpret and apply appropriate evaluation procedures in order to enhance motivation, to evaluate success of player development and to asses' program success. Assembling management information enables a coach to determine the effects of rules and procedures, skill development, and drills that apply to specific situations. This provides a coach with reliable information on the programs operational process. To be successful this process must be coordinated and detailed by developing and collecting written and/or electronic data that analyzes player development associated with practice and game statistical information. The final objective is to build motivation and morale. This is achieved by developing a feeling that each player involved in the team is respected for their contribution, by providing for individual recognition and opportunities that allows an individual, as well the team, to achieve a feeling of respect and success. To be successful these objective must internalize the habits necessary to select, interpret and apply the principles learned during training, i.e., the ability to use the skill needed for success effectively and efficiently.

In correlating volleyball skill acquisition to practice situations, it is critical to recognize the diverse components of motor learning and choose the appropriate principles that affect planning and instruction e.g. there is no two situation that occur during a game that are the same. Establishing practice goals and the tasks to be learned play an important role in efficient motor learning. Equally important, if practice is to be productive, the criterion skills to be learned must be determined. That is, what should the learner be able to do as a result of his/her effort in practice? There appear to be three important criteria goals that must be achieved if practice is to be maximized: long term retention, the proficiency to generalize motor skills and the ability to develop performance capabilities. Simply put, practice must generate generalized motor programs that produce long-term-retention and recall capability under varied and random conditions.

In volleyball, the goal of practice is to develop an ability to apply learned skills to variables found in the novel or random situations that occur in a performance environment. In addition to variations, such as speed, force and distance, the ability to react quickly and consistently to the changing conditions of competition is critical. To be more specific, practice, to be successful, must produce the ability to transfer skill executions (motor programs), developed in practice, to performance in game situations. Several variables that enhance long-term-retention and recall are game-like practice conditions conducted with faded feedback and automation based on random consist mapping specific to the activity being trained. As a result, the learner acquires generalized motor programs that are capable of being executed within the parameters (speed-distance-etc.,) required in a changing environment. To achieve this, a variable-random practice is necessary.

Practice organization is considered variable when there is a diversity of the same skill on each attempt. Variation occurs by changing the speed, force, distance and location of execution. Therefore, a varied practice, in volleyball, would include serving or hitting to different court locations on consecutive attempts. On the other hand, a random practice consists of switching from task to task in a random fashion. Random practice is most effective in providing the learner with the training essential for generating appropriate reactions to the ever changing circumstance experienced in competition by training those skills in practice. Generalized motor programs are necessary for retrieval of skills learned randomly. In volleyball, a random practice consists of passing different types of serves or hitting to different areas of the court in an irregular or unorganized manner on each attempt. Practices that are varied can be planned prior to execution while random executions occur by chance or haphazardly in relation the activities taking place in the environment.

To fit the ever changing conditions of the real world, a player is often compelled to continually get rid of an existing motor program and quickly instill a new program. As a result of the game characteristics of volleyball, practice must develop generalized motor programs which produce performance that can be adapted to varied, random and game-like conditions. Creating generalized performance capabilities facilitates future learning. This allows practice experiences to ease the transfer of skills acquired in practice to new and different circumstances occurring in the playing environment. In training general performance capability, practice should be highly variable and random with individual skill learning de-emphasized in order to stress multiple executions under game-like conditions. Random practice in skill learning improves retention by forcing the learner to constantly retrieve and recall different motor programs.

INSTRUCTIONAL MANAGEMENT FOR VOLLEYBALL TRAINING

GUIDED PRACTICE — An effective practice requires a comprehensive understanding and knowledge of the seasonal and daily practice schedule. This information gives the players and coaches' a general idea of the amount of time involved in each learning segment, in addition to total practice time. Practice can have a cumulative effect on performance and a quality program will be developed when practice consists of a series of positive and productive experiences. Practice is productive when high standards of behavior are required and displayed. An efficient and effective practice demands that the team, as well as individual players, never wastes practice time, maximizes every available opportunity to improve, and accepts responsibility for their actions. Lost minutes and hours can never be regained. Therefore, each player must arrive at to practice on time with a positive, supportive attitude. Each player should understand and appreciate the need for quality production during training. A coachable player is one who works hard, assists and encourages their team mates, hustles after every ball, helps maintain a proper gym atmosphere and follows instructions closely without argument. An effective practice should include the following factors:

- Date, time and location of each practice
- Dress and therapy procedures
- Daily team goals
- Team meeting
- Good communication skills
- Technical and tactical drills
- Competitive drills
- Conditioning
- Warm-up and Cool down

Dressing for practice, therapy and goal setting should not be considered as a part the formal practice and must be completed prior to the start of formal practice. The same practice uniform should be required of each player at each practice. This increases player responsibility and discipline. During the goal setting aspect of the pre-practice, players review the team and personal goals that have been established. In addition to goal review this period includes a brief review of the skills to be executed and visualizes their execution prior to practice. Athletes who are motivated learn best and execute the required procedures with greater success.

Motivated athletes are those who have established effective goals, understand and contribute to training procedures, and appreciate the opportunity to participate. The prime factors in effective instructions are:

- The skills of the coach.
- Intelligence and attitude of each player.
- The learning environment.
- The willingness to accept responsibility.
- The refusal to make excuses.
- Previous experience of players.
- Player readiness and ability to learn and execute skills effectively

A short team meeting ends the pre-practice period. This session reviews past events, future events and any other information relevant to practice, competition, school, and other important activities.

There are six basic steps in developing positive instructional management when planning an effective training session is as follows:

ANTCIPATORY SET: The objectives of the anticipatory set is to focus the player's attention on the tasks to be accomplished, review and relate expected learning to previous experiences, and to develop readiness and standards for instruction. This is a brief period that takes place at the beginning of practice. Establishing an anticipatory set could be achieved by asking questions such as: "Who will restate the key ideas of yesterday's practice before we expand on them today?", or "what are the key concepts that result in successful service execution?"

OBJECTIVE/RATIONAL: Objectives (goals) establish the relevance of present skills and tactics to future situations. Accomplishing objectives is important and useful in that they inform athletes of the end results of instruction and performance. Objectives/goals should be specific in content and focus on observable, expected behavior. For example: "We are going to learn the correct technique for executing the forearm pass, so that the results of performance are acceptable and perfected".

INSTRUCTIONAL INPUT: Consist of the information needed by each player to accomplish the stated objectives and goals. Once this is completed, the best means of dispensing that information must be chosen Example: lecture, video, demonstration, drills, etc.

DEMONSRATIONS/MODELING: Provides an accurate illustration of the finished product of the skills to be practiced. The skill modeled must be a precise example of correct execution by following the principles of modeling. Modeling the skill must be followed immediately by skill execution before information in short term memory is lost.

CHECK FOR UNDERSTANDING: Is achieved by observation and questioning players after performing a new skill. Example: Pose questions to entire group or call on individual players to answer specific questions as to the success and effectiveness of what is being taught will contribute to the learning process.

PRACTICE ORGANIZATION AND DEVELOPMENT: Practice must be well organized, intense and related to the level of performance capability.

TASK CLASSIFICATION

Skill acquisition (learning) and drill development for volleyball are based on three distinct types of skills: **discrete skills** — a skill with a beginning and end (e.g., the serve), **serial skills** — several discrete skills strung together (e.g., the attack which requires a pass, set and hit) and **continuous skills** — skill where action is continuous and has no recognizable beginning or end, (e.g., consecutive play action that transitions from offense to defense to offense, etc.).

In training discrete skills, the focus is on preplanning a production of movement that is brief and has a distinct beginning and end. Preplanning is important in early learning because it discourages modification while the skill is being executed. Because discrete skills have a definite end, evaluation (feedback) can take place immediately after the action has been completed. This increases the capability of players to identify performance errors by attending to their own response-produced feedback. Furthermore, since fatigue is not a problem when learning discrete skills, rest time can be minimized and the number of repetitions increased. The serve is a good a good example of a discrete skill. **Serial skills** are composed of several discrete actions strung together in which the order of execution is critical to success. These skills can be trained through either of the following types of practice: a series of **blocked executions** (repeated trials of the same skill), **varied practice** (variations in execution of the same skill) or **random executions** (haphazard consecutive trials of several skills). Part practice may also be effective in learning serial skills if the parts to be practiced are strongly interdependent. On the other hand, part-whole practice appears to most effective for tasks requiring low reactions but are less useful for skill procedures that require very quick actions.

Continuous skills are tasks that involve a series of ongoing modifications in execution, that is, they have no beginning or end. Focus, during execution, is on how to modify behavior (execution) based on the continual input of sensory information and environmental feedback. Learning ways to anticipate the regularity and probability of upcoming sensory information plays a major role in the process of effective continuous skill execution. However, fatigue tends to affect performance in continuous tasks and will require frequent active rest periods between trials. Keep in mind that rest between practice trails aids the development of continuous skills but is less effective when used in training discrete skills.

There is a range in variability in practice drill organization and intensity that should be considered in skill training. A low intensity type practice consists of blocked activities in which a skill sequence is repeated constantly, such as repeatedly passing the ball off the same type of serve from the same position on the court. Since blocked drills do not allow for a great deal of variation in responses, minimal practice time should be spent in this type drill. However, if used with discretion repeated practice of a skill, in a blocked drill, can often be very effective when a definite weakness is present that requires concentrated effort and many correct repetitions. As mentioned earlier, Instead of having a player perform continuous repetitions of incorrect serve he/or she can be removed to a specific area of the gym to strengthen and improve his/her serving technique and accuracy in a low intensity blocked drill. However, as players advance in skill ability, drills must become more game-like with varied and random sequences of executions.

Varying skill execution with three or four skills in a series has been shown to be more efficient than executing a single skill several times in succession. For example, it is best to pass the ball, then approach and hit the ball, block and transition off the net rather than pass 10 consecutive balls, then hit 10 consecutive ball, etc.). An intense, varied form of practice requires players to make extensive adjustments in technique; (e.g., a player approaches to attack from different angles, attacks different sets and executes a different shot on each attempt). This type of organization allows practice circumstances to be manipulated thereby demanding a variety of technical adjustments on each successive trail. To further illustrate, serving from a different position, attempting a different serve, or serving to an alternate location on each succeeding trial will provide a varied practice. Better still, it is more efficient to execute a serve under varying conditions in an organized and random fashion.

Recent research indicates that the quality of skill learning acquired through practice is profoundly affected by the amount of random and variable sequences in which different motor skills are performed. Varied and random skill practice has been shown to improve performance by requiring increased mental and physical effort. This increased effort forces players to work harder and concentrate longer. In fact, a randomized variable sequencing of practice trials has been shown to most effective because it requires a constant shifting of attention between numerous skills and thus is more game-like. In other words, the more variable and random the practice, the better a player learns to make the needed adjustments required to transfer motor skills from practice to game situations, i.e. recalling previously learned skills from LTM. Since learning is most efficient in variable, random type practice and drills, it can be concluded that a majority of practice time should emphasize this type of activity.

Random practice appears to help long term retention by increasing focus on the process of performing motor tasks, while block practice focuses on outcome. More specifically, exposing players to varying conditions forces them to use more cognitive skills thereby improving their long term retention. Motor learning studies (Schmidt) have concluded that players who are continually confronted with changing situation in a random fashion are forced to process relevant cues more acutely and with more thought, thus creating better understanding. That is, random execution require is a more complex cognitive process that demands a player generate new solutions in solving existing competitive problems. This is achieved by forcing the learner to repetitively retrieve different motor programs or develop generalized programs to fit the random and variable condition present in the environment.

INSTRUCTIONAL METHODS FOR IMPROVING MOTOR PERFORMANCE

INTRODUCTION: In forming an understanding of training theory based on the principles of motor learning and motor programming, decisions must now be made on how to apply these principles to practice organization. This is accomplished by outlining the objectives to be achieved; deciding upon the nature of the skills to be trained; and planning the appropriate learning environment. In planning an effective learning environment, the task to be executed (skills to be learned) and the principles by which they are taught must be analyzed to narrow practice focus and establish an efficient learning structure.

The most important premise in developing a training program is that players gain the ability to retain, recall and execute volleyball skills, with a reasonable degree of perfection, as a result of their practice efforts (Young). In other words, if the objective is to develop and teach specific skills to be retained for future performance, it is imperative that a practice structure be established that trains not only skill execution, but also skill retention and recall. In fact, to insure long-term retention and recall capabilities, the training sessions must be based on the principles of motor learning and tailored to be as specific as possible to the actual game situations that will be experienced. Coaches constantly complain that, although their players performed hundreds of repetitions reasonably well in practice, it does not carry over to game situations. This problem is most likely one of repetition without learning and retention taking place. However, recent studies indicate that the failure to execute learned skills may be one of recall rather than retention.

What coaches think as the best way to learn athletic skills is often the reverse of what has been found by experts in motor development to be the most efficient learning process (Schmidt-Kluka). Repetition, repetition, repetition, as employed in most practice situations is not substantiated by laboratory research as the most efficient method of motor learning. Practice for efficient learning is more complicated than mere repetition, which, in fact, may actually be harmful to learning in some situations. Therefore, if practice is to be successful, the tasks to be learned must be organized in a manner that facilitates learning, skill retention and recall. What must be established is the capability to recall skills as needed under the varying conditions found in competitive situations, i.e., an environment that is constantly and randomly changing. Thus, block practice with constant repetition, i.e., the same skill repeated many times in succession, may not provide significant retention and recall capability for a skill to transfer from practice to a competitive game.

Perhaps a definition of performance and learning would help us better understand why players perform well in practice without learning taking place. Performance has been explained simply as observable behavior, i.e. what we see a person do when a skill is attempted such as hitting, spiking, passing, etc... Learning in contrast is an internal phenomenon that is un-observable and can only be inferred by changes observed in behavior during performance. In order to make generalizations and inferences about performance and learning several characteristics must be identified. First, if learning is to take place performance should show improvement over time; and second, performance (proper skill execution) must become more consistent and skill execution less variable. Therefore, it can be inferred that if performance during game situation does not show consistency and improvement, learning has not occurred. Too make this even more confusing, learning can occur even if performance does not show it in practice. This can probably be explained by the fact that lack of motivation, boredom and fatigue often reduce the ability to perform in practice but may not stop learning (Schmidt).

MOTIVATION/GOAL SETTING/REINFORCEMTENT: — Motor learning is a gradual, complex process of change in movement patterns that can be enhanced by understanding the goal/s of the motor task to be performed and the improvement in movement that will result from achieving that goal. Although individual genetics cannot be changed, it may be possible to alter or control behavior and improve performance in certain situations, by modification of our value (behavioral) system through goal setting. Motor learning and performance are enhanced by the incentives that are created through goal setting and reinforcement. Thus, the higher the goal setting, motivation and positive reinforcement the greater the chance of learning taking place. Furthermore, goal setting and motivation may reduce the learning time needed to achieve skill acquisition by establishing direction and incentive.

Studies in motor learning suggest that motivated players learn faster and retain learned material longer (Schmidt-Young-Kluka). In volleyball, like all sports, there is a logical order of steps that must be followed to achieve a high level of intrinsic motivation. This order is fun, recognition or reward followed by self-actualized behavior (success). People usually involve themselves and remain motivated to participate in activities that are fun. Once an activity is no longer fun, learning and motivation decreases. For that reason, when a player reaches a certain level of performance ability, playing just for fun loses some of its interest and then recognition and reward become important devices for maintaining motivation. It must be noted, that reward and recognition provide only external motivation which is generally short lived and requires constant reinforcement. Therefore, to maintain and improve learning, the motivation to compete must eventually become self-actualized. To reach high levels of performance, self-actualizing behavior (the search for perfection) becomes the driving force behind the desire to perform.

GOAL ESTABLISHMENT: — An organized training and practice plan begins by outlining the overall goals to be achieved (Kluka-Young-Schmidt). As we have seen, goal setting enhances motivation, while, improving daily practice performance and drill execution. Therefore, effective goal development is a key factor in maintaining high performance standards that leads to an effective learning environment and successful skill acquisition. Goals that are specific, explicit, and measurable become more meaningful and achievable. Success and criterion goals should be established that are both challenging and attainable.

A goal-oriented practice that encompasses the specific objectives to be achieved, will provide focued learning and instruction. More specifically, each practice session should start by reflecting and focusing on individual and team areas that need improvement. This is best accomplished by reviewing daily team and individual training goals prior to the start of each practice. This action helps in mental preparation for that day's activities. Employing imagery techniques that mentally review the goals to be accomplished in the forthcoming practice has been shown to be a very effective learning and motivational tool. Furthermore, each training session should end with a review and evaluation of goal achievement. Reviewing success criteria helps in establishing new performance goals for up-coming practices. Player generated goals set the desired expectations while coaching goals determine the course of action and the means of attainment. High expectations established in a supportive climate allow players the freedom to be creative, to try, to fail, and to try again until success is achieved. The establishment of high individual expectations also forces the player to be accountable and responsible for his/her behavior and achievement (Lane).

VARIED PRACTICE: Research often indicates that organizing practice to develop consistent motor behavior could be achieved by practicing similar skills in a blocked form of practice. A blocked practice is one in which players practice the same skill with many repetitions. Once a motor program is developed players can then to begin practicing new skills under varied conditions. Although blocked practice is beneficial for inexperienced players in their initial performance trials, it becomes less affective in training automation and game like skills. However, research demonstrates that a combined blocked practice followed by random practice is best for sustaining retention, long term transfer and learning (Schmidt). It has been also concluded that maturity plays a significant role in the benefits received from random and varying practice. It seems that a blocked practice has little effect on learning and performance when decision-making and game-like situations are introduced that require instant analytical reasoning and critical thinking. Therefore, it must once again be emphasized that practice drills must be designed to include efficient match management, leadership and decision-making under varied and stressful conditions.

It is important to create a practice environment that demands diverse skills and repeated successful experiences that are similar but varied. By varying motor skills being taught during practice, players are able to link the skill being executed in one setting to other motor skills used in a different setting.

Variation in execution can be created by changing ball velocity, angle, direction, height and distance that closely resembles game performance. Thus, practicing in game-like situations where players must adapt to variation in the environment, random practice, enhances the retention of motor skills. For random practice to occur, drills must contain a minimum of three related skills (i.e. an attack drill must contain at least a pass, set and hit to be considered random. However, it must be emphasized that beginning players must develop an overall idea of how each skill should be executed in order for a varied-random practice to provide affective learning. Furthermore, when creating a practice environment that demands diverse skills be constantly repeated, it is important that experiences be provided that is varied but similar.

Questions are often asked, how much practice is too much and how should it be distributed within the practice time, in order for optimum learning to take place. To answer these questions, consideration must be given to the type of practice mass (no rest) or distributed practice (with rest intervals) will be used and when. Most research has concluded that learning is enhanced by interspersing intensive motor skill practice with moderate rest breaks (Schmidt). It seems that distributed practice aids neuromuscular innervations and long-term memory by providing time for the brain to adjust to change and make adjustments in body functions. Research further indicates that retention can be improved by mass or over-practice but can be negatively influence by the Law of Diminishing returns.

An additional, type of practice to be given significant considered is whole (teaching the whole skill) verses part practice (breaking the skill down into its various parts and practicing each part separately). However, research has concluded that part practice is best for beginning player or players having trouble executing the whole skill. Part practice is effective because of the limited information that needs to be processed. Part practice allows for alteration in speed and distance reducing the effects of temporal and spatial orientation. Possibly the best method of teaching a skill is the whole-part-whole method. In this process the player tries to execute the whole skill first to get a rudimentary idea of what the whole skill feels and looks like. Once this is achieved, the skill is then broken down into its various parts which are practice separately until a realistic degree of performance is achieved with each part. Once this is established, the parts are combined and practice as a whole making practice more game like in skill execution.

CHANGE: — In general, athletes change or modify their behavior - performance, only when they are forced to realize that the old responses to situations encountered are no longer productive (Braden). It has been concluded, that to maximize performance, players must respond automatically to situations as they arise in the playing environment. As players strive to compete at higher levels, the automatic responses that once brought desirable results frequently no longer work. For this reason, success at advanced stages of competition often necessitates that a player change and adapt to produce the new responses (skills) needed for efficient execution. Often, however, during an attempt to change, a loss of confidence occurs because changes in technique frequently result in unsuccessful execution and inadequate performance. The failure to achieve instant improvement creates a feeling of discomfort that hinders the desire to change. This loss of confidence causes players to return to the more reliable but less effective techniques they previously employed.

Ego appears to be the major psychological hindrance in the willingness to make the technical and tactical changes that lead to improvement. Internal forces restrict us when we are outside of our comfort zone. "Hey I was pretty good in high school and junior ball, so I don't want anyone messing with my arm swing" or "Man, I was better before I started using these new techniques" are statements often made by athletes who are having trouble with the changes required to improve skill execution. Unfortunately, victories or the feeling of success occur on occasion by sticking with what was previously known. This occasional success causes the continued use of poor technique for the fear of looking bad.

Regardless, the failure to change hinders the ability to push through that awkward, frustrating period needed to make the essential corrections that improve skill execution. It is, however, these technical improvements that will eventually allow performance to improve and increase the chances of sustained success. Change occurs when effort is made to accept feeling miserable after execution (that awkward feeling that accompanies the inability to execute effectively); because it's this mediocre feeling that accompanies learning new and advanced techniques that will eventually lead to higher levels of performance, achievement and success. Well, if not in the volleyball community, at least in the player's own mind.

Errors tend to occur at an increased rate when undertaking a change in performance technique. Making physiological changes in technique in order to reduce these errors is extremely difficult and painful because of the extended mental effort required to break long established muscle memory patterns, i.e. mental images. For instance, during practice, a player who has eliminated most of the incorrect extraneous and unnecessary movements when serving will often say, "Man, that doesn't feel right." This complaint occurs because muscle memory patterns (motor programs) are very strong and bad habits, once engrained, are hard to break.

Furthermore, working on a new skill such as the jump serve almost guarantees that execution will get worse before it gets better. The ability to execute a new skill with precision and confidence takes time and practice. Research suggests that it may take as many as 28 days and hundreds of correct repetitions to completely break a bad habit. Errors in performance occur because a player no longer has a handle on the old technique or complete control of the new technique. Consequently, in order to move to higher levels of play, an athlete must continue to keep at it long enough to get a kinesthetic feeling for the new technique:

Beyond actual change, a major challenge for a coach in achieving effective motor learning and skill acquisition is how to control the unpredictability of a player's reaction to the new and different circumstances as they arise during performance. The objective is to assist the athlete in reorganizing his/her point of view (values-perceptions) to fit more closer to reality (the actual situation) as it an happens. Therefore, to eliminate this unpredictability and resistance to change, an environment must be created in which new skill learning can occur and behavior modified without the loss of self-esteem until the skill execution can be perfected.

Because the perception of a situation varies among individuals, the information to be processed must be perceived as important to the individual performer if change is to take place. In other words, to change our point of view (interpretation or perception of a situation), the desired changes must be meaningful and relevant to the goals of the learner. Moreover, volleyball players must be convinced that learning follows a cyclical pattern and that in the early periods of skill development or attempts to improve an old skill, a temporary drop in performance will typically occur. In other words, to reduce a resistance to change, a player must be assured that his/her initial poor performance was not a result of the technical changes instituted, but probably due to a combination of the following factors:

- The Difference in timing or the addition of other environmental factors.
- Muscles, when being retrained, are unable to respond efficiently resulting in periods of poor performance.
- The conscious effort required to change and develop new motor skills will not achieve a great deal of success until the muscles can react with automatic reflex responses.

To achieve the best results, a coach should reassure an athlete that improvement and success can only be achieved by multiple, correct repetitions taking place over time. Likewise, it must be emphasized that a player's performance will eventually improve and surpass his/her current level of ability with continued correct technical execution and lots of quality internal and external feedback.

The objective of participating in a volleyball training program is generally based on the following factors: 1) to learn about the game; 2) to become a better volleyball player; and 3) to HAVE FUN. Fun comes with improvement, success and winning. You have never heard anyone complain by saying "Nuts I won again today." But, success and winning often require behavioral modification, in addition to technical adjustment. Change, in turn, requires commitment and discipline. Failure to charge or adapt to a dynamic new way of executing a skill or tactic, is a major physiological and psychological reason many players don't improve. On the other hand, the willingness to make positive changes in performance behavior may make them renowned in the annals of volleyball history.

SKILL MODELING: — in efficient learning, images are better than words; showing is better than telling, and too much verbal instruction may reduce learning. The first concern in teaching a skill is to ensure that the athletes are alert, motivated and ready to accept instruction. However, verbal explanations alone slows learning because the learner must remember the verbal images accurately, process the verbal information into visual images (pictures in the mind) and make an accurate connection while executing the desired skill.

The objective of modeling (demonstration/explanation) of a volleyball technical or tactical skill is to process for storage in Short Term Memory a clear mental image of correct execution. This is obtained through observation and the accompanying verbal feedback. Modeling is used to create the visual images that: first, allows learning to take place with images rather than words, and second, influences improvement of performance through body imitation. Modeling is most effective when an athlete is able to develop a mental image of the skill to be executed and can closely mimic the model. A model of performance is formulated and internalized when a performer can reflect on his or her sensory feedback information (visual, verbal or auditory) and compare it with the knowledge of the results concerning performance. In simple terms; a motor program begins to develop as a performer internalizes a model of acceptable performance.

Modeling, accompanied by a brief verbal explanation before skill execution, is an excellent instructional method and motor learning technique. The skill to be modeled should be demonstrated and explained by using short key words that emphasize the main execution points. Verbal cues enhance learning and encourage selective attention when they condense information, reduce words and provide a mental picture of the desired action. Verbal effectiveness is further increased if cue words are concise, frequently used expressions that are distinctive and colorful. Meanwhile, retention of movement is improved when verbal cues attach labels to specific movements.

The three-step-approach when initiating the attack will characterize the use of key words in relation to skill modeling. In explaining execution of the three-step-approach concise verbal cues must be presented that enhances the key points of: (1) right foot forward, (2) left/right, (3) together, (4) pendulum arm swing and (5) jump etc. provide excellent, concise verbal cues that can be used in conjunction with an approach model. In other words, key words are most effective when they depict good skill execution and correct performance movement. A simplified verbal explanation of serve execution could consist of three key words: step, toss and hit.

The following are several important key factors to consider when learning through modeling:

- The beginning and ending positions of the skill being modeled are the easiest aspect of movement to be remembered. Put your big guns here.

- Demonstrations should be frequent at the beginning of practice to instill the proper technique. thereafter, periodic demonstrations should be given that reinforce the image in LTM.

- Demonstrate skills from various positions so that the learner observes the model from varying angles and viewpoints.

- Demonstrate the technique under an assortment of varying conditions.

- The use of visualization immediately after a model demonstration may help reinforce a mental picture of correct skill execution.

- Skill execution should follow as soon after modeling as possible to insure retention in STM.

- A skill review in which the skill practiced is mimicked by each player should also take place at end of practice session to help consolidate learning and motor development.

GUIDANCE TECHNIQUES: The guidance techniques that can be used in teaching motor skills are visual, verbal or neuromuscular. Providing visual guidance means that instruction to athletes is based on a visual model in which you ask the athletes to do exactly what they see. Visual guidance requires that the participants have a clear view of the demonstration, that movement is performed rather slowly and that athletes immediately mimic the exact actions of the model. Feedback is provided to correct errors as they occur with an athlete immediately repeating the corrected action. Verbal pre-training provides an excellent method of combining timing cues for complex skill training. Verbal pre-training is the application of simple word cues-labels that help remind the athlete of what to do when executing a skill. During verbal guidance, athletes are asked to do exactly what is being verbalized. Although the cues presented can be either literal or figurative, they must be simple and clear. This enables an athlete to rehearse the skill verbally before execution. The cue words presented must be simple, direct labels that describe the movement or positions to be assumed by an athlete during execution.

Often, a verbal or visual model will not present sufficient understanding of image correctness to be an effective learning device. When this is the case, player manipulation, moving or guiding the player through the correct movement can be productive in establishing an accurate kinetic image or feel of the skill being executed. This is especially true for beginning players and slow learners. Manual manipulation and touching have been shown to produce educationally positive results and conveys a coach's personal interest in the player's improvement. Verbal cues along with manipulation are probably more effective than manipulation alone. However, there is one drawback to guidance techniques. This technique, if used too frequently may reduce the player's ability to evaluate his/her own execution when the coach is not present.

SPECIFICITY: — The law of specificity states that a reduction or simplification of the amount of information that must be processed by an athlete speeds learning. In skill development, specificity training limits the number of environmental cues a player needs to interpret, reduces the possibility of negative transfer and improve attention focus by boosting the ability to concentrate. Specialization in training is particularly important when practicing high speed activities that are similar to game situations. Creating and maintaining a high level of performance during competition, requires that the exact responses needed for success be isolated and practiced, specifically, those tasks essential to the position played. That is, the specific cues to be attended in game-like situations, must also be present during practice.

Specificity is achieved in volleyball with game-like drills and physical training activities that include specialized practice in the exact position to be played. When training for specificity, there are three components that must be considered: neuromuscular, position and energy specificity. Neuromuscular training must include the muscle groups and the muscle recruitment patterns required of the overall skills executed in the game of volleyball. The factors of spatial-temporal relationships and the force patterning to be learned should be considered along with the environmental factors present in game situations. Secondly, due to genetic factors, not all players possess the ability to execute all skills with equal proficiency and perfection. For this reason, training must be specialized to match each individual's ability to perform the specific skills of the positions played. Neuromuscular reactions are developed relative to the speed, trajectory and movement of the incoming ball and in relation to the specific foot, arm and body movement required of the position played. Consequently, players are able to concentrate on fewer tasks, resulting in better individual performance. Specificity in volleyball can best be illustrated by the development of the lebero who specializes in passing and defense.

The importance of serve receive accuracy in volleyball illustrates the need to train skills specific to the game and the position played. This means that, players who possess better passing skills become primary passers and focus their attention to the skills involved in passing. Assigning additional practice time to the skills to be learned and performed that are position specific will provide players with more repetitions at the skills of that position. This enables primary passers to get more practice at the skills needed to become even better passers. Similarly, those players who have limited passing ability can spend time practicing those skills at which they excel. For example, attackers who are relieved of passing responsibility are now free to concentrate this practice time on practicing their attack skills.

Finally, performance and learning are enhanced, if training is specific to the metabolic energy systems required to perform volleyball skills (aerobic/anaerobic). Two energy systems come into play in anaerobic training: activities of about ten-to-twenty-five seconds that depend on phosphates for energy and activities of ninety seconds to three minutes that require glucose to produce energy with the end result being a build-up of lactic acid. Although volleyball, is mainly an anaerobic energy system activity (training without oxygen) the aerobic energy system (training with oxygen) should be established first to provide a basis for anaerobic training. As a result, of training both the aerobic and anaerobic systems is important to optimal performance and therefore must be trained during practice. Aerobic energy training requires a continuous action of at least three to five minutes and depends on oxygen as the main source of energy. Once aerobic fitness has been achieved, the main aspect of training should be on anaerobic development. Training for anaerobic fitness in volleyball should consist of short intense periods of activity specific to the sport follow by a brief active rest period.

OVER LEARNING: — A relatively permanent change in motor behavior (performance) takes place and new motor programs developed and reinforced when skills are practiced repetitively over time. Research indicates that practicing at the same intensity over prolonged periods (mass correct repetitions) will significantly aid retention, but may only slightly improve performance. In fact, the importance of a high number of repetitions (over learning) may not be that it increases the permanence of skill acquisition but that it enhances performance by improving confidence and self-reliance in the ability to perform. However, the law of diminishing returns comes into effect with over learning and mass repetitions. There is a point in repetitive practice where the effort extended is greater than the learning that takes place. Therefore, the result of continued execution at this point becomes inefficient in light of time limitations and the ability to maintain effective concentration.

More importantly, an increased practice-to-time ratio can probably be achieved more efficiently by other methods of training. Remember, that the average effective concentration span for most players is about 15 to 20 minutes. With this in mind, it becomes evident, that continued practice of a specific skill, such as blocking, beyond this time period maybe less effective. However, to maintain motivation and learning a coach can change to a different drill in which blocking is a main component.

WHOLE-PART-WHOLE LEARNING. — Transfer of learning in volleyball may occur with either part-by-part practice of discrete skills (skill with a distinct beginning and end) and/or by the whole method of learning (training a series of related skills). The part method for skill learning divides the whole task into parts that are practiced separately until all parts are well learned. Once these parts can be executed separately, they are combined and practiced as a whole until the complete skill is learned. For example, the serve can be broken down into the toss, weight transfer, arm swing and ball contact segments that can be practiced separately. Research indicates that this procedure is most advantageous in early skill learning that has a high degree of complexity, a low organizational structure and consisting of parts that are highly independent. That is, part learning should probably be used when the skills are so complex that practicing in the whole method in early motor learning is very difficult or nearly impossible. For instance, when teaching advanced set techniques stationary set ability should probably be perfected before instituting the jump set.

Although part learning can be an effective learning tool, most of practice time should be in the whole method for skill learning (continued practice of the complete skill or a series of skills) executed in a game-like series. Practicing a task by using the whole method of learning appears to work best if the tasks to be learned are highly organized, intimately related and of low complexity. Attack tactics and team floor defense are examples of highly organized skills that can be learned efficiently by applying the whole method of learning. Intelligence, maturity and experience should be a contributing factor when determining whether to use the whole or part method. Evidence seems to indicate that players of high intelligence, an abundance of previous experiences and physical and mental maturity obtain greater benefits from practicing the skill as a whole.

With the above in mind when training volleyball skills, an effective method for learning a new complex skill or improving an existing skill could be through the whole-part-whole method. The objective-advantage of this process is that it teaches those aspects of a game that form a natural sequence of action and that have dependently formed parts (pass, set, hit)Training by the whole-part-whole method is capable of providing the best results with skills that can be practiced in any order or practiced separately. For example, the block can be taught as a whole skill or divided into the separate skills of movement, jump, arm action, etc. In this method, the whole skill is reviewed through an appropriate demonstration model that shows the skill component and qualities of movement (i.e., the precision in skill execution, the speed of movement, the force of the motor act, as well as body parts to be moved), This demonstration is followed immediately by each player performing a rough approximation of the skill/s in their entirety. After the complete skill has been introduced, it is then broken down into a sequence of related segments e.g. movement, jump, body and arm position that are practiced separately. Once these segments are methodically learned, they are then re-combined and practiced as a whole skill, hence the term whole-part-whole learning.

Research (Schmidt) suggests that at advanced levels, the greatest learning may take place when a series of inter-related skills are practiced as they occur in game situation. In keeping with the whole-part-whole method of learning, a series of skills can be practiced together, i.e. pass, set and hit, then broken down and practiced as an individual skill, i.e. passer's pass, setter's set, etc, and then reassembled and practiced as a series. Better still those players having difficulty with an individual skill, e.g., the pass, during team game-like situations can be isolated (removed from the drill) and allowed to practice that skill until perfected and then reinserted into the existing drill. This procedure retains drill continuity of execution, while the player having difficulty passing can receive individual instruction. Having observed the USA National Team (that was victorious in the Olympics) practice on many occasions, this seem to be a teaching method used on many occasions.

In concluding this section, a brief discussion should be made about progression. If learning is to be most efficient then simple progressions must be made that organizes material from simple thoughts and movements to those that are more complex. This is especially important in the introductory phase of learning when players can become overwhelmed and confused if techniques and explanations are beyond their ability to comprehend. Let's look at a simple to complex series of progression in teaching attack techniques. i.e., the approach, jump, arm swing, jump timing, ball contact and landing. A simple progression could be to execute this skill off a simple toss to a setter at the net by a coach. Once the skills mentioned have been perfected and become somewhat automatic, the more difficult progression would consist of teaching the seven basic, but most important, skills of the attack after a set from a serve reception to a passer who passes to the setter followed by a set to an attacker. The next progressions would be to execute the attack against a block, execution of multiple attack skills and finally the complete progression of execution in a game-like team situation.

LEARNING INDICATORS: The following are some indicators that can use to determine to determine if learning is taking place.

LEARNING OCCURS WHEN:
- Correct motor programs are recalled
- Skill is executed correctly and the outcome is successful
- Performance show improvement over time
- Improvement becomes more consistent
- Less errors occur
- Reduction in variation in execution
- Skills become generalized and automatic
- Develop a kinesthetic sense (KP-KR)

NO LEARNING OCCURS WHEN:
- Skill executed as planned but errors occur
- When attention is directed at the wrong sensory cues

- Information processing is incorrect
- Wrong motor program recalled but executed correctly
- Wrong motor program recalled and executed incorrectly

SUMMARY

Although coaching (teaching) can have an effect on individual physical performance and skill acquisition, the most effective learning takes place in a "preferred environment." A preferred environment creates an atmosphere in which the athletes with or without the coach's intervention, interact to effect learning and change. A preferred environment produces success by providing good role models, consistent experiences, and exceptional situations that allow an athlete to make quality informed decisions. By providing a multitude of superior experiences, a preferred environment creates situations in which an athlete increases skill learning through cooperation and discovery.

Since the ability to perform a skill is only indirectly related to the information and knowledge possessed, the most effective learning takes place when the coach, as a teacher, becomes an organizer, synthesizer and facilitator of knowledge rather than a mere dispenser of information. A successful coach provides an athlete with an organized structure or systematic arrangement of independent information and shows its relationship to the whole. By breaking down the elements of coordination from the complex to the simple, the coach synthesizes instruction so that it can be easily conceptualized. More specifically, skill acquisition is eased by the coach reducing the many factors involved in executing complicated motor programs. Therefore, the role of coaching is to improve motor learning by providing better volleyball experiences — in addition to dispensing more information.

The process of how we learn is believed to be as important as the product of learning. In fact, the coach who understands and uses the principles of motor learning in the education of his/her players, produces players who can think critically, evaluate their surroundings correctly, process information efficiently, and apply the skills learned to a variety of situations as they occur. The most efficient motor learning and thus performance occurs if the following principles of learning are adhered to during training. First, the law of readiness concludes that technical and tactical training must be commensurate with the level of ability and that readiness for training is mostly influenced by the factors of intelligence, experience and physical maturity.

The second, the law of effect suggests that learning takes place with greater efficiency when training experiences are pleasurable. Success creates the best learning situation when based on positive reinforcement and expected individual behavior. Finally, the law of exercise stipulates that exercise should be frequent for effective motor learning and training. Therefore, to be effective, training must, at the very least, consist of 65 percent active learning with non-active learning activities such as instruction, non-participation and rest kept to a minimum. Moreover, excessive conditioning that produces "extreme exhaustion" should take place at the end of practice so that learning is not restricted by fatigue. Several short periods of training are generally better than one long period, and the intensity of exercise must build to peak periods during practice. On the whole, a practice that ends on a positive note during a peak period produces the best training results.

Motor learning and skill execution require that an athlete perceive the environment correctly, attend to the right sensory cues and select an appropriate plan-of-action. Performance will not result in efficient motor learning if skills are conducted as planned but movement in execution is incorrect. Learning will also not occur if the skill execution is correct but the outcome of performance is unsuccessful. However, learning will take place if skills are performed as planned and executed correctly with a successful outcome. If information regarding skill execution is to be processed most efficiently, it should take place before the event. Skill correction and opponent analysis must also be given before or immediately after skill execution. Information presented during skill learning and execution tends to overload the player, reduce automatic responses, and thereby generate ineffective performance.

Consequently, coaches who holler instructions to players prior to or during skill execution only create confusion and hinder the ability to focus, relax and act reflectively. In addition, constant communication with players during a break in the action and during a time out overload players with information, which further diminishes performance. Perhaps, just a simple "we need a pass to get a side out" or "lets run middle X in transition" provide simple cues that will most likely result in successful skill execution once play has resumed.

Finally, perceptual efficiency in learning a skill is best achieved by reducing the task to be performed to its simplest and most productive form. Because information-receiving involves differentiating, identifying and recognizing from a variety of informational cues, practice and skill training must proceed from the most basic to the most difficult. More specifically, reception of small amounts of stimuli creates the best learning conditions for skill acquisition by simplifying the environment. Learning is further increased and training is more efficient if concise phrases or key words are used to explain skill execution.

For example, when designing learning procedures large amounts of information must be dealt with gradually from the simple to the complex. Brevity is best. Explaining serve execution with the words: "step, toss and hit" might better facilitate learning than a lengthy discourse such as "step to the target with the left foot, shift your body weight from the rear to the front foot, toss the ball 18 inches above the right shoulder, etc." This reduction of complex ideas into their simplest form prevents mental overloading during practice thereby improving skill learning, execution and performance while enhancing retention and recall ability.

Understanding how the motor system works and how skills are learned is important to both the player and coach if their objective is to maximize performance in highly competitive and stressful situation. Information to be useful must be both practical and applicable to the sport. If volleyball training is to be most efficient, competent skills must be taught and effective drills must be developed to meet the demands of competition. This requires a basic understanding of the scientific principles of motor learning and the biomechanics of human movement. For, if the scientific principles of skill acquisition are not instituted, training becomes merely trial and error learning which is unproductive in time expenditure and often leads to poor skill learning.

Simply put, two things seem to occur in preparation for executing a specific skill. This process requires a perception and selection of the appropriate data (what to attend to), an interpretation on how to process this data (what to do) and decision making (executing the skill) determines the action to be taken. This procedure results in a recall of an existing (correct) motor program for execution. New learning will occur if the results of performance feedback indicate that changes should be made. Based on the results of performance and feedback the existing motor program is reinforced or a new and more generalized motor program is developed. This modification of the existing motor program is retained in the nervous system to be recalled as needed.

Research performed by Dr. Sian Beilock of the University of Chicago found that thinking in great detail during performance is a recipe for poor skill execution. Extra time spent thinking gives a player extra time to screw up and gets in the way of what he should be doing. His research using brain scans found that when thinking too much about skill execution allows the prefrontal cortex, located just above the eyes, to begin controlling our conscious awareness and often screws up things that should be left to happen outside of consciousness.

Dr. Beilock's research found that players who have perfected and automated skill execution can overcome this problem of attending to much detail by reducing the free time between points. He concluded that by establishing relative short routines, such as a pre-service, actually hastens the action and prevents conscious thought from impeding unconscious execution. However, having reach these conclusion for the experienced player, it was concluded that inexperienced players need additional time to think about execution when trying to learn and prefect the movements needed for effective skill execution.

CHAPTER 5

Designing a Practice Session

INTRODUCTION

Training success in volleyball is based on understanding the principles of motor learning, physiology, sports psychology and biomechanics and the ability to relate them to the player development. Efficient training occurs when a player can control the sequences of movement needed to complete the tasks (skills) demanded by the situation confronted. The experience, ability and insight of the coach are important in deciding what skills to teach and drills to use at the various stages of motor skill development and learning. Efficient practice design should also consider when a player is ready to progress to the next stage of development. Furthermore, when working with individuals as well as the team, consideration must be given to differences in player ability and learning styles. The type of practice and motivational level will determine how an individual and the team obtain volleyball ability. This in turn will the influence the amount of practiced trials needed, the rate and level of learning achieved by the performer.

Practice organization and drill design must accomplish three basic objectives needed for successful skill execution and application to be achieved. The first objective is to train players to effectively execute the motor skills of volleyball, i.e., sound mechanical technique, so that attention can be directed to the tactical execution in relation to the ball and the opponent. This includes the ability to:

- Control speed and accuracy in execution.
- Ability to automate execution.
- Execute under random and varying conditions.

Second, motor skills must be consistently applied to the requirements of competition. The ability to apply motor skills to the demands presented by game situations:

- The ability to quickly perceive and select relevant data.
- The appropriate choice of tactics/strategies (decisions).
- The skill to adapt tactics to circumstances as they occur in an ever changing environment (plan-of- action).
- The talent to select and perform the correct motor program with imagination and creativity.

In volleyball, game condition and rules limit the ability of a coach to intervene and control situations that occur during play. Once an athlete becomes involved in a game, he/she must have the ability to manipulate the variables of: concentration, self-control, movement correction and the ability to adapt to changing situations as they occur. Therefore, the techniques and tactics to be used in competition must be trained in practice if positive results are to be achieved. For example, it's absurd to require disciplined behavior and proper execution of a player, when his/her first encounter with such demands is during a match. Therefore, all forms of game behavior must be taught and practiced prior to match play under similar stressful conditions found in competition. Otherwise, what you get are players who execute with style and technique during warm-up but fail to measure up under conditions of stress.

This was evident in the 1996 NCAA women's volleyball championships, as a group of coaches attempted to determine the outcome of each match by who won the warm-up (looked the best). The subjective results were that there seemed to be little correlation between who performed well during the warm-up period and the outcome of the match.

The third factor in practice organization is psychological preparation that develops the correct mental attitudes, behavioral patterns and characteristics that will lead to improved individual performance and team success. The coach is the architect of a progressive process that outlines a rational and systemic approach to the game. The objective is to establish mental guidelines that bring players to a point where they can perform to their maximum ability at the appropriate moment during competition.

There are five factors that need to be considered in developing a well-planned program of instruction: (1) **inventory** — determines the present physical and mental ability of the team to select a starting point (Arnot-Gaines); (2) **forecasting** — outlines the objectives and determines the expected performance goals; **(3) planning for instruction**— selects the subject matter to be taught i.e., skills and tactics; **(4) implementation** — establishes a plan to achieve the desired goals, i.e., drills and practice agenda; and (5) **control** — assesses training effectiveness by measuring performance improvement, i.e., analysis and evaluation of performance execution during practice and match play.

In developing a practice plan, a coach **inventories** present conditions (i.e., technical/tactical experience level|/physical development etc.) of individual players before attempting to teach a new technique or change an incorrect technique. In attempting to modify an existing skill or instilling a new execution procedure, several researchers (Martins/Doldge) have suggested that a coach should consider the following factors when modifying technique:

- Is the present technique unsuccessful?
- Would continued use of the technique lead to injury?
- Is the technique being used cosmetically embarrassing?

Before instruction begins, the coaching staff should determine (inventories) each player's present state of development (readiness) and experience level (maturity) by reviewing the length of previous training and competitive experiences both as a starter and as a substitute. This would not only include the length of previous training, but the level of participation and type of competition by both starters and substitutes. Additional information about a player's ability level can be obtained by reviewing physical and psychological test results and by subjective and objective evaluation of individual technical and tactical skill performance. Maturity, more than age, has been shown to be an important indicator when determining readiness to learn and perform. In setting the goal or objective of instruction, a list of each player's strengths and weaknesses will help in deciding which skills need the most work and their respective order of importance. To determine the training needs of a team. Information must be gathered and evaluated in terms of the factors that most affect a team's performance. This is obtained by taking into account the physical attributes of speed, strength, size, in addition to mental ability (intelligence, behavioral factors, etc.) in performing volleyball skills (Spooner).

Having determined the relative performance ability and experience of each individual player and the team as a whole, a **forecast** is made to estimate possible season's accomplishments and objectives. These objectives should be outlined in specific performance statements that determine the conditions, standards and tasks necessary for accomplishing individual and team goals. Standards (performance goals) establish the training conditions and tasks necessary to achieve the performance success goals.

PLANNING AND ORGANIZATION FOR INSTRUCTION

This section includes the selection of subject matter (skills) and instructional methods (drills) that will allow for optimum development of individual motor abilities and team tactics. Having determined the skills to be taught, an outline of the needed skill and drill progressions can be resolved so that instruction can be organized into a meaningful context that runs from simple to complex. In addition to the mental and physical factors that affect performance, consideration should be given to age, gender and playing experience. Identifying these factors is crucial in determining the type and amount of training required to achieve the chosen goals.

A logical progression of activities should be developed that matches the ability and fitness of each athlete with the activities planned. In addition to school work, consideration should be given to employment requirements, social activities and personal needs when making training decisions. For example, in-depth concern should be given to the demands on time and individual needs of beginning players in comparison to advanced players. Outside activities will take longer and be harder to resolve for inexperienced players. Extensive consideration must also be given to the season, time in season and the caliber of the opponent when planning for instruction.

Table 1

General Athletic Factors That Influence Success In Volleyball

When developing an efficient volleyball training program, the physical and mental factors required for successful performance must be identified, evaluated and programmed into practice organization. Player evaluation serves three distinct functions: first, as a source of motivation for the individual athlete and team; second, to discover the present level of fitness and ability; and third, to detect and select the best athlete. This can be determined by measurement of data that pertain to actual athletic proficiency. The following is a brief outline of the basic factors that must be considered in effective player training and development. Page 71 contains a form for calculating general athletic factors.

MUSCULAR ABILITY	ARTICULO-MUSCULAR RANGE - FLEXIBILITY
• Jumping ability (height-quickness-timing) • Strength • Power	• Back/forward stretch • Attacking arm flexibility
PERCEPTIVE-KINETIC QUALITIES • Coordination/agility/balance • Motor precision • Speed of reaction/movement • Temporal orientation	• VISION • Acuity • Convergence • Binocularity • Eye dominance
ATIAL ORIENTATION • Hand-eye coordination • Court orientation • Ball to body relationship • Ball to court relationship • Body to court relationship	ANTHROPOMETRIC DATA • Height • Weight • Standing reach • Percentage body fat
MOVEMENT PATTERNS • Upright movement • Low movements • Lateral movements • Foot patterns	ORGANIC ENDURANCE • Aerobic fitness • Anaerobic fitness

Anot/Gaines

IMPLEMENTATION OF AN INSTRUCTIONAL PLAN: Pre-practice (prior to actual skill execution) information should be provided vocally and by demonstration that contains general rules and movements require in executing a skill. A performer must have an idea (mental picture) of how to execute a skill and a frame of reference of correctness in order to evaluate performance. An instructional plan begins by combining the planned instructional methods (drills) with a tentative practice and competitive schedule in order to instill the desired behavioral patterns at the appropriate time. The skills and tactics to be taught must be implemented and adapted into a system of play that fits into individual as well as the team's ability to achieve. In addition to what is to be taught and practiced, this schedule determines when instruction is to take place and the time allotted for each practice situation. Factors to be accounted for are training load, number of training days, the caliber of the opponent and most importantly the stage of development of the individual players and team. Also included in this instructional plan, is the development and preparation of the practice site and securing needed equipment. Safety should also be built into an instructional plan. Periodization is an excellent means for implementing the goals of instruction. **See Table # 1 General Factors the influence Success**

CONTROLLING THE PRACTICE ENVIRONMENT: In controlling the practice environment, it is essential to maximize time and the content of each practice. This is accomplished through analysis and evaluation of the effectiveness of each practice session. Maximization of the training process requires a constant measurement, analysis and evaluation of performance results as compared with the established goals. A controlled practice environment allows a coach to compare present performance with preseason expectations as a means of determining areas of progress, which can lead to reducing deviations and gaps in planning, and to adjust training time. This organization will allow for deficiencies and problems that arise in technical and tactical execution to be corrected as they occur.

ESTABLISHING A PRACTICE ATMOSPHERE

The season in progress (pre, competitive, or offseason) will determine the objectives (what needs to be learned), the content (what is to be taught) and the organizational structure (how it is to be presented). These factors will vary in importance depending upon the requirements of each training season, restrictions placed on specific training periods by various governing bodies and upon player needs. For example, the preseason will have a different time frame, organizational structure and goals, etc., when compared with the other training seasons. As a result of these factors, a coach should be meticulously prepared for each training period by designing a well-organized seasonal, weekly, and daily plan that describes a course of action and reinforces the desired behaviors.

ORGANIZATION: — Research demonstrates that athletes cannot function under conditions of peak performance 100 percent of the time. Furthermore, it should be noted that volleyball players will probably only peak about 5-6 times during the competitive season. Thus, it is imperative that a yearly training and competition plan be organized that will maximize team and player effort when it is most needed. In today's highly competitive game of volleyball, there is a constant demand for more practice time. With this in mind, a yearly, weekly and daily time frame should be developed so that each training period meets the time need and the allotments allowed.

Weekly and daily plans should be revised or upgrade existing plans at the beginning of each new practice week that sets forth the daily activities and is designed in increments that achieve intermediate and long term seasonal goals. A weekly practice schedule should be arranged and organized mainly for maximum skill instruction and behavior modification within the time allotted to each practice situation. All functions to be included in a weekly and daily practice time frame must be outlined with a precise organizational design, routines, and discipline. The first consideration of design is to determine each player's strengths and weaknesses and what the coach can or cannot control.

Examples of factors a coach cannot control are: facilities and equipment limitations, time, player availability and inherent physical ability. However, consideration must be given to these components before an efficient time frame and practice content can be adopted. The components in determining what a player can or cannot do might consist of his/her:

- Physical capacity to perform.
- Technical ability.
- Tactical knowledge.
- Competitive and mental behavior (motivation).
- Knowledge of game theory.
- Past volleyball experiences.

Periodization as a system for organizing practice and competitive activities is an excellent method for planning the total volleyball year and provides the best chance of goal achievement. By careful planning for the important events, a coach not only determines when he/she wants a team to peak, but can also reduce the risk of injury and psychological burnout, i.e., training and competing under constant and intense pressure. Periodization can also be used to organize individual practice sessions as a means of controlling physical fitness and technical skill acquisition while reducing the chance of injury, boredom, and loss of motivation. Progress in physical performance, requires efficient skill acquisition, improved learning of advanced tactical strategies, and the execution of many correct repetitions. Individual players should strive for uninterrupted training that extends over the entire year. The lack of some sort of year-round planned volleyball or cross training will result in a decrease in performance in the areas of physical ability, technique, will power and mental toughness. In addition, a full concentration on the most important points, analysis of performance, error detection and correction, and frequent rests are required. This is accomplished by establishing a training load that can be adjusted to each individual's capacity to perform thereby maintaining a balance between training load and recovery. Periodization allows for this adjustment in training load.

Periodization sets aside active recovery periods to take place at several occasions throughout the year. An active recovery period should occur for about four weeks at the end of the competitive season and for about six to eight weeks at the end of the spring training season. These relatively long periods are set aside after the end of both the competitive and spring seasons to allow the body and mind to recover and re-generate. This concept breaks the volleyball year down into four phases: preparation, pre-competition, competition and the off-season periods. Each phase will vary in length depending on the restrictions imposed by the various governing bodies, facility availability, and the particular needs of the program. Through yearly periodization, an efficient volleyball training plan can be developed that controls the duration, intensity, frequency, and content of individual and team workouts and competitive events. In this way peak performance effort can be achieved for the most important in-seasons competitions. Since coaches must work under the rules set-down by most governing bodies; in some instances, team organized off-season volleyball specific training often cannot be required.

Preparation is a phase of training that consists of a short period allotted for organized individual and team physical training and technical development. The main purpose of the preparatory period is characterized by providing both team and individual player time to prepare, on their own or in small groups, physically and mentally for the up-and-coming pre-competitive and competitive seasons. Training during this period consists of developing physical fitness and strength while reviewing basic technical skills. This is the time to make necessary technical changes as well as perfecting and automating existing skills. In addition, technically, this is the time to reestablish kinetic, spatial and temporal skills and to develop a strong aerobic base so that anaerobic development can be the fore most point of emphasis during the pre-competitive season. Furthermore, individual as well as team benefits will be derived from the increase in physical fitness (strength and endurance) and the technical skill improvement developed in the preparation phase of training.

The pre-competition season should be divided into two phases of training: In the first phase emphasis is placed on individual and team technical training, in addition to continued physical conditioning. Sprint training works good here. If new tactics are to be instituted during the coming competitive season, they should be introduced at this time to both new and returning players. It's important to remember that the intensity and type of training during the preparation and pre-competition period has significant effects on the ability to perform at high levels during the competitive season. Although previously learned skills are re-introduced at this time, new technical and tactical skills should be the main point of emphasis. The main focus of this practice period is to achieve perfection of technical skills in preparation for the start of the formal phase of the pre-competitive season.

The formal phase of the pre-competitive training period consists of highly organized individual and team practice. Strength training should begin to taper off as the competitive season approaches. Although the load is reduced, intensity can be increased. Aerobic training should also be greatly reduced so that more quality time can be devoted to training the volleyball specific anaerobic energy systems and for tactical skill development. Research indicates that well conditioned athletes can often maintain the status quo with just 2 or 3 days of intense physical training per week. The formal team pre-season is a most critical period for instilling the discipline, focus, cooperation and team spirit required to survive during periods of intense competition and fatigue. In a nutshell, this period not only provides technical and tactical preparation, it is also a time for developing the competitive instincts that are necessary to win conference and national championships. Several low pressure match dates should be scheduled as a means of practicing new skills, instilling competitive behaviors and evaluating individual and technical and tactical progress in game situations.

A **competitive season** is generally divided into three stages: non-league, league and post season play. Although winning is important, the main emphasis of the non-league stage is to prepare the team technically and tactically for league and post-season play, while continuing to prefect and make automatic those aspects of the game developed during the pre-season. Determining when to peak means analyzing the schedule to determine the most important events and adjusting training accordingly. Aerobic and strength training during this period is generally for maintenance.

This is the time when it is important to peak for certain major opponents. The ability to handle physical and psychological stress differs among athletes and must be given careful consideration when determining training load. This includes such factors as maturity, gender, type of nervous system, personal obligation, athletic capacity, skill level and health. These factors can interact to determine the length, amount, and intensity of training. Furthermore, adaptability and the ability to recover after long and arduous workouts, tournament and highly fatiguing individual matches must be considered when planning the load and recovery requirements of training. Considering these variations, it seems mandatory that the training load be diverse to meet the demands of individual training if performance is to be maximized. It would also appear sensible and beneficial in practice organization and player development to group players into working units according to their loading capacity, e.g., players who can handle higher training loads could be placed in positions that provide more intense repetitions. Likewise, starting players who are highly active during competition may need reduced loads at various times during training to allow for recovery. Meanwhile, substitutes and specialists can be given additional practice time due to the reduced playing time during matches.

Improvement in performance capacity requires that players be challenged - extended systematically with a steady increase in training load. Therefore, maximizing intensity and the amount and length of activity is indispensable to increasing performance capacity. Each practice must positively affect physical conditioning by creating fatigue that borders on exhaustion. However, research indicates that periods of high load to exhaustion must be followed by a sufficient period of active rest recovery. A problem exists in that research has not been able to determine what is the best time and length of an adequate rest interval. Research has also had a hard time in determining the affects of fatigue on motor skill learning. Several fatigue and performance studies (Schmidt-Young) indicate that the higher the level of fatigue the greater it affects performance. However, low to moderate levels of fatigue has little or no affect on learning but seems to decrease performance. Therefore, a coach must determine what aspects of performance are most affected by fatigue. Research indicates that speed is mostly affected by physical fatigue while accuracy is more impacted by mental/cognitive fatigue. Research further indicates that learning a new skill while exhausted can lead to inefficient and ineffective performance.

A training load consists of the amount, length and intensity of performance. Research indicates the higher the load, the longer the period needed to recover. Some research suggests that organism tends to recovers quicker under conditions of active recovery, i.e. some movement, rather than by complete inactivity. For example, at the completion of a very intensive drill that causes temporary fatigue, players seem to recover quicker in activities of a short interval with a minimum load. That is, in a spike and block transition drill, a quicker recovery will occur if the intense activities of spiking and blocking are followed by a short active rest period or a drill of low intensity such as the serve.

As the playing season progresses, the training load and practice structure increases in importance. If the objective is to have fresh players ready for peak performance during competition rather than in practice, then consideration must be given to the ratio of training load to practice time and effort. When preparing for single match play, the best ratio may be 1:1 that is one day maximum load followed by a day of low load. However, if a team is being prepared for extended tournament play perhaps a 2:1 ratio would produce optimum performance. Exercise physiologists seem to agree that the volume and intensity of the training load ought to relate to the type of activity stressed during competition. For example, if an up-coming competition requires that a skill should be stabilized and perfected then the coach should create controlled and diversified practice conditions. These conditions will force an athlete to continuously adapt physically, physiologically and psychologically, under game-like conditions with high volume and high intensity. Training at high levels of intensity and load are essential in developing the will power and physical fitness considered necessary to compete effectively at a high level. On the other hand, if the training session pertains to skill acquisition (motor learning) and tactical training a lower volume of repetitions of high intensity is probably best. Research indicates the 60 seconds rest intervals may provide adequate recovery.

The off-season is a time of active rest and recuperation in which a player should spend some time in physical activities other than volleyball, i.e. a period when no organized player training should take place. In addition to relaxation, these "active rest" periods are a time for cross training (e.g. participation in other sports such as tennis, soccer, and racquetball). It is also a period to re-assess personal and team progress to determine areas of weakness and strength in preparation for the up-and-coming pre and competitive seasons. Goals and plans can then be directed at re-building areas of weakness while improving areas of strength. This active rest period also offers an excellent time to read and study about volleyball. Although a period of relaxation and time away from volleyball is needed, overall physical fitness, aerobic conditioning and strength training should be intensified.

Intensive individual and team training should be reintroduced several weeks prior to the start of the formal team pre-season. As the pre-season approaches, players who want to maximize their ability and enhance their chance for success during the competitive season should set aside sufficient time to re-introduce themselves to physical conditioning and volleyball fundamentals. In addition to the need for cross training, there is a need to optimize individual strength (anaerobic) fitness. The preparation and off-season offers this opportunity.

With the time limitation placed on volleyball training, time management becomes one of the most encompassing factor in developing a successful training plan and will determine to what extent performance can be maximized. Murphy's Law states that "everything takes longer than expected". Therefore, a team must maximize every opportunity to seek improvement by never wasting a day, an hour, or a minute of training time. Practice activities are limited to the time available and based on the amount of time that can be controlled by the coach. Usually, time will be limited to the restrictions imposed by the national governing body, league and/or school, and by facility availability. Daily practice time is generally organized in 2.5 and 3.0 hour blocks and varies with the season in progress and the stage of training. Time utilization can be monitored by developing a time analysis chart to determine the optimum length of time needed to cover all aspects of training and to maximize quality effort **(See Table # 2 Practice Time Analysis)**

TABLE 2

TIME ANALYSIS CHART				
PRACTICE PERIOD				
Preseason: Date to / Time to				
Pre-league: Date to / Time to				
League: Date to / Time to				
ACTIVITY	PRE-SEASON	PRE-LEAGUE	LEAGUE	POST-SEASON
DRESS/THERAPY/ TAPING	Player Specific	Player Specific	Player Specific	Player Specific
DAILY GOAL SETTING/IMAGERY	10 min	10 min	10 min	10 min
DISCUSSION/TEAM MEETING	10-15 min	10-15 min	10-15 min	10-15 min
WARM UP • Movement • Stretch • Skill Activity	15 min	15 min	15 min	15 min
TECHNICAL DRILLS • Individual technique • Team Technique • Movement skills	80 min	75 min	55 min	45 min
TACTICAL DRILLS • Attack • Defense • Transition	30 min	35 min	40 min	30 min
COMPETITIVE DRILLS • Scrimmage • Doubles, triples,	15 min	15 min	30 min	30 min
CONDITIONING DRILLS • Aerobic • Anaerobic • Jump training	20 min	15 min	15 min	15 min
COOL DOWN • Review goals • Set new goals	5 min	5 min	5 min	5 min
TOTAL PRACTICE TIME	3.10 HOURS	2.9 HOURS	2.75 HOURS	2.6 HOURS
THERAPY/SHOWER	20 MINUTES	20 MINUTES	20 MINUTES	20 MINUTES

ESTABLISHING A POSITIVE TRAINING ENVIRONMENT

A successful volleyball program that is well-organized, with a clear sense of direction, realistic limits and reasonable expectations will establish a climate that encourages group and individual productivity. The most successful training occurs in an environment that is positive, supportive and in surroundings where the players feel comfortable. The behavior concepts of attitude and commitment greatly affect the atmosphere under which training is conducted and operates. In other words, a training plan must strive to create an environment in which participants enjoy what they are doing and the team enjoys working together. The training environment sets the tone for practice by portraying the team's attitude and personality, which in turn develops attitudes and behaviors that will carry over to game situations. A practice area that is neat, clean, and well organized will project a business like image and help in establishing a positive training environment.

In the initial phase of developing a practice scheme, the coach must identify the areas of concern in individual and team development, that is, what needs to be learned or reviewed, the specific goals to be accomplished, and the strategies to be used in addressing these concerns (plan-of-action). Research shows that during the early phase of planning, players should be involved in some manner when setting goals and outlining training activities. Player involvement increases awareness and commitment to the projected activities. Experts have concluded that including players in some aspects of decision-making is also an extremely effective motivational and leadership tool. If the participants are to make effective contributions to practice or drill success, behavioral standards, routines and limits under which training takes place must be outlined and thoroughly understood and enforced.

Practice will be effective, if reasonably enforced behavior guidelines are instituted that require non-volleyball activities to be eliminated during on-the-court practice activities. The volleyball court must be considered a sanctuary limited exclusively to volleyball training activities. All other activities and emotional problems must be eliminated or resolved before entering this sanctuary. Incredible amounts of time are wasted by players who use volleyball time to discuss personal problems, school and other activities.

THE INFLUENCE OF THE COACH: — Although player's behavior has the greatest influence in making practice effective and successful, the learning quality of practice and overall team behavior is significantly affected by the actions and conduct of the coaching staff. More specifically, the outcome of a training program is dependent on the organization, communication and leadership ability of the coach/s. For these reasons, when outlining-the-factors to be incorporated into a volleyball training program, the ability of the coaching staff must be given vigilant consideration. To be effective, efficient, and successful, a coach must possess the following qualities that establish a coach's credibility:

- A sound philosophy of coaching.
- A well-developed set of teaching and learning principles.
- Affective teaching techniques.
- An outline of acceptable team behavior as well as goals and roles for each individual involved.
- A substantial knowledge of the technical and tactical skills required as well as their application to their chosen sport.
- The possession of an in-depth understanding of the principles of motor learning, bio-mechanics, exercise physiology and injury prevention and treatment.
- Personal creativity and imagination.
- Excellent organizational and communication skills.
- The ability to execute (model) the skills being practiced.
- An in-depth knowledge of each player's personal strengths and weaknesses.
- The ability to evaluate individual skill and team performance.

Foremost in establishing an effective practice and learning environment is the personality of the coaches. How a coach interacts with the world plays important role in controlling the behavior and tempo of practice. In particular, the effectiveness of training is influenced by the body language (posture, movement, facial expressions, etc.) and voice inflection (positive, encouraging, quiet, loud, fast, etc.) displayed by each coach. Coaches are also a major factor in deciding how individual athletes and the team feel about the training process. The influence of a coach on the quality of practice and team behavior is also affected by his/her creativity, i.e., the willingness to try new ideas and flexibility, i.e., the ability to adapt to new and unexpected situations as they arise. A sensitivity and understanding of the daily ebb and flow of emotion, desire, concentration, and the physical condition of each player, as well as their own, also plays an important role in creating a successful training environment. Empathy is a key to effective player relations.

PRACTICE ATMOSPHERE. — Developing an effective and efficient practice environment is a responsibility of both the coaching staff and players alike. The attitude by which the coaches and players approach each practice session has a tremendous affect on the mood and tempo of practice. Often the success of a practice session is unconsciously determined by events that occur before practice, in the players' locker room, or coach's office prior to the start of practice. With this in mind, each player assumes an obligation for making the practice session a success. Therefore, each player must come to practice with a positive, supportive attitude. All players must also understand and appreciate the need for quality production in training by making every contact on the ball to the best of his/her ability. Competent learning situations occur when players prepare mentally for practice by focusing on areas that need improvement and by establishing performance goals that achieve those objectives. A coachable player is one who works hard, helps and encourages his/her teammates, hustles after every ball, helps maintain a proper gym atmosphere, and follows instructions closely without argument.

A coach also develops an effective training atmosphere by his/her ability to establish and control the mood and tempo of training. As stated previously, the ability to control the training environment is either enhanced or impaired by the body language (posture, movements, and facial expression) and voice inflection of the coach and/or the players. Furthermore, addressing problems as soon they arise with compassion and understanding helps to institute a positive atmosphere. Finally, by catering to the specific characteristics of the team, drills can be created to reflect, affect, and enhance the personalities of those involved in the program. Establishing a positive-competitive mood and tempo plays a significant role in determining the effectiveness of the learning environment by reinforcing the desired behavior in each practice situation. That is, an effective practice mood/tempo is initiated by designing drills and competitive situations that strengthen expected behavior and by the players and coaches' attitude.

PRACTICE BEHAVIOR. — The accomplishments of any team in competition are planned for and built by the behavior established during training. If it is true that players make practice a success or failure, then player behavior must be established and maintained that is both effective and efficient. Positive mental and emotional conduct must be instituted that reinforces consistent individual and team behavior. This might include such factors as: work ethic, competitiveness, and a general positive feeling about training. Likewise, success is achieved by instilling in each player: (1) a positive, supportive attitude, (2) an understanding and appreciation for what the coaching staff is trying to accomplish, and (3) a realization of the need for quality production in training.

To initiate the appropriate behaviors, a coach can use a player's personal motivation (why they want to participate) and peer pressure to create a consistent application of specific standards and expectations. Consistency in effort and behavior are key ingredients that blend players together into a team. Thus, it is through practice that the coaching staff takes a group of players with wide ranging personalities, abilities and desires, and molds them into a cohesive unit.

The following are a list of attitudes and procedures that influence practice behavior.

ATTITUDES THE AFFECT BEHAVIOR

- Work to make practice fun.
- Participate in practice and each drill with enthusiasm.
- Prepare mentally for practice.
- Focus on areas that need improvement.
- Be willing to sacrifice and always give maximum effort.
- Encourage teammates during a fatiguing drill.
- Always leave practice on a positive note.
- Make the gym a sanctuary-leave your problems outside.

PROCEDURES THAT GUIDE BEHAVIOR

- Be on time to every practice.
- Aid in setting up practice equipment
- Complete non-practice activity prior to the beginning of practice.
- Neatly fold and store practice gear not being used.
- Report all injuries or illness immediately.
- No setting during practice unless O.K. by the coach.
- Jog or run at all times during practice.
- Learn names and organization of each drill.
- Assume drill responsibilities and execute effectively.

Effective behavior is established by the routine activities that take place in practice as well as other areas of daily life and must be consistent with team expectations. The desired behavior displayed by the team in the course of training, travel, in the classroom, during game situations, and on other occasions must be taught and reinforced during practice. Moreover, the establishment of desirable behavioral guidelines requires a commitment by both the coaching staff and the players to be effective. Furthermore, if specific behavioral patterns are to be instilled, behavioral control and emotional control (by both the coach and the players) must be insisted upon at all times in practice and non-practice situations. In addition, no demands should be placed on an individual player that is not also expected of all players and the coaching staff.

Accountability, responsibility, and commitment offer the best real life learning guidelines and flexibility in dealing with team behavior. Establishing these principles as expectations to be achieved by each player reduces the coaching staff's direct responsibility for the action of players. As young adults, each player must make a commitment to responsible behavior and should be held accountable for his/her actions in relation to teammates, the school, and the coaching staff. Once the desired behavioral patterns have been communicated and the policies established, each player becomes responsible for their success or failure in training, school, social life and, ultimately, to the team's success in competition. Behavioral expectations (routines) supply behavioral guidelines that regulate expected behavior or can be used as a set of specific training rules. Behavioral guidelines are established and enforced by the coaching staff with the cooperation and input of the players. However, the final decisions always rest with the coaches. **See a sample of Routines pp.64-67.**

CHAPTER 6

Daily Practice Design and Organization

INTRODUCTION

Considerable thought, creative thinking and analysis should go into planning each daily practice schedule. Perhaps a short, but intense brain storming session by the coaching staff will produce new ideas in practice organization and content. Items to be considered include: the general structure of practice drills, time allotment to each activity, previously learned and new skills to be introduced, team development and warm-up and cool-down activities. In addition to facility limitations, player accessibility and governing body's requirements put severe restrictions on the amount of time available for training. These limitations demand that practice time be extremely organized and strictly regulated to ensure sufficient coverage of technical, tactical and competitive skills as well as behavior modification. The time required to prepare for non-on-the-court practice activities varies between players. Included in these activities would be: dressing, therapy, daily goal review, team meetings and showering. These activities should take place outside of formal practice activities. Each practice should also contain some form of visualization that can be used to review previously learned skills and the skills to be included in the days practice.

A daily practice schedule outlines the training structure, determines the content time scheme, and establishes a beginning and ending time frame of each training session. Once the duration of practice has been determined, time can be assigned to each activity. However, daily training routines should be flexible enough to conform with seasonal training needs and problems as they arise. A drill that is not achieving the required goals should be changed or canceled. In addition, the time allotted for practice should be decreased slightly and gradually throughout the season to allow players more time for rest and study. This reduction in training load is also necessary as the league and post season play approaches to keep players fresh and to limit physical and psychological wear and tear (burnout) caused by the long competitive season. The actual practice session begins with a short team meeting to cover administrative details, to review upcoming practice activities, discuss technical and tactical guidelines, and review the goal-objectives of practice and if needed, to cover scouting reports. A team meeting should also discuss procedures for drill execution and end with some form of team motivational activity or message.

A brief but intense warm up should precede all physical training activities (drills-conditioning). In addition to light patterns of movement and stretching the warm up period should include some form of skill activity to review previously learned skills and create practice motivation and intensity. This could include Queen/King of the court, 3on3-2on2 loser out drills. Many of these activities can be found in the drill section. Likewise, practice ends with a brief cool down, a preview (evaluation) of the day's practice, followed by setting of new performance goals for the next practice. During preseason and pre-league play, anaerobic conditioning drills can be dispersed throughout practice. However, as the season progresses, conditioning drills can be relegated to the end of practice. Research (Schmidt) indicates that although fatigue does not affect learning, exhaustion does and should not be a factor when training tactical, competitive and fine motor skills. Furthermore, the chance of injury is seriously increased during periods of overexertion and exhaustion.

Time allocation and prioritization depends on individual and team experience and ability level. Early in the pre and competitive season technical skills will be the main point of emphasis and consume the largest portion of available training time. Tactical and competitive skills can be introduced at this time but should play only a minor role. As the season progresses, the amounts of time necessary to train tactical and competitive skill gradually increases. Accordingly, with the approach of league play, a majority of practice time should be spent in competitive/tactical team play. As previously noted, the major amount of aerobic and strength training should take place in the off-season and pre-season. Once competitive play begins conditioning should be strictly for maintenance with high reps and minimum load. The following is a typical outline of the activities to be covered and their order of appearance.

PLANNING AN EFFECTIVE DAILY PRACTICE SESSION

NON-ON-THE-COURT ACTIVITIES

Prior to on-the-court activities, a non-formal period should be set aside for players to review individual and team performance goals and to re-examine previously learned skill through visualization and imagery. This is a quiet time where individual players can briefly review and visually rehearse technical skills and tactical demands required. Through visualization, a player's daily goals can be reconciled with the technical and tactical objective of the upcoming practice.

TEAM MEETING:— A team meeting should initiate a practice session. This is the time to briefly discuss practice agenda, goals and organizational structure. Procedures for training new skill executions or reviewing existing skills and concepts should be discussed at this time. Administrative duties, scouting reports and instilling practice motivation should also be incorporated. Team meetings are also an excellent opportunity for feedback and input from players and coaches on ways to improve practice which helps improve player motivation and reinforce performance.

ON-THE-COURT ACTIVITIES

WARM UP: Most research indicates that practice should begin with some form of light movement and stretching patterns prior to intense physical activity (e.g., a brief run, jumping rope, or volleyball specific movement exercises without the presence of a ball, etc.). This period is designed to raise body temperature in preparation for stretching exercises. This movement activity is followed by an intense full range of motion stretch (static/pnf) of all major muscle groups to increase flexibility. However, this is not a period for socializing. Stretching is followed by a brief period of rehearsing/reviewing skills that are volleyball specific or game related, (e.g., ball handling, spiking and blocking movements, defensive movements and/or agility development that includes a ball). The objective of this activity is to mentally prepare players for practice, to reinforce previously learned skills and to develop practice intensity. As skills improve and the season progresses, short competitive exercises can be used to increase intensity and motivation and set the tone for practice.

REVIEW PREVIOUSLY LEARNED SKILLS: —An advanced training session should begin with an emphasis on reviewing either a single skill or multiple skills under specific game-related conditions. Execution usually consists of two or more players concentrating on two or more skills. A drill reviewing serving/ passing technique is a good practice opener and provides an additional warm up. The next phase of this review adds a set and attack to this passing drill. This is an excellent a time to work on perfecting and reinforcing previously learned individual techniques with continuous, block or continuous type skill activities and combination drills, (e.g.,3-on-3 and 6-on-6 drills) can be executed in a variable and random order. Evaluation of skill execution in these drills should be based on standard performance criteria (e.g., consecutive correct attempts/accuracy to target).

INTRODUCE NEW MATERIAL: — Since learning occurs best prior to the onset of fatigue, new techniques and tactics should be introduced, modeled, and demonstrated early in the practice session. Likewise, the best results are accomplished by commencing skill execution with lead up activities that progress from easy to difficult. In other words, begin with discrete-type training and gradually add random and varied trials as ability improves. A high number of correct repetitions that gradually progress toward game speed and game-like conditions are the goal to be achieved. The basic learning format is to first develop a rough approximation of a skill followed by perfection, automation and finally competitive development.

TEAM DEVELOPMENT. — The basic objective of this phase of training is to develop game-like behavior. This is achieved by a series of discrete skills, continuous and serial drills performed in a varied and random fashion. However, emphasis should be on competitive drills that are 6/6 oriented and with a degree of difficulty equal to or greater than that found in competition. The main purpose is to develop individual and team ability in technical execution, with tactical efficiency, under stressful conditions. Tactical success is a top priority of team development. Therefore, individual technical instruction and review should take place outside the main drill action. Drill activity should not be delayed to review poor individual technical execution.

PHYSICAL DEVELOPMENT: — Although conditioning and fitness can be established by drills of high intensity conducted during practice, the end of practice is a good time for a short an intense workout that is geared to increasing or maintaining the fitness needed for executing volleyball skills. Included here are aerobic, anaerobic, plyometrics, and strength development. Moreover, when improving physical conditioning the best results occur if these activities are combined with the skills used in volleyball, e.g., instead of just running sprints back and forth across the court the player would repeatedly pass a hard hit ball or serve. Passing the ball is followed by sprinting a predetermined distance and back to the starting position.

COOL DOWN/PRACTICE REVIEW. — This is a time to slow down and return the body processes to normal and consists of less intense movement and stretching. It is also a good time to review goal achievement and to evaluate practice results. Based on this review, new team and individual goals are developed for the forthcoming practices and competition.

SUMMARY

Practice organization must take in to account that skill development has many components, some of which are verbal, motor or muscular. Verbal cognation is the important factor in the early stages of learning. However, since verbal examples are difficult to translate into action, practice should begin with simple skill fundamentals drills which involve a small number of joint movements and limb coordination. The goal of beginning skill training is to develop a rough approximation of skill execution. Developing motivation is critical at the early stages of learning in order to give the learner a good reason for learning skills. Motivation at all stages of learning can be enhanced with videos and photos describing a motivational event or by having a skilled player demonstrate simple and complex skills. This could include both how to execute the skill and how not to execute a skill. Keeping with the whole-part-whole method of learning preliminary attempts should be made at executing the complete skill first. Once these attempts have been concluded, the coach breaks down the skill/s to be taught in meaningful and easy to understand segments (blocked practice). Guidance techniques where the coach moves the player in the correct movement patterns seem to be very helpful in this early stage of learning. Practice must be constant with a single skill variant. Once the various parts of a skill can be executed with a reasonable amount of accuracy, the skill can once again be practiced as a whole.

Training objectives/goals provide the main organizational elements to be emphasized in relation to the volleyball tasks to be performed. Drill development and selection should be based on performance and behavioral objectives that are creative, demonstrative, instructive, and innovative. Effective and efficient drill design maintains consistency with the practice objectives, and the goals to be accomplished. These objectives and goals should be specific, attainable, quantitative and measurable. In addition to the skills to be instituted, each drill should outline the behavioral changes desired and establish experiences that develops the individual and teams ability to perform at their maximum ability. Practice design should have specific routines that are simple in structure, limited in scope, and easy to understand and execute. The design components to be considered in drill construction include: organizational structure, efficient operational procedures, informational content, skill evaluation, success criteria, and environmental factors. This organization begins with a checklist of every skill to be taught, evaluation of procedures and success criteria that measure improvement. In addition, an allowance must be made for individual differences in physical ability, experience, age, maturity level and existing skill level. A check list of every technical and tactical skill to be taught must be developed. Samples of dill development can be found in Drill section of this project.

Examples of three practice outlines are included on the following pages as examples of various training periods and skill emphasis that correspond with seasonal demands. These schedules can be used to vary practice intensity and variety that coincides with the seasonal time frame. Meanwhile, as player ability improves, emphasis is placed on different aspects of training. For example, during the first week of the preseason, individual technical skills, basic multiple skills, and simple tactical abilities are introduced and trained. In the second week of preseason and early in the pre-league, less time is spent on individual skills and more emphasis is placed on multiple and team game-type skills. With the approach of league play, primary emphasis is placed on multiple and team tactical skills. As the season progresses, team and tactical skills can be moved to an earlier portion of practice while individual skill training, if needed) can be moved to the end of practice or varied throughout practice.

Having said all this, previous experience, maturity and athletic ability are the most factors to be considered in developing any practice, training or drills.

ROUTINES: THE KEY TO MAXIMIZING PERFORMANCE

INTRODUCTION: Many of the problems associated with performance at very high levels of intensity are caused by the psychological stress that occur either prior to or during performance. However, many performance interrupters can be reduced by establishing systematic rituals or routines that prepare a player for every aspect of performance. Rituals or routines can be used prior to practice, a game or even before each point to improve the chances of success. Players have a greater chance of achievement in a match if they formulate regular routines or patterns of behavior that regulate: when and how they eat, exercise, practice, visualize, etc. There is no doubt and common sense suggests that rituals regarding, eating habits, rest and sleep play a major role in how a player handles stressful situations and workout intensity.

Routines serve two basic functions: Recovery and Preparation. Recovery involves physically recuperating from the tension created and the energy expended during play. Players with well defined rituals seem to react to pressure and stress more efficiently. Short, positive self-affirmation statements can be used to reinforce a successful play or relieve the self-doubt and negative energy that accompanies mistakes in performance. Likewise, brief moments of relaxation can be used to relieve tension and stress built up during play. As soon as they have recovered emotionally and physically, players can begin to prepare for the next series of action. Optimum preparation time invested in mentally selecting a plan of action or strategy to be used when play resumes usually results in the desired performance. Routines direct focus to the adjustments needed to attack the opponent's weakness by maximizing player strengths while eliminating their weaknesses. This process involves mentally reviewing techniques and rehearsing the next skill execution. Rituals, once established, should be executed basically the same way each time.

Using the serve as an example, Dr. Sian Beilock's research found that player's who took too much time preparing to serve committed more errors. This extra time provided them with the opportunity to worry about screwing up and prompted them to think which alter their service execution leading to a botch service toss. Brain scans of the prefrontal cortex showed it don't work as fast which hinders conscious thought. Have said this, new players need extra time to think about what to do when executing volleyball skills. However for experienced players, this extra time can be eliminated with pre-activity routines which limit thinking time.

Research (Groppel-Leohr) in tennis suggests that those who employ a plan to control non-active time through pre-set rituals have a greater chance of winning the next point and ultimately the match. Tennis players have for years gone through set routines prior to serving the ball and during breaks in play. Like tennis, volleyball has a series of sequences which require planning to provide for efficient use of non-activity time. Tennis player bounce the ball off the racket, bounce the ball off the floor many time with the non-serving hand, visualize successful skill execution and voice a positive affirmation before serving. I have noticed that most players are using these techniques to ready and relax themselves prior to the serve. Basketball players have for years used established routines prior to shooting a free throw. They rehearse shoot technique before receiving the ball, bounce the ball, spin it around in their hands, and repeat a positive affirmation before shooting the ball.

Pre-established routines create a game plan for regulating behavior during the natural breaks in play. By eliminating unnecessary details, training and game organization is greatly improved. By the way, so is the chance of being successful. The following are several examples of simple routines that prepare players for practice, before skill execution during practice and game situations. They can be effectively used during a time out and breaks between play to relieve stress, prepare the player for skill execution and to improve motivation and confidence. Routines can be used to provide a few brief moments for reviewing technical and tactical execution. As previously stated, athletics cannot be thinking about technical and tactical execution during play. Once play has begun skill execution must be automatic and unconscious responses.

The practice and game rituals to be described here are divided into to the following categories: (1) preparation prior to performance (2) activities instituted when play is halted (time outs) and (3) routines that can be used prior to the start of each point. Pre-performance routines should include a goal setting and visualization session. These rituals can be accomplished by reviewing the goals and structure of a practice session prior to implementation. Having a set pattern of behavior prior to performance will eliminate the worry about being on time, forgetting equipment and handling personal needs. Most athletes find it beneficial to spend a quiet time prior to practice and competition. This restful period can be used reviewing goals, visualization or just relaxing to reduce stress.

Rituals executed when action is halted provide time for reducing stress, visualizing, instilling motivation or executing a pre-skill routine. Areas in which rituals or routines help to improve performance are pre-skill execution routines. Pre-skill routines such as, a pre-service and pre-reception routines, have proven very useful to players having difficulty executing specific skills efficiently. When used properly this type of behavior can be applied to institute a improve performance, improve concentration and focus and preparing the player for execution of specific skills or tactic. For example, instituting a set pattern of behavior prior to beginning the serve will enhance consistency and accuracy in serve execution. Players who do not have well-established mental and physical rituals prior to serving the ball increase their chance of making an error. In volleyball today, it costs the team a point.

Very little thought and planning is given to how to effectively use the time when the ball is not in play. To solve this problem, routines can be instituted to cover this free time when no action is occurring. Unnecessary details can be eliminated and training and game performance improved by establishing regular, well-trained routines. According to educational research, learning is more effective if players know in advance how the structure of practice and drills are organized and the procedures to be followed in skill execution and performance. With this in mind, routines must be developed that provide behavior guidelines during such situations as pre-match preparation, game performance, practice behavior, and drill execution. Practice time can be directed towards what to do during the short period of time when no on the court action is taking place. These routines will hopefully carry over from practice to game situations.

Discipline, motivation and learning are best achieved by instituting consistent practice and game routines. It is these routines that create the disciplines that in turn lead to efficient performance. Furthermore, activities are generally easier to administer and usually more successful when players follow pre-determined practice and game procedures. There are two factors, time and structure, that are most important in developing efficient and consistent routines. If the time allocated and structural design of each activity is consistent, behavior will also be consistent. For example, without effective routines, time that could be utilized learning volleyball skills is wasted by the constant need to learn new drills, expected behaviors and training procedures. Often by creating and enforcing efficient routines, additional time will be available for spotting and eliminating problems, observing skill execution, or providing for individual players and team instruction. Efficient routines also improve time management by delegating responsibility, that is, "who" is responsible for warm-up, keeping time, instruction, evaluation, drill operation, court set up, etc.

TABLE #3

PRE-PRACTICE ROUTINE

PERSONAL PREPARATION
- Make a list and prepare equipment needed for practice the night before
- Meals
  1. Eat high carbohydrate meal the night before (pasta, etc.)
  2. Eat breakfast
  3. Eat light meal at 12:00—Bring fruit to practice
  4. Pre-hydrate by drinking **4 8 oz** glasses of water a couple of hours prior to practice
- Goal development
  1. Review personal goals
  2. Visualize goal achievement

PRACTICE APPAREL
- Each member of the team will be dress in assigned uniform of day
- All gear brought to court will be stored neatly behind team benches
- All playing apparel will be placed in players bag upon removal

PRACTICE PREPARATION   15 Min.
- Be dressed, in the gym and ready to go at practice time
- Socialization-therapy period must be completed prior to court time

MENTAL PREPARATION   10 Min.
- Visualization/review goals/mental rehearsal (bring goal sheet)
- Institute relaxation/positive affirmations procedures

TEAM MEETING   15 Min.
- Review practice procedures
- Review information discussed at previous meeting
- Institute Discuss new information

PREPARE COURTS FOR PRACTICE   10 Min.
- Set up courts
- Count and air balls
- Bring all necessary to equipment to court
- Set up clock

WARM UP ACTIVITIES   15 Min.
- Line agility-PRP-Approach—3 min.
- Flexibility 8 min.
- Skill activity 5 min.

FORMAL PRACTICE   2-3 HR.

TABLE #4

PRACTICE ROUTINE

DRILL ACTIVITIES -	**2-3 HRS.**

- Be on court and ready to practice at assigned time
- Move quickly to assigned court position during drill
- Light jog at all times during practice
- Communicate each time you touch a ball
- No setting during practice unless requested by coach
- Practice will be strictly timed
- Practice will end when performance goals have been achieved

BREAK ACTIVITIES - Active rest	**3 Min.**

- Pick -up all balls prior to break
- Hydrate- 1/4 quarter bottle of water at each break
- Visualization/relaxation (may be seated)
- Discuss previous and up-coming action
- Record -review goal achievement
- Don't be last person into team on court at the end of a break

DISMANTLE EQUIPMENT: at conclusion of skill practice (captains)	**10 Min.**

- Take down nets and poles if necessary
- Pick up and count balls
- Return equipment to storage areas

PHYSICAL TRAINING -	**30 MIN.**

- Move quickly to training area and exercise as required
- Anaerobic interval training (TTHS) 30 minutes
- Anaerobic conditioning (weights-MWF) 25 minutes

COOL DOWN -	**10 Min.**

- Light movement - flexibility exercises
- Review goals achievement
- Set new goals

TABLE #5

ON THE COURT MATCH ROUTINES

OPENING CEREMONY
- Assume position at team bench
- Take an active interest in activities - National Anthem

BETWEEN POINTS
- Meet quickly at center court for team cheer and positive affirmations
- Listen to setter for play call
- Quickly assume offensive or defensive position on court
- Reaffirm play call with setter/coach
- Quickly communicate required information
- To relax take deep breathing through the diaphragm
- Institute pre-skill routine- visualize next possible sequence of action
- Prepare for skill execution with positive affirmation

TIME OUTS
- Come immediately to bench
- Hydrate (drink a 1/4 bottle of water)
- Deep breathing to relaxation
- Communicate quickly with teammates
- Visualize next possible sequence of action
- Listen to instruction from coach
- Quickly take attack or defensive position on court
- Reaffirm play/defense with setter/coach
- Institute pre-skill routine
- Prepare with positive affirmations

BETWEEN GAMES
- Take position on bench
- Hydrate-energy intake-banana/orange
- Use deep breathing to relax
- Communicate with teammates
- Listen to strategy from coach
- Visualize
- Assume court position for next game

TABLE 6

GAME DAY PRE-GAME PREPARATION ROUTINE

EQUIPMENT
- Complete the check list of equipment needed for game
- Pack the night before away games
- Towel and toilet articles for away games

MEALS
- Eat high carbohydrate meal the night before (pasta, etc.)
- Eat 2-3 hours before game and pre-hydrate with 4 glasses of water
- Eat some fruit 30 prior to match

PRE-GAME SCHEDULE

ARRIVAL TIME
- Be dressed, on the court and ready to go 70 minutes before start of game
- All therapy/treatments must be completed prior to court time

COURT BEHAVIOR
- Dress in assigned uniform of day
- All gear brought to court will be stored neatly behind team benches
- Warm up bottoms to be removed prior to start of warm-up period
- Non-participating players stay active by encouraging teammates and by completing statistical requirements
- Non-starting players stand at end of bench

CHECK FACILITIES: familiarize yourself in unfamiliar surrounding by checking:
- Lights
- Court
- Net
- Boundaries
- Ceiling

TEAM MEETING	**10 minutes**
MENTAL PREPARATION	**10 minutes**

- Visualization/review goals/mental rehearsal
- Institute relaxation/positive affirmations

PHYSICAL WARM-UP

• Line agility-Block step	5 minutes
• Stretch	5 minutes
• Individual pepper	3 minutes
• 3 player pass with toss over net	5 minutes
• Team pepper	5 minutes
• Team hitting with toss over net	8 minutes
• Shared serve	2 minutes

TABLE #7

THE PRE-SERVICE ROUTINE

The objective is to development a set pattern of behavior prior to beginning the service action which will improve service success through improved consistency and accuracy.

The following procedures should be used as bases for establishment of a pre-service routine.

PRIOR TO BALL POSSESSION

1. Concentration on instruction from coach
2. Read the opponents reception pattern to determine who and where to serve
   - Determine the number and location of primary passers
   - Focus on areas not covered by passers
   - Pinpoint the seams between passers

UPON BALL POSSESSION

1. Take several deep breaths-shrug shoulder and shake arms and hands
2. to aid in relaxation
3. Manage stress with positive reinforcement/self affirmation
   - "I am a good server"
   - "This serve will be in court" or "to designated area"
4. Stabilize concentration
   - Concentrate on instructions from your coach
   - Focus attention on the ball to eliminate irrelevant cues (outside distractions such as crowd etc.)
   - Center attention on ball by looking for valve stem-place middle finger of holding hand on stem
   - Choose service strategy-whom and where to serve

5 Establish readiness through visualization
   - Picture ball in your hand
   - Rehearse entire service motion in your mind
   - Visualize a successful serve

AFTER REFEREE'S WHISTLE

1. Take another deep breath to relax
2. Re-institute positive self talk
3. Make eye contact with target to establish sense of collective purpose and serve direction
4. Toss the bail— complete service motion and serve a winner

TABLE 8

PRE-RECEPTION ROUTINE

Establishing a routine of early preparation prior to service will allow the primary receivers to establish focus, assume assigned court and body position and direct attention to the task at hand — passing the ball to the target area.

PRIOR TO BAII POSSESION BY OPPONENT — 15 seconds

1. Meet a center court to instill positive reinforcement

2. Move quickly to the assigned reception position in relation to end lines, sidelines, net, other players and rotational order.

3. Assuming a serve receive court and body posture immediately after the previous play has ended
   - Concentrate on attack instruction from coach/setter
   - Organize a passing strategy.
   - Repeat skill cues, e.g. elbows locked—thumbs together

4. Review relaxation routine:
   - Take several deep breathes-bigger out breaths than in
   - Counting the number of breaths
   - Shrugging shoulders - shake your arms
   - From the crouched position, sway back and forth to stay relaxed

6. Remove self doubt, fear and insecurity by repeating POSITIVE AFFIRMATIONS.
   - "I am a good passer"
   - "This pass will be designated target area"

7. Visualize a perfect pass to the target area

UPON BALL POSSESSION — 5 seconds

1. Read the server
   - Focusing on the server's distance from and location on end line and court
   - Check court prior to serve to improve depth perception (Spatial-Orientation)
   - Recognize the position of server's shoulders and lead foot.

2. Stabilize concentration
   - Quickly review instructions from coach/setter
   - Focus attention by eliminating irrelevant cues (outside distractions)

3. Review passing strategy

AFTER REFEREE'S WHISTLE — 5 seconds

1. Repeat positive affirmations

2. Take another deep breath to relax

3. Make eye contact target to establish sense of court position-location of target area

4. Establish readiness through quick visualization

5. Focus on the ball toss as the servers makes contacts

6. Maintain focus on the trajectory and velocity of serve

7. Verbalize the type and location of pass

8. Verbally reward yourself for a good pass

Appendix

SAMPLE OF DAILY PRACTICE SCHEDULE

The following are samples of practice schedules organized to fit the 3 phases of motor learning Cognitive, Perfection and Autonomous (automatic) and the 3 classification of drill development. Introductory/Cognitive-Advanced/Combination—Automatic/Competition. Each practice session contain drills that correspond to motor learning and drill classifications covered in manuscript. There are organization box at the top of each page. These organization boxes consist of sections that include the date of practice, session of practice, the duration (time allotted for practice session) and the starting and completion time of each practice. The time necessary for dressing, taping, therapy or any personal preparation take place outside formal practice.

The three following sections outline the physical and mental factors that prepare player with the ability to perform the skills and tactics needed during all levels of performance. The first section consists of a Team Meeting/Announcement which provides a rough idea the subjects to be covered during that meeting. The second section charts the goals set for this practice to impart motivation and direction. The last session is a summary of the factor that prepares players physically for the activities that take place during the practices session. This warm period consists of a short phase of activity which raised the body temperature and gets the blood flowing. Once this is completed players should do some form of stretching to prepare the muscles for strenuous physical activity. This section ends with a short volleyball activity drill that either reviews a previous skill or that develops team and player motivation.

Each section of the practice organization is given a time limit which should be followed as closely as possible to comply with the time limits needed to accomplish the tasks at hand. The time follows closely with the school, league, governing body and any other factors that might limit the time available for practice.

The major portion of practice sets forth the behavioral, physical skill and tactical training drills. Every set of drills contains a multitude of activities that cover individual, team, competitive technical and tactical skill training. The practice session ends with a short conditioning session and closes with a cool down period in which body is returned to normal and new goals or objective are established.

Contained in each drill are suggestions of the type of practice and skill that is being used in the drill.

TABLE #9

PRACTICE SCHEDULE #1

INTRO/COGNATIVE/VERBAL LEARNING DRILL

DATE: 2-1-12   SESSION: Morning   DURATION: 9:00--12:00   TIME: 3:00

40 MIN.

TEAM MEETING-ANNOUNCEMENTS.

15 min.

1. DISCUSS BUSINESS OF TH DAY   4. DISCUSS PRACTICE OBJECTIVES
2. DISCUSS FUTURE ACTIVITIES   5. REVIEW SKILLS TO BE EXECUTED
3. REVIEW PREVIOUS PRACTICE   6. EXPLAIN COGNATIVE DEVELOPMENT

PRACTICE GOALS,

10min.

1. INTRODUCE SERVE-PASS-SET-ATTACK TECH.   3. DEVELOP TEMPORAL/SPACIAL OREINTATION
2. ESTABLISH COGNATIVE UNDERSTANDING OF SKILL EXECUTION

PRACTICE PREPARATION-WARM-UP

MOVEMENT: LINE AGILITY   5 min.
1. FLEXIBILITY: PNF –DYNAMIC STRETCH   5 min.
2. SKILL ACTIVITY; 3 PLAYER PEPPER   5 min.

INDIVIDUAL TRAINING ACTIVITY.

50 MIN.

1. SKILL EMPHASIS: - SERVE: FOOTWORK-ARMSWING TECHNIQUE   15 MIN.
   A. DRILL: SHORT SERVICE   Blocked Practice-Closed Skill
   B. DRILL ORGANIZATION
      1. DEMONSTRATE STEP- TOSS AND HIT
      2. PRACTICE STEP-TOSS- ARM SWING BALL CONTACT
      3. SHORTEN COURT TO REDUCE PHYSICAL STRENGTH REQUIREMENT
   C. BREAK   2 MIN

2. SKILL EMPHASIS: LINEAR FOREARM PASS FOOTWORK/ BODY/ARM TECHNIQUE   15 MIN.
   A. DRILL: FOREARM LINE PASS   Blocked practice-Closed skill
   B. DRILL ORGANIZATION
      1. DEMONSTRATE FUNDAMENTALS OF FOREARM PASS
      2. EMPHASIS FEET TO BALL-BODY-ARM POSITIONING
      3. PASS WITH CONTROL/ACCURACY TO STATIONARY TARGET
   C. BREAK   2 MN.

3. SKILL EMPHASIS: APPROACH AND RETREAT/ ATTACK TECHNIQUE   15 MIN.
   A. DRILL: 3 /4 STEP APPROACH ,   Blocked practice-closed skill
   B. DRILL ORGANIZATION. DEMONSTRATE APPROACH/RETREAT TECHNIQUE.
      2. EMPHASIS ON PROPER APPROACH -RETREAT FOOT WORK
      3. LAST TWO SETPS MUST BE RIGHT LEFT-HEEL TOE
   C. BREAK   2 MIN.

TABLE #10

PRACTICE SCHEDULE #1

INTRO/COGNATIVE/VERBAL LEARNING DRILL

INDIVIDUAL SKILL ACTIVITY   MIN.

4. SKILL EMPHASIS: JUMP-ARM SWING - LANDING TECHNIQUE   20 min
   A. DRILL: INTRODUCTORY SPIKE   Blocked practice- Simple Skill

   B. DRILL ORGANIZATION
      1. DEMONSTRATE PROPER JUMP/ LANDING TECHINQUE
      2. COACH TOSS ES AT THE NET
      3. ATTACK FROM STANDNG JUMP -- 1 STEP--2 STEPS---3 STEPS APPROACH
   C. BREAK: 2 min.

5. SKILL EMPHASIS ARM SWING -ARM EXTENTION-WRIST SNAP FOR TOP SPIN   10 min.

   A. DRILL: WALL HIT   Blocked Practice-Closed skill
   B. DRILL ORGANIZATION
      1. DEMONSTRATE/XPLAIN SKILL TECHNIQUE--ORGANIZATION-PURPOSE
      2. BALL HIT OFF FLOOR INTO WALL--RE-HIT BALL OFF WALL INTO FLOOR
      3. REPEATLY-HIT BALL OFF WALL INTO FLOOR
   C. BREAK   2 min.

6. SKILL EMPHASIS: BALL LOCATION APPROACH-ARMSWING-LANDING   10 min.

   A. DRILL: SELF TOSS AND HIT   Blocked Practice-Discrete Skill
   B. DRILL ORGANIZATION
      1. DEMONSTRATE/EXPLAIN FORE ARM SKILL TECHNIQUE
      2. SELF-TOSS HIT BALL OVER NET TO OPPOSITE PLAYER
      3. COMPLETE SKILL OF APPROACH-JUMP-ARM SWING-LANDING
   C. BREAK   2min.

7. SKILL EMPHASIS: OVERHEAD PASSING TECNIQUE   10 min.
   A. DRILL: OVERHEAD LINE PASS   Blocked Practice-Closed Skill
   B. DRILL ORGANIZATION
      1. DEMONSTRATE/EXPLAIN OVERHEAD PASS TECHNIQUE
      2. BALL PASSED BACK AND FORTH OVER NET FROM TEN FOOT LINE
      3. DEVELOP KINESTHETIC FEEL -SPACIAL AND TEMPORAL ORIENTATION
   C. BREAK   2 min.

CONDITIONING: M-W-F SPRINT TRAINING / T-TH STRENGTH TRAINING OFF SEASONS   15 MIN.

COOL DOWN   10 MIN.
   1. ACTIVITY/FLEXIBILITY: LITE RUN/WALK –STATIC STRETCH
   2. REVIEW PRACTICE GOALS/SET NEW PRACTICE GOALS

TABLE #11

PRACTICE SCHEDULE #2

COMBINATION/AUTOMATIC PERFECTION LEARNING DRILL

DATE:_____ SESSION:_____ DURATION:_____ TIME:

		40 MIN.
ANNOUNCEMENTS		15 min.

1. <u>REVIEW GOALS FOR DAY</u>   4. <u>EMPHASIS SKILL PERFECTION</u>
2. <u>SUMMERIZE DAYS ACTIVITIES</u>   5._____
3. <u>DISCUSS ADMINISTRATIVE DETAILS</u>   6._____

PRACTICE GOALS   10 min.

1. <u>PERFECT EXISTING SKILLS</u>   3. <u>INTRODUCE NEW COMBINATION SKILLS</u>
2. <u>IMPROVE SERVE/PASS/SET/HIT TECH.</u>   4. <u>DEVELOP CONATIVE UNDERSTANDING</u>

WARM UP   15 min.
1. MOVEMENT: <u>LINE AGILITY</u>   <u>5 min.</u>
2. FLEXIBILITY: <u>PNF –DYNAMIC STRETCH</u>   <u>5 min.</u>
3. SKILL ACTIVITY; <u>PASS/SET/HIT</u>   <u>5 min.</u>

MULTIPULE SKILL ACTIVITY   **45 MIN.**

1. SKILL EMPHASIS: <u>REVIEW SERVING TECHNIQUE-ACCURACY</u>   15 min.
    A. DRILL: <u>AREA SERVE</u>   <u>Blocked Practice-Closed Skill</u>
    B. DRILL ORGANIZATION
        1. <u>IMPROVE FLOATER SERVE PERFECTION/ACCURACY</u>
        2. <u>BASIC SERVE TECHNIQUE AND MECHANICS</u>
        3. <u>PRACTICE PRE-SERVICE ROUTINE</u>
    C. BREAK   2 min.

2. SKILL EMPHASIS: <u>PASS ACCURACY AND TECHNIQUE</u>
    A. DRILL: <u>FOREARM PASS</u>   <u>Blocked Practice-Closed Skill</u>
    B.DRILL ORGANIZATION
        1. <u>SERVE RECEPTION TECHNIQUE TEMPORAL/SPACIAL ORIENTATION</u>
        2. <u>PRACTICE LOCATION TO BALL WITH HOP STEP</u>
        3. <u>IMPROVE PASSING ACCURACY TO TARGET ZONE</u>
    C. BREAK   2 min.

3. SKILL EMPHASIS: <u>OVERHEAD PASSING TECHNIQUE</u>   **15 MIN.**

    A. DRILL: <u>ROTATION OVERHEAD PASS</u>   <u>Blocked Practice-Closed Skill</u>
    B. DRILL ORGANIZATION
        1. <u>ESTABLISH PROPER HAND AND BODY POSITION</u>
        2. <u>TO DEVELOP QUICK MOVEMENT TO CONTACT POINT</u>
        3. <u>TO UNPROVE OVERHEAD PASS ACCURACY</u>
    C. BREAK   2 min.

TABLE #12

PRACTICE SCHEDULE #2

COMBINATION/AUTOMATIC PERFECTION LEARNING DRILL

MULTIPLE SKILL ACTIVITY   45 MIN.

1. SKILL EMPHASIS: <u>APPROACH-JUMP-HIT TECHNIQUE PERFECTION</u>   <u>15 MIN.</u>
   A. DRILL: <u>REPETITIOUS HIT</u>   <u>Constant Practice-Discrete Skill</u>
   B. DRILL ORGANIZATION
      1. <u>TO TEACH APPROACH AND RETREAT FOOTWORK</u>
      2. <u>DEVELOP HITTER/SETTER TIMING</u>
      3. <u>INSTILL PROPER ARM SWING TECHNIQUE</u>
   C. BREAK   2 min.
                                                         30 MIN.

2. SKILL EMPHASIS: <u>ATTACK TO BLOCK TO ATTACK</u>   <u>15 MIN.</u>
   A. DRILL: <u>BLOCK-RETREAT-ATTACK</u>   <u>Variable Practice-Discrete Skill</u>
   B. DRILL ORGANIZATION:
      1. <u>TRANSITION TO ATTACK AND BLOCK</u>
      2. <u>IMPROVE MOVEMENT SKILLS</u>
      3. <u>IMPROVE BLOCK AND ATTACK TECHNIQUE</u>
   C. BREAK   2 min.

3. SKILL EMPHASIS: <u>READING THE ATTACK BY BLOCK AND FLOOR DEFENSE</u>   <u>15 MIN</u>
   A. DRILL: <u>BLOCK DEFENSE</u>   <u>Constant Practice-Discrete Skill</u>
   B. DRILL ORGANIZATION
      1. <u>DEVELOP THE ABILITY OF THE BLOCK TO READ ATTACK</u>
      2. <u>IMPROVE DEFENSIVE SKILLS IN REACTION TO THE BLOCK</u>
      3. <u>TO INSTILL BLOCK DEFENSIVE COMMUNICATION</u>
   C. BREAK

4. SKILL EMPHASIS: <u>REVIEW DIG MOVEMENT-CT. POSITIONING TECHNIQUE</u>
   A. DRILL: <u>NO BLOCK DIG THE BOX</u>   <u>Continuous Practice-Discrete Skill</u>
   B. DRILL ORGANIZATION
      1. <u>LEARN DEFENSIVE CT. SPATIAL POSITIONING IN RELATION TO ATTACK</u>
      2. <u>IMPROVE LINEAR AND NON-LINEAR ARM TECHNIQUE</u>
      3. <u>READ ATTACK BODY-ARM-HAND POSITIONING</u>
   C. BREAK.   2 min

CONDITIONING: <u>M-W-F SPRINT TRAINING / T-TH LIGHT WEIGHTS</u>   15 MIN.

KOOL DOWN
   1. ACTIVITY/FLEXIBILITY: <u>LITE RUN/WALK –STATIC STRETCH</u>
   2. REVIEW PRACTICE GOALS/SET NEW PRACTICE GOALS

TABLE 13

PRACTICE SCHEDULE # 3
COMBINATION/AUTONOMOUS LEARNING DRILLS

DATE:_____ SESSION: _____ DURATION: _____ TIME:

0 MIN.

ANNOUNCEMENTS.   15 min.
    1. _____ 4. _____
    2. _____ 5. _____
    3. _____ 6. _____

PRACTICE GOALS   10 min.
    1. <u>TO AUTOMATE PREVIOUSLY PREFECTED SKILLS</u> 3.<u>IMPROVE ATTACK. DECISION MAKING</u>
    2. <u>IMPROVE TACTICAL DECISION MAKING</u>   4._____

WARM UP   15 min.
    1. MOVEMENT: <u>LINE AGILITY</u>   <u>5 min.</u>
    2. FLEXIBILITY: <u>PNF –DYNAMIC STRETCH</u>   <u>5 min.</u>
    3. SKILL ACTIVITY; <u>SERVE- PASS- SET DRILL</u>   <u>5 min.</u>

MULTIPLE SKILL ACTIVITY

45MIN

    1. SKILL EMPHASIS: <u>**TRANSITION TO ATTACK**</u>
        A. DRILL PLAY ACTION <u>**3 ON 3 TRANSITION**</u>   **Random Practice-Serial Skill**   **15 Min.**
        B. DRILL ORGANIZATION
           1 <u>**READ THE TYPE OF SERVE-SPEED-TRAJECTORY BEFORE CROSSING NET**</u>
           2. <u>**COMMUNICATION AND MOVEMENT TO POINT OF CONTACT**</u>
           3. <u>**ASSUME PROPER COURT- BODY - ARM-HAND POSITION**</u>
        C. BREAK   2 min.

    2. SKILL: <u>**EMPHASIS READING THE LOCATION OF SET AND BLOCK**</u>   **15 min.**
        A. DRILL: <u>**READING THE BLOCK**</u>   **Variable Practice-Cognative Skill**
        B. DRILL ORGANIZATION
           1. <u>**SETTER TRANSITIONTO TARGET AREA-- SETS A HITTABLE BALL COVER**</u>
           2. <u>**DETERMINE BEST SET OPTION-BASED ON GAME SITUATION**</u>
           3. <u>**EXPAND-NARROW VISION DEPENDING ON BALL LOCATION**</u>
        C. BREAK   2 min.

    3. SKILL EMPHASIS: <u>**DEEP COURT ATTACK SKILLS**</u>   **15 min.**
        A. DRILL: <u>**DEEP COURT VOLLEY**</u>   **Random Practice-Complex Skill**
        B. DRILL ORGANIZATION
           1. <u>**IMPROVE DEEP COURT ATTACK TECHNIQUE/TACTICS**</u>
           2. <u>**TO IMPROVE SPACIAL/TEMPORAL ORIENTATION WITH 10' LINE**</u>
           3. <u>**REVIEW DEFENDING DEEP COURT ATTACK**</u>
        C. BREAK   2 min.

TABLE 14

PRACTICE SCHEDULE #3
COMBINATION/AUTONOMOUS LEARNING DRILLS

TEAM TRAINING ACTIVITY   60 MIN

1. DRILL: <u>THREE POSITION ATTACK VS DEFENSE__Random Practice-Serial Skill___</u>   20 min.
   A. TECHNICAL EMPHASIS
       1. <u>IMPROVE ATTACK TACTICS</u>
       2. <u>IMPROVE BLOCK TACTICS</u>
       3. <u>PRACTICE FLOOR DEFENSE TECHNIQUE</u>
   B. TACTICAL EMPHASIS
       1. <u>READ THE BLOCK AND SET APPROPRIATE SET</u>
       2. <u>READ BLOCK AND FLOOR DEFENSE AND ATTACK TO OPEN COURT</u>
       3. <u>IMPROVE SETTER/HITTER COMMUNICATION SKILLS</u>
   C. BREAK   2min

2. DRILL: <u>MIDDLE TO LEFT SIDE TRANSITION</u>   <u>Random Practice-Serial Skill</u>   20 min
   A. TECHNICAL EMPHASIS
       1. <u>AUTOMATE MOVEMENT TECHNIQUE-TRANSITION MIDDLE TO LEFTSIDE</u>.
       2. <u>IMPROVE SETER/HITTER ATTACK TACTICS</u>
       3. <u>CREATE INTENSE GAME LIKE SITUATIONS</u>
   B. TACTICAL EMPHASIS
       1. <u>SET QUICK SETS MIDDLE AND OUTSIDE</u>
       2. <u>MIDDLE ATTACKS AT LEFT OR RIGHT ANGLE TO BLOCK</u>
       3. <u>DETERMINE BEST SET OPTION IF BALL IS BLOCKED- RETURN OVER NET</u>
   C. BREAK   2 min

3. DRILL <u>FREEBALL TRANSITION</u>   <u>Random Practice-Serial Skill</u>   20 min
   A. TECHNICAL EMPHASIS
       1. <u>TWO HAND OVERHEAD PASS ON ALL BALL LOBBED OVER NET</u>
       2. <u>DEVELOP THE TECHNIQUE FOR TRANSITION FROM MIDDLE TO OUTSIDE</u>
       3. <u>PASS BALL WITH LOW TRAJECTORY</u>
   B. TACTICAL EMPHASIS
       1. <u>RUN QUICK OFFENSE IF POSSIBLE</u>
       2. <u>PLAY THIRD HIT OVER NET TO DEEP COURT</u>
       3. <u>INSTILL GAME LIKE SITUATION AND STRESS</u>
   C. BREAK _   2min

CONDITIONING: M-W-F SPRINT TRAINING / T-TH LIGHT WEIGHTS   15+ min.

COOL DOWN
   1. ACTIVITY/FLEXIBILITY: <u>LITE RUN/WALK –STATIC STRETCH</u>   10 min.
   2. REVIEW PRACTICE GOALS/SET NEW PRACTICE GOALS

Glossary

The definitions presented here are based on the information mainly presented by Dr. Richard Schmidt and the various motor learning experts used to research this project.

Automatic processing —Information processing that is based on unconscious responses which are fast, not attention demanding and often involuntary.

Autonomous stage of motor learning — An advanced stage of motor learning in which movement -information processing is automatic (without cognitive thought)

Augmented Feedback— feedback received from body movement

Bandwidth Feedback — Feedback where only errors in execution are corrected

Blocked Practice — Practice in where many consecutive trials of a single skill are executed

Closed Skill — The execution of a skill where learning takes place in an environment that is constantly the same that allows for advanced movement organization

Cognitive Skill — A skill in which decision making and intellectual processing are the major determinants for success

Complex Skill — Skill that requires a coordination of many body part overtime that to produce movement

Constant Practice — An environment in which only a variation of a single skill is practiced

Continuous skill — The practice of a skill where movement takes place continuously and has no recognizable beginning or end

Discrete Skill — Brief skill action which has no beginning or end

Distributed Practice — A scheduled practice in which the rest period between trials are long in relation to the trial

Error detection ability — the capability of a player to self-detect errors by analysis of responses produced by feedback

Extrinsic Feedback — Internal feedback that occurs as a result of external movement

Faded Feedback— A process where a high level of Feedback is given early in learning and reduces gradually as practice continues

Delayed Feedback — A period of time to occurs after execution until Feedback given

Generalized Motor Program — A combination consisting of many motor programs that allows simplification of these programs so they can be executed automatically

Guidance –A process used in practice to physically-verbally direct a learner through skill execution to reduce performance errors

Instantaneous Feedback — Feedback give immediately after performance occurs

Intermittent Reinforcement — Feedback that is given randomly or given only occasionally during performance

Intrinsic Feedback — Self given feedback as a result of performance or movement

Knowledge of Performance (KP) — Describing the movement patterns produced by augmented feedback

Knowledge of Results (KR) — Augmented feedback given verbally after performance that describes the success of movement in meeting established goals

Mass Practiced —Massed Practice — Practice in which the amount of rest scheduled between skill executions is relative short in comparison the length of execution

Mental Practice — Learner imagines successful skill execution without overt physical practice through visualization or imagery

Modeling — A system of facilitating understanding and learning through the use of an analogy or demonstration that produces the correct skill execution

Motor Learning —A relative gain in performance capability due to a set of internal processes associated with practice and performance

Motor Skill —The movement component that is the primary determinant in the success of skill execution

Motor Stage — Second stage if motor learning in which learning becomes increasingly consistent due motor program development

Parameters — The values such as speed, force and amplitude that influence movement in a generalized motor program

Part Practice —The breaking down of complex skill into parts so they can be practice individually

Prescriptive Feedback — Feedback that leads the learner toward self feedback

Progressive Part Practice — The gradually integrating single skills into larger skill units that eventually become the whole skill

Random Practice — A process where several skills are executed in a random order over consecutive trials

Retrieval Practice —Using random practice to retrieve motor programs- parameters from long-term memory

Serial Skill — A skill composed of several discrete skills strung together in which the order of execution is critical for success

Simple Skill — A skill involving a number of joint movements which require limited coordination among the limbs

Stimulus-Response (SR) Compatibility — The relationship between a stimulus and the assigned response

Summary Feedback — Information given about skill execution after the skill or performance is completed

Variable Practice — Practice which has many variations of the skills to be practiced

PART 2:
THEORIES AND
PRINCIPLES OF DRILL DESIGN

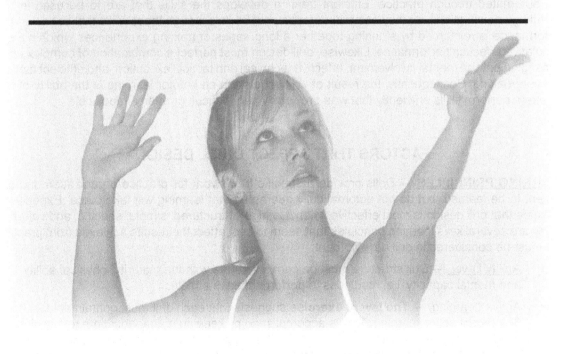

CHAPTER 1

Theories/Principles of Drill Design

"If you cannot win make sure the one ahead of you breaks the record"

INTRODUCTION

If it is true that we represent an accumulation of our experiences, then volleyball coaches must develop guidelines that create a series of positive and productive experiences based on high standards of behavior, in which individual player as well as team success is achieved. The intricate nature of the modern game of power volleyball demands a mastery of varied technical and tactical skills that occur at tremendous speed. For these reasons, volleyball training is a long-term, progressive, and systematic action that requires constantly changing game phases that places unusual demands on individual performance within a team concept.

The major objectives, i.e., the specific concepts that you want volleyball players to know or do, are provided thorough efficient practice organization and drill development. Motor learning and skill acquisition only occur or are improved when the natural ability to perform a skill is perfected and automated through practice. Efficient training develops the skills that are to be used in the specific game situations, as they occur during competition. It is though these drills that behavior and performance is reinforced by stringing together a long series of training experiences which have a cumulative effect on performance. Likewise, drill design must perfect a combination of complex units demanding precise mental involvement, effective technical and tactical execution, and efficient tactical decision making. Consequently, the result of skill acquisition and motor learning is the ability of the athlete to perform skills efficiently that was previously very difficult or nearly impossible.

FACTORS THAT AFFECT DRILL DESIGN

LEARNING PRINCIPLES — Drills provide a specific framework for practice organization and the content to be learned, but do not automatically guarantee that learning will take place. Experience indicates that drill design is most effective when it is highly structured, simple, specific, and variable. Below are several keys learning principles that seem to best affect the results achieved from practice and must be considered in drill development:

- Ability Level. — Drill structure must be commensurate with the maturity, physical ability and mental capacity, i.e. readiness to perform of each athlete.

- Active Learning. — **The law of exercise** suggests that each drill must contain at least 65 percent active learning. This is accomplished by keeping managerial time (explaining drills, giving directions, etc.) and non-active learning (instruction, non-participation time, rest periods, waiting to perform, shagging balls, etc.) to a minimum.

- Learning Efficiency. — The most efficient learning takes place at the beginning and end of each drill. Therefore the most important aspects of a drill should take place during these periods.

- Perfection. — An extreme degree of excellence must be achieved according to a pre-established standard of correctness in skill execution. Skill perfection is a key ingredient for consistency and automation in performance. However, consideration should be given to individual diversity in the ability to execute and perform

- Motivation. — Goal setting, fun, interest and variation in drills are excellent motivational techniques. Each drill and skill execution must end on a positive note.

DRILL COMPOSITION: The establishment of an organized structure for teaching new skills and tactics while maintaining previously learned skills through constant review and practice is a major factor in efficient drill design. To assure practice effectiveness, drills must have a purpose, stress the variables to be emphasized and designed with an organizational structure that will accomplish the desired results. Effective drill design provides for a plan of action, establishes the regimen or routines to be followed, and sets forth the expected behaviors to be achieved. In addition, when designing drills methods for evaluating performance must also be instituted to ensure drill quality and continuity. This type of format provides an intensity that will establish and maintain optimal effort without disrupting the learning process when developing a new drill or using a pre-existing drill.

Athletes will react in game situations in direct relation to how and what they have accomplished in practice. Therefore, if effective learning is to occur, efficient drill design and development must consider the factors that affect motor performance as they relate to match play. Successful performance is based on effective motor learning, retention and recall that is a direct result of competency in four major areas: input of data, adept decision-making in relation to that data, proficient output (performance as a result of that data), and precise feedback. The end result of input, decision making, output, and feedback are new and relevant techniques (motor/perceptual skills) that arise as products of individual and team creativity, imagination, and inventiveness.

Input is the perceptual selection and attention given to the appropriate data from internal and external sources. In other words, recognizing what is to be learned. In addition to a player's own awareness of his/her body position, posture, movement and muscle sense, input encompasses a sense for the flight and velocity of the ball in relation to the court, the position played and the action of one's teammates. Input also includes recognizing the behavior of the opponent prior to and after contact with the ball.

Decision making consists of selecting and planning the appropriate motor responses to fit the environmental situations encountered, i.e., the organization of what has been perceived and translated into a plan of action. These judgments include the interpretation and processing of information based on a perceptual comprehension of the situations confronted. Once sensory information has been interpreted, decisions can be made as a direct result of this data. The end result is the recall of generalized motor programs generated from previous training experiences that will lead to effective skill execution.

Output is the execution of the movements required in performing a skill, i.e., a combination of input and decision making to create skill performance. Output is the result of selecting the appropriate motor program (technique) and executing that skill in relations to a team's system of play.

Feedback is the evaluation of skill execution to change performance behavior through the correction of inappropriate actions and by reinforcing correct behavior.

GOAL DEVELOPMENT: — Development and/or selection of appropriate drill/s are determined by the practice objectives (goals), the behavioral changes desired, and the tasks to be achieved. Performance goals provide the needed motivation for better technical and tactical control, evaluation, and feedback. Objectives should be set that are achievable in that failure hinders the learning process while success breeds success. Research indicates that intrinsic goals that are performance orientated develop a sense of purpose and provide the best incentive, inspiration, and inherent rewards.

Performance success is best achieved through measurable objectives that are assessed and evaluated either subjectively or objectively in relation to a pre-determined performance standard.

Meeting these objectives is assessed either by the participating players and/or the coaching staff as to their technical and tactical efficiency. In other words, each drill should have a clear set of performance goals (generalized statements of what the athlete or team is expected to learn/achieve) that pertain to each game situation being duplicated in the drill. This would include such factors as conditioning, skill development, tactical considerations, etc.

SKILL INTRODUCTION — When introducing a new skill, learning is most efficient if athletes are informed of what they are to learn and why it is important before they attempt skill execution. In addition, showing and interpreting how the components of a skill or skills are related to the established goals will give the performer a good internal model and a clearer idea of why and how the skill ought to be performed. Each skill should be introduced, explained and demonstrated via the use of a theoretical model. This demonstration consists of the elements to be mastered at each stage of development. A skill model or demonstration sets forth the tasks to be achieved while stressing the most important cues through the use of key words. Although key words are effective as reinforcement, it must be understood that the ear is only 1/10 as effective as the eye. Hence, learning is most effective by seeing and doing.

The effectiveness of the demonstration process when introducing a new skill can be increased by instituting the following procedures. First, begin each drill with an example, demonstration or specific model of the skill to be performed. This supplies the players with a correct mental picture of the desired movement. Second, employ verbal pre-training techniques consisting of simple and direct phrases or cue words that identify the sequence of steps to be taken. An explanation of the significance of cue words in solving the task to be performed or the skill to be executed will also enhance learning. And last, immediately after a skill model has been demonstrated, visualization can be used to recreate a mental image of the skill and to reinforce correct skill execution. The following are several verbal pre-training techniques (key words or cues) that will reinforce skill execution:

- Demonstrate the skill with emphasis on a key word or cue
- Visualize skill execution with emphasis on key/cue words
- Practice the skill with feedback based on key words or cues
- Reinforce positive behavior with short phrases, key words or cues
- Repeat key words until an association is developed between the key words and skill being executed

It is extremely important during the introductory process of motor learning, that athletes are visually shown and orally reminded of the movements required during each step of skill execution. For example, learning the three step approach to attack can be visually demonstrated while providing the simple and concise verbal sensory footwork cues of "left, right, together, jump" to reinforce the visual demonstrations. The athlete now has a mental structure and kinetic image of how the skill is to be performed and the sequence in which the component parts are to be implemented. In addition to outlining the mechanics of movement needed to execute a skill accurately, an advanced skills' model should present the tactical information needed to integrate technical skills into a system of play; (e.g., hitting down the line against a cross court block requires efficient technical execution of the spike in-conjunction with the tactical ability to read and react to the location of the block and floor defense).

Demonstrating a new skill can sometimes be restrictive or inadequate because motor skills, when demonstrated, are often executed too quickly for complete comprehension — especially for the inexperienced player. Pictorial diagrams are often less obstructive and will assist the learning process by providing the athlete with a visual background of how the motor skill should look when being performed. These visual images help associate visual and mental perception with the motor movement sequences required. Pictures series, filmstrips, videos, instruction cards, handouts, and error diagrams can also be used to integrate the skill model with motor skill practice and theoretical instruction. The end result of modeling is an increased reinforcement of the correct movement concept demanded in executing various skills.

In conclusion, modeling is an excellent method for providing players with a visual example of the skill being executed. Players should be grouped so that vision and communication is adequate. The model should be performed so that it can be viewed from the front, back and side. In addition, players can mimic the model giving them a kinetic fell of how the skill is executed. The skill modeled should be repeated and mimicked by the player at the end of a drill to provide a review and reinforcement of skill execution.

SKILL DEVELOPMENT: — Skill acquisition is accomplished when the athlete can identify (perceive) and interpret relevant environmental cues, establish and recall the appropriate motor program and initiates the skill required successfully. Through instruction, demonstration or any other means available, a coach must instill a structural framework and sequence of experiences in which the component parts of a skill are performed repeatedly in a manner that promotes motor learning and successful execution. For this to take place the athlete must have a clear and complete visual image or idea of what is involved in skill execution.

In skill development, it must be remembered that beginning and unskilled learners have difficulty handling complex situations. Consequently, drills must be simplified if skills are to be performed properly. The instructional complexity of a drill and the number of cues used are limited to those that are essential to successful execution and related to individual skill level. To do this, a coach must present a step-by-step picture, beginning with what the athlete already knows about skill execution. As players achieve higher levels of ability, experience and knowledge, more complex game-like drills can be instituted. Regardless, remember the KISS principle, Keep It Simple Stupid, to achieve the most efficient learning and ultimately the best performance.

Research (Schmidt) indicates that learning, therefore drills, ought to form a gradual, natural progression from simple movements to simplified technical skills to complex game situations and, finally, competitive play. In progressive drills, a player does not proceed to the next technical or tactical level until he/she has mastered the preceding skill. In order for a drill to progress and proceed efficiently, each player must understand what is expected of them in terms of performance quality and do their best to perform each skill at the required level or at a higher degree of execution than demanded in competition. To be more specific, early training should take place without the tactical demands of competition. Similarly, complicated technical development should be based on specific motor sequences executed under the pre-set conditions demanded in a simplified game-like performance. Moreover, extensive basic instruction in technique must precede complex units requiring highly skilled physical execution, in-depth mental involvement, and sophisticated tactical decisions.

Technical execution can be enhanced and perfected by first previewing material already mastered, i.e., repeating previously learned skills briefly before a new skill is attempted. This is accomplished by demonstrating the skill at the beginning of a drill, and by briefly reviewing these skills at the end of each drill. To illustrate: in learning to spike in a pass-set-and-hit drill, perhaps, the pass and set should be quickly reviewed first. To be more specific, if spiking down-the-line is the instructional goal to be achieved, perhaps the approach, arm swing and jump should be reviewed and practiced first. After this technical review, the complex action of mid-air shoulder rotation when hitting the line can be demonstrated and practiced. Each drill should end with a review of the steps required to execute a successful line attack.

Consensus among authorities in motor learning (Schmidt-Young-Kluka) seems to indicate, that individual technical execution should be corrected only during the technical phase of training. That is, during tactical performance, individual technical motor skill execution should limited. Competitive play is not a place to make specific technical corrections like: "elbow first on the attack arm swing; elbow's locked on the forearm pass," etc.). Tactical situations (team play) offers a period in which to make mental resolutions (error correction) concerning the accuracy of tactical decisions in relation to the objectives of the motor skill being performed and the tactics required to execute effectively. In reality, because of the loss of practice time, team drills should never be stopped to make an individual technical skill correction. Thus, if inaccurate skill technique persists during tactical execution, the player should be removed from the drill and the proper technique rehearsed outside the main drill. This allows for tactical drill continuation and reduces disruptions in the learning process for the remaining team members. Furthermore, the player who needs to review technical execution is provided a simpler environment in which to concentrate their attention on executing with proper technique.

GAME-LIKE DRILLS: — Drill design should first concentrate on building a diverse repertoire of basic skill progression that relate to the specific technical aspects required during performance. In addition to improved technical performance, well-designed drill progressions produce an effective learning atmosphere for developing the game-like perceptual and decision-making qualities that make integration of volleyball-specific skills into game situations possible. Furthermore, it is in game-like drills that a player learns to perfect skill technique according to the tactical requirements of the game. Court awareness, spatial considerations and temporal coordination can best be established with teammates and the opposition by creating training conditions similar to those found in competition. The following are several factors that must be considered when designing game-like volleyball drills.

- Drills are not a series of isolated skill executions strung together, but a progression of specific game phases that resemble possible game situations.

- The tactical requirements of a drill are to prepare players for the specific game tasks to be performed under the constantly changing conditions of competition.

- Game-like drills must provide for correct spacing (spatial orientation) in relation to the net, player movement and court positioning.

- All skills within a drill must be executed with game-like speed, agility and dynamics, thereby forcing players to adapt their action (movement) to temporal requirements found in a variety of game situations.

Modeling and visualization can play an important role in a drills ability to teach quick stimulus-response compatibility. **Stimulus-response compatibility** is the degree to which an athlete sees a particular cue or event in the surroundings as belonging to, or being related to a specific plan-of-action. These two processes aid in establishing a relationship between the event taking place and the action to be taken in response to that event. For example, when a blocker reads the direction of the set to the left side (stimulus), he/she learns to react immediately to the cues present by moving to the right (response). In addition to physical practice, mental practice will also improve the relationship between environmental events and the desired physical reactions. Having athletes watch and emulate successful athletes can also help in teaching stimulus-response compatibility.

To train the mental and physical process of tactical skill execution under game conditions, drill design should take into account the functions of perception, decision making, information processing and imagination (creativity). The application of the required skill/s to isolated game-like situations dictate that a player attend to environmental demands, make the proper movement decisions specific to the position played, after he/she evaluates, comprehends and processes the information available. This cognitive activity consists of the ability to perceive and process information through selective attention as to the flight of the ball in relation to a player's specific position, posture, and movement, and in association with the position and action of teammates and opponents. During match play, nearly all situations are influenced by the actions or reactions of an opponent. Remember this all takes place all most instantly.

Game-like drills should present a variety of problems to be solved that are derived from corresponding game situations. The problem(s) to be solved should conform to simplified game conditions that require players to perform the appropriate skills in a technically and tactically correct manner. Based on the problem/s to be solved, data is selected and the appropriate technique chosen in accordance with the team's systems of play (tactics). The best tactical solution, specific to the movement skills demanded of the position played, is then chosen. This can best be illustrated by the following example: an opponent is blocking the line in a perimeter defense to take away a team's attack strength or to cover up for a weakness in their defense. Tactical decisions must be made instantly as to where and how to hit or tip the ball to an open area of the court successful against the opponents type of defense, A drill is then designed that forces the attacker to read the position of the block and back court defenders, and hit or tip the ball to the open areas of the court. In order to produce game-like situations, drills should include an active opponent of equal or greater ability than they will face in competition. Therefore, the core of the training process should consist of game-like situations that incorporate the idea of the big plays or important points.

Training complex game skills for competitive type situations requires athletes to practice under intense levels of physical and psychological stress. This allows the player to experience and adapt to a variety of stressful situations requiring tactical decisions, while executing diverse technical skills. For example, game intensity can be achieved by establishing volleyball game-situation scoring as the major emphasis of a drill to create stressful, game-like conditions. By pre-setting the game score prior to beginning a drill, added weight can be given to each situation resulting in increased pressure to perform with precision and accuracy; *(e.g.,* pre-setting the score to a 18-23 in favor of the opponent creates a stressful environment that demands performance accuracy and intensity of effort in order to overcome the opponents advantage. Setting the score as 23-21 could be used to instill the concept of how to close out a game or match.

A game-like drill sequence has three parts: (1) **a preceding action, i.e.,** a skill execution that occurs before the main action, (2) **the main action,** and (3) **the concluding action.** Each drill should incorporate one main skill or action related to a game situation, in accordance with the skill objectives to be achieved. When executing the skills required by a drill, the player involved in the main action would play the same role as presented in a game situation while other players play supporting roles, i.e. servers, passers, blockers, etc. This break-down of drill sequencing must also consider the function and task to be completed in relation to the position played. For example, a drill emphasizing passing should begin with a movement to the ball (preceding action), the execution of the pass (main action), and then movement to either an attack position after the pass or a coverage position after the set (concluding action).

THE LAW OF SPECIFICITY: — A key to efficient individual performance in today's high speed, competitive volleyball is specificity in training. To achieve game-like specificity, each practice drill must be as close to game conditions as possible and all cues that are present in a game must also be available in the drill. As game pressure and intensity increase, it is important that the exact responses required for success in competition be isolated and practiced. It must be remembered that high levels of arousal, found in intense competition, tend to bring out the best-learned responses when specificity has been part of practice.

Moreover, during performance in an open skilled (continuous task executions) it is crucial that technical skill execution be automatic, so that attention can be distributed in the constantly changing demands of the environment. Thus, the player who practice digging shots specific to a single assigned position will probably be more successful than a player who training includes execution at a variety of positions. Therefore, technical and tactical skills must be trained specific to the game of volleyball and in relation to the position played. This simplifies the demands of execution while increasing the number of reps that can be accomplished. For example, each athlete must receive precise skill practice specific to the role, position played and tasks to be executed; (e.g., a defensive player trains in an assigned base court position contingent on his/her ability to execute efficiently within the defensive system). In summary, the objective is to continually train the specific muscle groups (motor skills) being used with the exact movements (motor programs) and the same velocities and special relationships required of the skill activity being duplicated. That is, a player who is assigned to play middle back defense, practices the skills and tactical reads specific to that position until they are perfected and can be executed automatically without conscious thought. Thus, the institution of the lebero.

Except for the serve, volleyball is a sport that requires continuous task execution (skill or task with no beginning or end). Therefore, when developing or selecting drills to improve motor skills specific to volleyball, it must be determined if the skill to be learned requires a previously programmed automatic response — **a closed skill,** or if it requires the ability to perceive, interpret and react to cues as they occur in a changing environment — **an open skill.** In closed skill training, emphasis is placed upon technique that conforms to a prescribed standard of performance. For example, the performance of a specific volleyball skill, such as the serve, requires a single response in a closed skill environment and demands that skill execution be constant and predictable with the required movements planned in advance.

However, once the ball has been served, individual players are confronted with the need to make multiple continuous responses (decisions) in an open skilled environment. In an open skilled environment game situations are constantly changing, making it nearly impossible for players to plan responses prior to execution. Passing, setting, attacking, blocking and defensive actions require the ability to combine several motor acts into a sequence of movement patterns (generalized motor programs). These motor programs must be capable of being appropriately manipulated and altered as environmental cues are perceived, identified and interpreted. The keys to executing skills specific to an open-skilled environment are creativity, imagination and flexibility (factors we need to teach). Efficient performance of open skills also demands that errors and extraneous movements be minimized or eliminated. Understanding effective spatial and temporal organization is also important in creating a well-coordinated and integrated production of skill patterns in open-skilled situations.

REPETITION – Retention and recall are the keys to skill development and performance success. Often coaches and players repeat a skill many times with the assumption that if enough reps are executed, a player will eventually learn to execute the skill correctly. Although trial and error learning through constant repetitions may play a role in skill acquisition, it is often inefficient and time consuming. However, trial and error learning can be a useful teaching tool if it produces innovative and accurate tactical and technical execution. When learning volleyball specific motor sequences, fault correction and refining perception of movement may be more important than executing large numbers of repetitions. Although thousands of correct repetitions are required if motor learning is to be stabilized, refined, perfected and made automatic, mere repetitive drills without the correct mental attitude, internal motivation, feedback, reinforcement and a knowledge of performance and results will lead to limited success. Efficient performance occurs only if repetitions are correct technically and tactically on each execution. Consequently, when practicing technique, the movement skills and the body coordination needed to performing large numbers of repetitions will be effective only if accuracy in execution and motivation is maintained over time. To achieve the best results, skill repetitions within a drill should include movement in relation to the quantity of contacts **(number of correct repetitions)** and the quality of contacts **(the degree of perfection).** Furthermore, motor accuracy must be demanded even when fatigue is present.

In summary, motor learning is a product of a person's ability to store information about motor skills into memory through repetition so that they can be recalled and executed automatically when needed. **Over-learning** — or extensive, repetitive practice — will place information into long term memory from short term memory if the following factors are remembered and programmed into training and drill design.

- The number of points that can be retained quickly at one time is around seven—check your phone number.

- Much of the information to be learned will be lost within about 60 seconds if the opportunity to practice or rehearse physically or mentally is not readily available.

- When presenting a new skill, practice only that skill for a considerable period before introducing other activities

- Instruction about how to perform a skill is best remembered if accompanied by a descriptive phrase or key word.

- Remember that the ear is only 1/10 of the eye and that seeing is believing. With this cliché in mind, modeling and skill demonstrations may be an efficient learning technique.

Bear in mind, the number of repetitions performed should be set by the tempo and intensity of the movement desired. In less strenuous activities, such as the serve, pass and set — where accuracy is the prime consideration — low intensity drills with continuous movement and numerous correct repetitions should predominate. However, the opposite is true of drills emphasizing tactical considerations and intense movement demands. These types of drills demand a slower pace (fewer repetitions) while maintaining a relatively high intensity level, e.g. transition from defense to attack.

PRACTICE DISTRIBUTION — In addition to the consideration of physical ability, playing experience, training level, drill pace, intensity and the number of repetitions the quantity and length of rest periods should be programmed into each drill and practice session. To maintain motivation, accuracy and lessen fatigue during periods of extended execution, practice must provide for variety and active rest. For example, (e.g., passing can be practiced for longer periods if the drill structure, type and intensity are random, varied and interspersed with active rest periods). Moreover, motivation is improved by drills that are flexible, varied, interesting, and conducted under the relaxed conditions of praise and reward rather than criticism. To motivate and maintain maximum effort, practice should begin with drills consisting of a high number of repetitions of low-to-medium level of exertion that gradually build in intensity and load. The objective is producing a practice that ends on a high activity and emotional note. Research (Schmidt-Neville) indicates that learning is promoted by drills that alternate between long and short activity periods and between periods of high and low intensity. These studies further emphasizes that by progressively decreasing the length of activity (number of repetitions) and the intensity of concentration imposed on the players increases the chance of learning taking place throughout the entire training period. Although the number of repetition may be reduced slightly, high physical intensity should be maintained over the course of a drill and practice.

Within each drill, the intensity of movement and length of each rest period is determined by the characteristics of play and the objectives of the drill. Intense play action such as attacking, blocking, and court defense should be practiced in short bursts of approximately ten – plus continuous repetitions of about fifty to seventy seconds in length, followed by a short, active rest period after each series (anaerobic interval training). For instance, in a serve, pass, set and hit drill sequence, the high intensity skill of hitting the ball should be interspersed with a low intensity drill such as the serve or pass. Depending on the intensity level of the activity, the work load of a drill should generally be distributed evenly over a period of at least twenty minutes but no longer than thirty minutes in duration.

A performance schedule in which the practice time is less than the rest period is considered a distributed practice. Studies (Schmidt-Young) in sports physiology and motor learning have shown that performance scores are generally higher under a distributed practice. This indicates that a higher frequency of active rest intervals to activity exercise intervals will reduce fatigue and increase the total volume of exercises that can be performed with accuracy. Thus, following the interval principle, each activity calls for a ratio of between 1:2 to 1:4 activity to rest periods (e.g., following the 1:2 ratio formula, a sequence of intense actions that lasts for 30 seconds should be followed by a 1 minute rest period). This rest period does not mean that the drill intensity is reduced or that active participation stops. What is indicated is that the participants involved in the main action are replaced by someone who was involved in a lower intensity of activity or who has not been taking an active part in the drill. In this scenario, a passer would replace a hitter or the setter would set a different attacker. Active rest means that a rest period should one of movement and rather than sedentary behavior.

To improve or teach a specific skill, the overall training period devoted to developing a single skill can be lengthened to provide for additional individual repetitions. However, in order to maintain motivation, this extension must fit within the recommended time and interval guidelines. As an example, to increase the number of passing repetitions possible during practice, the overall time committed to passing can be extended with several different passing drills of approximately 15 to 20 minutes in length rather than one drill of 40 minutes. Thus, the time devoted to passing has been lengthened without exceeding the time limit recommended for each independent drill. Competitive play and activities that involve high perceptual and conceptual material (tactical decisions) should take place early in a practice. Learning may be reduced if these activities are practiced after exhaustion and boredom has set in. However, research (Schmidt) seems to indicate that simple fatigue does not appear to hinder learning. On the other hand, group activities can be practiced for longer periods than individual tasks because of fewer individual repetitions and more frequent rest periods. Similarly, athletes who are more experienced and competent in their sport can effectively practice an activity for longer periods than the less skilled. Likewise, older players are able to practice for a greater length of time than younger inexperienced players. This is possible because experienced and higher skilled players use less energy during skill performance. Finally, progressively decreasing the length of concentration and intensity demands of practice periods as the playing season progresses seems to be advantageous to learning and may aid in injury prevention and burnout. If practice time is shortened, intensity should be increased.

SKILL EVALUATION: — Once the skill technique, a plan-of-action and the goal to be achieved have been introduced, explained and demonstrated, the athlete must now attempt to execute the skill. To better understand the results of performance and its causes, most drills and practice time should include an in-depth evaluation and analysis of performance. If effective learning is to occur, the efficiency of an athlete's performance must be evaluated by either the athlete, the coach or by a combined effort. This performance evaluation attempts to determine whether movement was executed as planned and if the technical and tactical goals were accomplished. To be successful, each drill task must achieve a reasonable degree of accuracy in relation to the established goals. Through observation and recording of repeated attempts at execution, a reasonable evaluation of performance can be made. Based on this feedback, a modification or improvement in skill execution should occur. If learning has taken place, a change or improvement in skill execution should be observable during subsequent performance. In evaluating skill performance, the main objectives are to:

- Provide the coach/player with a knowledge of player/team progress
- Assist in player self-evaluation of technical and tactical execution
- Determine player/team consistency and accuracy in execution
- To identify and correct individual and team execution problems
- Assist the coach in predicting future competitive behavior and training needs
- Act as a guide for improving coaching skills
- Determine the effects of training content and motivational techniques used

Knowledge of the improvement in execution is accomplished through the use of reinforcement and feedback. Several internal and external options are available for presenting effective feedback. Possible analytical measures of player performance include personal feedback about movement sensations (muscle sense), comparison of theoretical goals with execution, and the comparison of a player's self-assessment of performance with the coach's correction analysis. This data provides either a **knowledge of performance**, i.e., was the movement executed as planned, did it look right and/or did it feel right and a **knowledge of results** (accuracy of execution) to determine if the predetermined goals were accomplished i.e., did the athlete score a point, did he/she win the match or stop the opponent from scoring.

Feedback can also be given concerning tactics, by measuring and evaluating correct movement sequences in relation to the reactions of opponents and teammates. In analysis of technical mistakes or incorrect tactical decisions, it is essential to ask the players questions about the reason for their action and/or decision. Questioning the player will enable the coach to determine if the players' perception of the situation was realistic, correct or incorrect. This type of inquiry also provides the coach with an excellent opportunity to reinforce learning. Presenting tactical feedback can best be explained by using the following situation. In setting a ball to an attacker, the setter quickly sets a difficult back set, off a bad pass, to a weak hitter. Discussing, with the setter, the proper set to be used and location of the set in this situation will lead to the development of critical thinking, self-analysis and problem solving skills in future situations.

Execution correction cannot take place until a player realizes the cause(s) of his/her mistakes and compares them with the correct patterns of movement. Merely determining that an error has occurred is not sufficient enough information to affect learning because players are, generally, unable to link this information with their sense of movement. Optimum correction is possible only when a player can mentally compare his/her own performance with the ideal skill execution. This can often be accomplished by using mental imagery. To achieve the best results, comparisons and feedback should be given as soon after the skill execution as possible. Constructive— not destructive criticism — should be given in such a manner that the player will accept and benefit from any criticism about performance.

This is perhaps a good place again to review constructive criticism-positive feedback and destructive criticism/negative feedback. Although all feedback and criticism should be presented in a positive and constructive manner, it is sometimes necessary to be negative about performance. Often for learning to occur, negative feedback, knowing what you did wrong, must be given to reach a positive solution. A positive form of negative feedback occurs when a players is told that his/her actions are not effective and must be changed if execution is to improve. Following this form of feedback with a positive affirmation assures the player that he/she is capable of success. Negative criticism loses any positive effects when is becomes personal and destructive to ego development and detrimental to learning.

Remember, errors in technique and tactics should be corrected as soon as possible by providing a player with diametrically opposed situations; (e.g., jumping too early for a spike should be corrected by explaining the need to delay the approach or by offering an alternative that delays approach movement). Individual key words, cues or short phrases can be developed to support the action or behavior sought. An example would be the often used phrases: "good play," "good hit," etc. Although motivational, these phrases are not explicit or specific enough to provide adequate feedback. To be effective these key phrases must have a qualitative or quantitative value "That's the way to move to the ball", "your speed on the approach was excellent", and "set the ball about a foot further inside" provide better examples of specific feedback and positive reinforcement.

Feedback is subject to the limitation of short-term memory and selective attention. Therefore, it is particularly important for athletes to pay close attention to the feedback they receive. In particular, a coach or the player may want to draw attention to a unique movement or situation that occurs during practice. By doing this, selective attention is manipulated to ensure that the feedback will enter into short term memory. Once a skill has been attempted, there are four types of information about performance that can be stored in short-term memory:

- The original movement goal of the skill to be executed
- A plan of action
- The actual way in which the skill was executed (knowledge of performance)
- The outcome of movement (knowledge of results)

In conclusion, an active role must be taken by the coach to ensure that each drill provides for correct technical execution; furnishes the appropriate solutions to tactical problems that arise; and instills motivation, mobilization and stimulation for each player. Beginning or inexperienced players will only be able to receive and process a limited amount of information. Thus, drills for beginning or novice players should be designed to provide progressive learning and gradual consolidation of simplified volleyball-specific motor skills into complex, game-like skills (motor programs).

The truer the standard of correctness of instruction, especially during early motor learning, the more efficiently an athlete will execute in later performance. If original learning is incorrect, inefficiency in execution will persist and become exceedingly difficult to correct, because these incorrect habits are constantly being reinforced during practice. Therefore, until skill execution is perfected and becomes automatic, the coach must provide for controlled skill execution with correct and adequate feedback and reinforcement when correcting performance. Practice drills must be designed not only to teach new skills, but to constantly reinforce previously learned skills thereby improving the athlete's ability to recall and retrieve previously learned motor programs through continued review and constant correct repetitions.

SUMMARY

Practice organization must consider that teaching motor skills has many components, some of which are oral, motor or muscular. Oral cognation is the important factor in the early stages of learning. However, since verbal examples are difficult to translate into action, practice should begin with simple skill fundamentals drills that involve a small number of joint movements and limb coordination. The goal of beginning skill training is to develop a rough approximation of skill execution. Developing motivation is critical at the early stages of learning in order to give the learner a good reason for learning skills. Motivation at all stages of learning can be enhanced with videos, photos and other techniques describing a motivational event or by having a skilled player demonstrate simple and complex skills. This could include both how to execute the skill and how not to execute a skill.

Keeping with the whole-part-whole method of learning preliminary attempts should be made at executing the complete skill first. Once these attempts have been completed, the coach breaks down the skill/s to be taught in meaningful and easy to understand segments (blocked practice). Guidance techniques where the coach moves the player in the correct movement patterns seem to be very helpful in this early stage of learning. Practice with unskilled players must be constant with a single skill variant. Once the various parts of a skill can be executed with a reasonable amount of accuracy, the skill can once again be practiced as a whole. Drill development must take into account the 3 phases of motor learning: cognitive-perfection-automatic.

Training objectives/goals form the main organizational elements to be emphasized in relation to the volleyball tasks to be performed. Drill development and selection should be based on performance and behavioral objectives that are creative, demonstrative, instructive, and innovative. Effective and efficient drill design maintains consistency with the practice objectives, and the goals to be accomplished. These objectives and goals should be specific, attainable, quantitative and measurable. In addition to the skills to be instituted, each drill should outline the .behavioral changes desired and establish experiences that develops the individual and teams ability to perform at their maximum capacity. Drill design should have specific routines that are simple in structure, limited in scope, easy to remember, understand and execute. The design components to be considered in drill construction include: organizational structure, efficient operational procedures, informational content, skill evaluation, success criteria, and environmental factors. This organization begins with a checklist of every skill to be taught and evaluation procedures and success criteria that measure improvement. In addition, an allowance must be made for individual differences in physical ability, experience, age, maturity and existing skill ability. A check list of every technical and tactical skill must be developed. Table's # 1 and 2 provide an elementary technical and tactical check list that can be added to or subtracted from in order to fit individual needs. These check list are offered as examples and you may have other technical or tactical skills to add.

Table 1
Technical Skill Check List

SERVING
- ❑ General Fundamentals
- ❑ Pre-service routine
- ❑ Floater
- ❑ Spin
- ❑ Jump

LOCATION
- ❑ Perimeter zones
- ❑ Short zones
- ❑ Seams

FOREARM PASSING
- ❑ General Fundamentals
- ❑ Communication
- ❑ Pre-serve reception routine
- ❑ Types of forearm passes
  - ❑ Linear
  - ❑ verhead
  - ❑ Non-linear
  - ❑ J pass
  - ❑ Run-throughs
  - ❑ Sprawl

OVERHEAD
- ❑ General
- ❑ Attackers
- ❑ Deep court set   ❑ Right side set
- ❑ Free ball

- ❑ Setters
  - ❑ Set   ❑ Off net sets
  - ❑ Setter   ❑ Rotational sets
  - ❑ Front sets   ❑ Forearm sets
  - ❑ Back sets   ❑ One hand sets
  - ❑ High (15/95)   ❑ Collapse sets
  - ❑ Fast (14-33-53-73-93)   ❑ Play action sets
  - ❑ Quick (32-52-72)   ❑ Out of net
  - ❑ Left side run-throughs ❑ Jump sets

❑ Attacking the pass
- ❑ Spike ❑ Tip
- ❑ Left-handed dump ❑ Reverse tip

FLOOR DEFENSE
- ❑ Fundamentals (Balanced court and body position)
- ❑ On help court position
- ❑ Communication
- ❑ Emergency positions
- ❑ Sprawl
- ❑ Dive
- ❑ Extension-slide-barrel roll
- ❑ Pursuit and relay
- ❑ Net recovery
- ❑ Run-throughs

ATTACK
- ❑ General Fundamentals
- ❑ Communication

- ❑ Types of attack
  - ❑ High sets (15-95)
  - ❑ x court
  - ❑ Line

- ❑ Quick sets
  - ❑ Quick inside (32-52-72)
  - ❑ Slide outside (73-93)

- ❑ Medium tempo
  - ❑ Inside (33-53-93)
  - ❑ Outside (14-93)

- ❑ Alternate attack
  - ❑ Tip-slam dunk
  - ❑ Off-speed
  - ❑ Wipe off
  - ❑ Back court a-b-c
  - ❑ Inferior sets

BLOCKING
- ❑ General Fundamentals
- ❑ Timing
- ❑ Communication
- ❑ Types of Blocks
  - ❑ Attack
  - ❑ Control
  - ❑ 1 person
  - ❑ 2 person
  - ❑ 3 person

- ❑ Emergency positions
  - ❑ Block and replay
  - ❑ Attack the over set
  - ❑ Playing ball out of net
  - ❑ Playing ball off block
  - ❑ Playing tip

- ❑ Fronting the attacker

- ❑ Hand position
- ❑ Penetration
- ❑ Closing seams
- ❑ Sealing the net
- ❑ Movement to the outside
  - ❑ Cross over Step
  - ❑ Slide
  - ❑ Mini Cross Over

Table 2

Tactical Training Check List

SERVE

- ❏ Location
  - ❏ Deep (1-5-6)
  - ❏ Cross court (1-2)
  - ❏ Line (5)
  - ❏ Short (2-3-4)
  - ❏ Seams
- ❏ Speed and trajectory

SYSTEMS OF ATTACK FORM SERVE RECEPTION

- ❏ 2 person (court-position-responsibilities)
- ❏ 3 person (court-position-responsibilities)
- ❏ 4 person (court-position-responsibilities)

TTACK TACTICS

- ❏ Setting Tactics
  - ❏ Establishing a break point
  - ❏ Reading the defense
- ❏ Altering the attack
  - ❏ Angle
  - ❏ Timing
  - ❏ Location
- ❏ Attacking the block
- ❏ Attack zones
  - ❏ Parallel
  - ❏ Horizontal
  - ❏ Vertical
- ❏ Attack signals

SYSTEMS OF ATTACK
- ❏ Play action
- ❏ Outlet series
- ❏ Free ball spread
- ❏ X or Crossing patterns
- ❏ Tandem series
- ❏ Slide series
- ❏ A/B back court series
- ❏ Transition to attack
- ❏ System of attack coverage
- ❏ 3/2
- ❏ Middle
- ❏ Modified 2/3
- ❏ Back court attack

BLOCKING SYSTEMS
- ❏ Read/react
- ❏ Line/Cross
- ❏ Commit
- ❏ Modified (2-4/2-1-2)
- ❏ Balanced
- ❏ Unbalanced
- ❏ Individual tactics
- ❏ Reading the attack
- ❏ Attention focus

FLOOR DEFENSE SYSTEMS
- ❏ Systems
- ❏ Court Perimeter (2-4)
- ❏ Rotational (2-1-2)
- ❏ Court positions
- ❏ Base
- ❏ Recognition
- ❏ Reaction
- ☒ **Defensive movement**
- ☒ **Parallel movement**
- ☒ **Theory of centrality**
- ☒ **Areas of responsibility**
- ❏ Switching

CHAPTER 2

Drill Development and Drills

INTRODUCTION

Operational procedures, how to get it done, create a relationship between the types of skills taught, the task to be accomplished and the methods to be used for achieving technical and tactical skill acquisition. A coach must decide what objectives a specific drill or set of drills should achieve. Once the objective of practice have been determined, existing drills can be selected or a new drill developed that trains the skills needed to meet these objectives. The coaching staff then sets the patterns of movement, rhythm and the amount of activity required. In addition, a drill must also be adaptable to teaching a single skill or a number of techniques simultaneously. Finally, a clearly stated purpose, a set of operational rules and a system of scoring (evaluation) must be adopted. Drills should follow a logical progression from simple to complex so that the athlete will gradually advance at a steady pace to the level of skill performance required in competition. Drill operation should promote a combination of elements found within a sequential order of play, while demanding cooperation among all players and the mental capacity to resolve technical and tactical problems. The following are several operational factors that will improve the learning process and increase drill efficiency:

- Keep unnecessary components out of the drill
- Control the drill process by on-the-court structured player movements
- Regulate the speed of movement, strength of application and resistance required in drill execution to the player's physical and mental ability
- Keep instructional groups small
- Increase motivation by creating competition between groups
- Stop a drill while intensity is high
- End all drills on a positive note
- End each drill before fatigue and boredom affects the outcome (limit drills to 15 or 20 minutes

Effective drill procedures demand productivity in time management. Efficient time management is calculated by comparing the time available to the optimum amount of time needed to maximize effort and learning. Time segments should be planned and allot to each drill based on the total amount of time available for drill administration and the approximate length of time anticipated to execute the predetermined skills and achieve the objectives, and performance goals. Drills should not exceed 15-20 minutes in length in order to maintain motivation and eliminate the chance of boredom. Research indicates that 20 minutes is the limit of attention span and concentration before the Law of Diminishing Returns sets in. Having chosen the type of drill or drills needed to meet these limitations, a time commitment can then be calculated for each drill and the desired number of repetitions can be determined. Once time factors are resolved, the repetitions available should generally be equally distributed among all players. Furthermore, the quality not the quantity of repetitions creates a more effective learning environment.

Remember, routine procedures that are well-trained, enable a drill to progress rapidly and operate with efficiency and precision while maximizing practice time. Routines also improve learning efficiency by allowing players to spend time learning skills instead of learning drills. Administratively, routines are most effective when they are thoroughly explained to the players, understood by each participant and adapted to meet specific individual and team needs and abilities. Since long verbal examples are difficult to translate into action, verbal instruction should be relative short-simple.

In addition to the number of players needed to operate a drill effectively, player movement, positioning and the role of each player directly or indirectly involved must be defined and outlined. The path and circulation of the ball can be controlled by establishing a starting point, i.e., where each drill repetition begins, the specific return point of the ball and the endpoint. The starting point should always be at least one position before the skill to be taught; (e.g., if the skill to be trained is the overhead set, the drill could begin with a toss to the setter or better still by a serve to a passer who passes to the setter. Decisions must also be made about how movement is to occur (circular, waves, group, random subs, position, front to back or by game rotation). In addition to when players will rotate or be replaced, time limits, and performance criteria also need to be planned.

Player-centered rather than coach-center drills are more realistic, game-like, and will lead to faster learning. A key to efficient operation of player-centered drills is for the coach to remain out of the actual drill execution; coaches are for coaching. Better drill operation and learning ensues if the coach is available to supervise, instruct and offer feedback. This is difficult to achieve in coach-centered drills without stopping or seriously affecting the time and conditions of drill efficiency. Players should, or on occasion student assistants, assume the roles of tossers and hitters thereby forcing each player to learn the skills of tossing, handing a ball to the tosser/hitter, shagging, and protecting teammates from injury. However, coach-center drills can be effective, when there is a need to control the accuracy and tempo of a drill.

Coaches should also not be actively involved in on the court pre-practice and game procedures and warm-up activity. Coaches do not toss, hit or set during a game, so to be game-like, players should perform these responsibilities. This requirements force players to take an active role in game management, assume leadership and acquire the skills needed to perform effectively. As a result, they must learn to execute the ball handling techniques needed to operate pre-game or practice drills activities (toss, hit, shag, and feed, etc.). If a player cannot hit the ball accurately in drill situations, how can he/she be expected to execute effectively and accurately in a game situation when under intense pressure. On the other hand, an active role should only be taken by the coach in competitive drills to exert game-like pressure and to provide the conditions under which game task are to be completed. The following are a list of player skills that contribute to an efficient practice.

- Shag (pick up all balls) to protect fellow players from injury
- Learn how to toss and serve accurately
- When feeding, assist the tosser/hitter by placing ball on their left hip so that the efficiency and pace of each drill can be maintained-right hip for left hand players
- Players should learn the name, time limit, initiation, and organization of each drill so they can start quickly and progress smoothly

SUCCESS CRITERIA: Success criteria outline the conditions and methods for achieving perfection in drill execution and performance. Matching goal achievement with some form of skill execution through the establishment of success criteria enables the coach and players to measure and evaluate performance improvement, while producing positive feedback and reinforcement. Success goals can include the number of timed responses, the number of consecutive attempts, the number of successful responses and/or total repetitions. Whatever the scoring system used in determining success, it must be simple enough not to distract a player's attention away from the focus of the drill and achieving competitive effort. Since volleyball is a game in which a score is kept, a game-like mind set can be established by setting game score related performance goals. In order to maintain game-like competition all drills must be planned to end at the score dictated by the rules of volleyball (i.e., the game ends at 25 points with a two point cap). In team drills, success criterion should be related to the game score with points scored for each successful execution.

Game scoring situations can be established that start play at different points along the scoring continuum, e.g., 10-10, 15-18, 20-23 etc., to create game-like situations that occur during competition. These could include: fast scoring games, big and little points, handicaps, minus scores, wining point burdens, and wash drills. Regardless of the starting score, game-like drills should always maintain game scoring and end with regulation scoring. The performance objective of game scoring situations is to develop the ability to play under pressure, how to rally when behind and the confidence to close out a match when ahead.

Quantitative methods of assessment provide an objective process for evaluating performance for future preparation and as a means of making corrections in current skill execution. Several factors included in arriving at these assessments of skill execution could be based on the following criteria:

- Timed executions and the number of successful repetitions
- Total number of consecutive successful repetitions
- Effort extended
- Hitting Percentage-errors-kills —service accuracy-aces-errors
- Number of balls dug and accuracy of execution
- Number of stuff blocks, blocked ball, touched balls and errors
- Number, accuracy, and success of each type of set

By recording the number of correct accurate and inaccurate responses, objective measurements can be employed to collect qualitative data regarding performance goals. This type of measurement can be used to verify technical and tactical efficiency by comparing individual performance to optimal standards of performance. A factor to be utilized as qualitative data might include the basic criterion of accuracy, i.e., the accuracy of the pass to the target zone during conditions of stress would be a good example. Qualitative data regarding accuracy could also consist of:

- The number of accurately performed skills
- Percent of accurately performed skills
- Consecutive number of accurately performed skills.

An effective and efficient method of collecting qualitative data would be for the coach or teammates to rate each player during performance or immediately upon completion of a specified skill or drill, practice or match. This type of evaluation could be accomplished by using a simple Likert scale of 0-10. Based on this scale, performance is assessed as to how well the player being reviewed performed: (1) in comparison to past performance, (2) in comparison to others in the drill, and (3) in comparison to an optimum standard of performance. These recording devices also present visual representations that can help identify psychological and physical trends and tendencies in individual behavior that might otherwise go unnoticed. A simple table, chart, or graph could be developed to record the results of performance and posted so that players receive immediate feedback. However, if scores are going to be posted some method of identification should be established to protect player's identity-integrity.

REMEMBER: Practice makes perfect only when you practice what is perfect over time.

DRILL CLASSIFICATIONS

Drill selection for training skills is simply a matter of determining practice goals and choosing or developing drills that achieve these objectives. Establishing a repertoire of drills to fit every learning situation begins with the development of a system of classification. Although there are a multitude of drills designed to fit the various situations encountered in volleyball training, most should fit within three major categories: (1) introductory/cognitive, (2) Combination/Automatic, and (3) Advanced/ Competitive. These drill classifications are discussed below as they relate to the corresponding principles and phases of motor development previously discussed.

INTRODUCTORY/COGNATIVE DRILLS: — Introductory/Cognitive (I/C) type drills correspond best to the preliminary stage of skill development. The main purpose of I/C drills is for players to discover and coaches to instill basic skill mechanics and effective motor patterns while developing a familiarization with the basic techniques of volleyball. This would involve simple skills that have a small number of joint movements in which minimal coordination among limbs is required. In addition, a background (cognitive) understanding of how skill/s is to be performed, how they are to be executed and why, is also established through explanation, demonstration and repetitions.

The major emphasis of I/C drills is to establish elementary or basic skill executions. These skill executions would include movement patterns, timing, and spatial relationships in conjunction with the court and the ball. The objectives of this type of drill is: (1) to improve overall physical preparation; (2) to execute simple motor skills by improving efficiency in foot movement and body position; and (3) as a lead up to the more intensive training found in advanced and competitive drills. Evaluation is based on measurable objectives in terms of the ability to execute and the technical form displayed during performance. However, only a rudimentary standard of performance need be demonstrated for success to be achieved and advancement to more complex drills.

In (I/C) drills, athletes are placed under artificial conditions in which skill execution is kept simple and constant. Blocked drills that teach simple skill execution can be used and geared to the basic principles of positioning, dynamics of direction and timing of body movement in relation to the ball and court. I/C drills should be uncomplicated in their organization, structure and the motor ability needed for efficient execution. Player action and movements are controlled by requiring a progressive and sequential combination of skill segments. By controlling and regulating the conditions under which body movement and court positioning occur, the coach can maintain consistency in direction, spatial orientation, and temporal progression of movement. Simple progressions allow for a gradual increase in the volume of training intensity (frequency and length of activity-action) as well as the consolidation and stabilization of motor skill fundamentals.

The type of drills that relate best to the cognitive/introductory stage of learning include: teaching drills that are moderate in pace, methodical, mechanical and specific to the movement pattern required, i.e., mechanics related (not game related). All movements are closely scrutinized by the coach as to correctness of response. These basic individual motor skill drills are usually single discrete skills units executed in a blocked drill (serve, pass, set, etc.) that emphasize efficient execution of one motor program. However, several single skill motor programs can be grouped together during the later stages of development, e.g., when blocking, the crossover step, jump, arm position etc., are generalized into one motor program encompassing the entire blocking action. In addition, several skills can be grouped together by combining the pass, set and hit into a more generalized motor program. Introductory drills include individual drills; partner drills (pepper) and small group coach-oriented drills. Line drills can be used at this stage of development to provide simple multiple repetitions once the basic movement patterns have been developed. However, line drills can often not be time friendly.

ADVANCED/COMBINATION DRILLS: — In drills of this type, the major focus is on the technical elements of movement that promote skill acquisition, stabilization and perfection of specific motor abilities. Accuracy in execution, precision of movement, consistency in performance, and sequential movements are the major goals to be achieved by **Advanced/Combination (A/C) drills.** In specialized drills, the athletes are placed under conditions where they must execute one specific skill continuously (skill with no beginning or end or several discrete skills (skills with a recognizable beginning end) in a combined sequence under variable or random conditions until precision of movement and performance consistency is achieved. Although the main purpose is to promote the stabilization and consolidation of basic technical skills; modifications, if done in a systematic and kinetic manner can be introduced to increase skill complexity in preparation for tactical execution. Varied and diverse skills that require specific game-like execution can be initiated in random fashion once players have sufficiently mastered (perfected) the basic movement skills required in executing technical skills. However, a relatively high standard of performance must be maintained within the capacity of the athlete before moving on to **C/A** type of drills. In addition to developing new skills these, drills can be used to retrieve motor programs from long term memory for review and execution improvement.

Combination drills synchronize the actions of two or more players in executing several skills in a sequence to coordinate movement while perfecting individual technique specific to the position played. Each player in the drill executes the same skill repeatedly under variable and/or random sequencing until mastered, (e.g., dig a ball, transition to attack after the dig and repeat the attack). This type of drill is characterized by a high number of repetitions that continually progress toward game speed. The motor, perceptual, and tactical skill requirements of a combined drill can be gradually introduced and increased as long as a high quality in execution and performance accuracy is maintained. Increases in drill difficulty can be achieved by extending the parameters of the physical distance to be covered, ball speed and length of drill intensity.

Like specific drills, combined drills are very limited in the situations and solutions from which an athlete has to choose. Therefore, major emphasis is placed on one role or one technical element, with the other players involved in the drill being auxiliary to the main performance; i.e., if the main role in a combination type pass-set-and-hit drill is to perfect attack technique, the passer and setter play only secondary roles. On the other hand, this subsidiary role offers an excellent opportunity for auxiliary players to reinforce-review previously learned pass and set techniques. Automation, accuracy and perfection are the key elements that lead up to competitive/automatic drills execution. The objective is to prefect skill execution so that performance will eventually take place automatically without conscious thought. Individual and team tactics in preparation for competitive drills can be gradually added as soon as players are able to execute technical skills with automatic reflexes and responses.

Formation of multiple skill drills characterizes this category. Their objective is to create an ongoing series of action sequences that integrate the basic skills by constant repetition of a single skill, or by a constant repetition of a sequence of action employing a series of skills under-game like conditions. They generally involve two or more players performing in a variable and random mode. Rapid fire/fast tempo, game-like drills with many ball contacts performed in a short period of time, under increasingly stressful conditions are the basis of this category. Triad drills with three players and flow of play drills that blend two or more skills help to develop a relationship between players, court awareness, and the required game-related movements.

COMPETITIVE/AUTOMATIC DRILLS: — once the basic individual technical and tactical skills have been stabilized, perfected and become automatic, highly technical and tactical variation in conditions of skill execution and performance can be instituted. A repertoire of individual and team tactical solutions can then be introduced to form competitive skills that can be executed automatically. When executing competitive drills, technical skills are combined in a sequential order to form a series of generalized tactical motors programs that are position-specific, function specific and demand the cooperation of a number of players; (e.g., a blocker assumes his/her designated position at the net and performs a coordinated block specific to that position and in coordination with other blockers, floor defenders and the attacker.

In competitive drills, cooperation and complicity among players is essential to accomplish the tasks of speed in execution, rhythm of play, and spatial-temporal orientation. These factors take place in conjunction with a player's relationship to the court, to teammates and to the actions of an opponent.

Movement demands must be similar to those used in competitive situations and involve the integration of one or more skills into a system of play (tactics)

Competitive/automatic drills are primarily aimed at coordinating the individual actions of a team to strengthen their ability to execute tactics specific to the positions assigned and the situations encountered in competition. This type of drill calls for motor, perceptual and memory skills in realization of the tasks to be completed. Individual components like: passing, spiking, etc., are combined into team skills that are integrated into a team process. As players become more experienced, larger blocks of time should be spent in practicing competitive team skills — such as transition to attack after a block or dig — where to attack the ball in relation to the block and floor defense.

The tactical demands of performance in C/A drills must be consistent with situations encountered in competition. This can best be illustrated by describing the process of attack from serve reception. Although attacking the ball is an individual process, it requires the assistance of two or more players, specifically, the passer and setter, who interact in a sequence or series to execute an attack. Thus, the individual skills of passing, setting and attacking combine in a coordinated and cooperative effort to complete the team action of serve reception to attack.

Competitive drills are modified and controlled to mirror the skills needed in competitive game situations. The circumstances confronted in performance calls for the merging of one or more skill into a system of play, while calling for tactical decision making to resolve competitive problems as they appear. In modified drills, such as 2/2-3/3/6-6 type games, the rules can be altered by the coach to create the desired competitive conditions. As an example, these changes may demand that players play all positions and assume both offensive and defensive responsibility. Competitive situations can be improvised that require game-like skill execution, develop tactical intelligence and serve as lead-up activities to 6/6 games. Controlled drills can be used to present problematic situations, in which the players must focus on partial phases of the game, (e.g., movement to defensive from an attack position relative to the specific position played or attacking the ball down the line against a cross court block). In addition, high pressure drills can be developed that place added demands upon players to perform up to or greater than a preset standard, thereby creating a physiological and psychological overload (stress) for the players to overcome.

Game drills can also be used in practice to verify technical and tactical efficiency under conditions that are consistent with those encountered in competition. Game-like drills that teach skills within specific court boundaries (in relation to the net, teammates and the opponent) will develop the important physiological skills of visual/motor timing, peripheral vision, feel for the ball and temporal anticipation. Drill, court, and space compatibility are developed by conducting drills on the court and in relation to the spatial and kinesthetic awareness required during competition. To develop individual game skills under competitive conditions, emphasis is placed on complex game-like drills and practice games. However, performance rather than winning is generally the objective of this type of drill. The ultimate competitive drill is team play under game-like conditions. Remember; employ tactically only what you can execute technically.

INSTRUCTIONAL DESIGN

Instructional design organizes the information to be learned, trained or practiced, and outlines the procedures needed for achieving efficient performance. Instructional design includes the number of repetitions, rest time, the coach's role and the drill variants available for effective learning. The purpose/objective of a drill will be determine by the instructional content, (i.e., technical, tactical skills, etc.) to be emphasized in the training process. Instructional content also includes success criteria, skill evaluation and environmental factors. Meanwhile, the role of informational content, i.e., what the drills are supposed to teach, clearly determines the tasks to be undertaken and the amount and type of activity to be incorporated.

Most successful coaches either develop their own drills or redesign existing drills to fit their training needs. Except for the very basic drills in the introductory stage of motor learning, all drills should be conducted so that most of the action takes place back and forth across the net under game-like conditions. The following administrative factors are necessary for efficient drill organization.

- **Name**. Each drill should have a means of easy recognition and identification. This can be achieved by a short name or catch phrase that is easy to remember and indicates what the drill is designed to achieve.

- **Type of Drill.** Drill selection is eased when the skill/s to be trained can be associated with the most efficient drill. Consideration must be given to determine if the conditions of performance require either a player-centered or coach-centered drill. Other conditions for drill selection might be the perfection and automation of technical, tactical and competitive skills.

- **Intensity**. Intensity of movement is an important criterion for determining effort extended. The intensity demand selected must be specific to the goals to be achieved. However, a ratio should be established between activity and rest

- **Skill level.** A drill should outline a training skill level. This should correspond to the varying stages of motor learning. Physical ability is a major factor in determining drill complexity and intensity. Maturity, age, experience and the level of previous competitive play are most important in determining the skill level needed to execute the chosen drill effectively

- **Equipment.** The primary piece of equipment needed is an adequate number of volleyball's to conduct a drill efficiently. It is assumed that the nets, poles, etc., are readily available and in good working condition. However, coaches' boxes and ball carts are also necessary for conducting a well-run practice. If a drill requires any miscellaneous equipment, it should also be specified and accounted for.

- **Personnel.** The number of players available for practice often determines what type of drill can or cannot be used. The personnel needs for effective drill execution should not only include those involved in skill performance, but shaggers, tossers and hitters, etc. Injured players or assistants can often be used to perform many of these activities.

- **Objectives.** The desired behavioral patterns needed to achieve the goals of a drill must be established if a drill is to be effective. These goals should be discussed with the players prior to starting a drill as a means of determining performance criteria. More importantly, these objectives should relate to performance and outline the means of instituting the criterion for success. Performance standards can be assessed by either qualitative or quantitative measures.

Having established administrative procedures needed for effective operation, the next step is to describe the behavioral factors that determine what is to be practiced and how it is organized.

- **Coaching Points:** Each drill outline should summarize and emphasize several specific aspects of the skill to be learned. These are brief statements about technical or tactical concepts that are important to efficient skill execution and performance success.

- **Concentration Keys**: There are generally several key words or cues that can be used to emphasize the coaching points or main aspect of the skill being executed. These keys words or short phrases also enable a coach to provide quick verbal feedback and reinforcement without creating information overload.

- **Rotation**: Establishing a rotational order (circular, linear, front to back, game, etc.) allows for quick and efficient drill operation by eliminating lengthy delays in player movement to a new position or out of the drill. Rotation takes place upon completion of designated performance goals, e.g., time limit - number of repetitions - number of correct repetitions -game score, etc.

- **Performance Goal/Scoring**: Each drill should have a basic success criteria or performance goal/s to be achieved before drill execution can end, rotation enacted, or player advancement to the next phase. For example, in individual skill execution of the underhand pass, ten accurate passes to the target must be executed to complete a player's evolvement. In a multiple skill drills, ten passes, sets, and hits must be accomplished before the players can rotate. When executing competitive drills, a team must score the required number of game points (win by two points) to end the drill.

- **Sequence of Action**: This segment outlines, in detail, the beginning and ending positions and sequence of movement of each player in relation to the court, path of the ball and other players. In addition, the duties of the shaggers, tossers and hitters should be explained.

- **Diagram:** A diagram provides a visual picture of what the drill is trying to achieve. This Included location of the players on the court, the starting position of each player, and a sequence of action and player movement. An efficient diagram will show the rotation of players, each player's position in relation to court boundaries, and the beginning and ending positions of players involved in the main action as well as the role of secondary players. In addition, the position and movement of shaggers, feeders and location of coaches' boxes and ball carts are outlined. Player movement relative to the path of each player and the ball should also be shown.

- **Symbols:** A symbols chart must be included that shows the roll of each player in addition to the position of ball carts, coaching boxes and score board etc. In addition this list of symbols designates player location and movement, ball movement, equipment and position of auxiliary players.

- **Drill Variations**: Many drills have slight variations or changes that can be made in the degree of difficulty or that provide slight adjustment in how the drill is conducted. Drill variations maintain motivation and interest by manipulating instructional content and time limits while maintaining specific skill execution and routines. For example, variation can be added to an attack drill by adding blockers and backcourt defenders and by replacing a toss to the setter with a serve to a passer. Similarly, a coach-centered drill can be replaced with a player centered drill. Often several drills can have an order of progression to another drill which could include simple to complex, single to multiple skills etc.

- **Rest Periods**. Frequent short rest periods and time imitations are necessary to facilitate maximum performance in tasks that contain continuous and open skills which are unpredictable, unstable and unorganized. However, there is less need for frequent rests when teaching discrete skills where short rest periods have little effect (the serve is a good example).

DRILL STRUCTURE

The basic structural components of a drill are theme, tempo, and logical progression. A theme is based on clearly defined, measurable, and attainable goals and behavioral objectives. For example, if the theme of a practice is to train transition skills, then the drill chosen should provide an abundance of transitional experiences (repetitions). These experiences might include transition from attack to block transition from block to attack, offense to defense transition or transition from attack to attack coverage.

Drill tempo establishes the maximum effort and intensity for success in competition. The pace of a drill is either geared for low intensity (learning), high intensity (overload) or game intensity (competition). Drill tempo is controlled by raising and lowering the physical demand of performance, while controlling the variables of volume and intensity. By varying the duration, rhythm and speed of performance, a balanced physical output can be established throughout a drill and practice session. Drills that are rhythmic pace and routine in structure reduce delays, prevent cool down and create interest and motivation while limiting lapses in concentration. In order to maintain pace and rhythm, the following are several factors that are unacceptable and should be excluded from drill design.

- Poor organization
- Late comers to practice
- Slow moving players
- Lengthy explanations/demonstrations
- Excessive feedback or reinforcement
- Lack of motivation
- Fatigue and boredom

Individually designed drills are limited by the actual physical capacity of the player, readiness to perform, skill level, and will power of each athlete in addition to the knowledge and experience of the coach. Likewise, the load-volume-intensity should be designed to demands performance at a high level, while considering individual and team readiness. Keeping these concepts in mind, drill design should consider the following factors:

- Player age and experience level
- Volume of previous training
- Quality and number of previous competitions
- Technical skill efficiency
- Tactical capacity and aptitudes
- Tactical intelligence
- Physical capacity and development

Drills can be programmed and structured to develop the proper attitudes and mental power for self-improvement (motivation). Instilling proper attitudes requires the institution of cooperation, commitment, discipline, cohesiveness, a common spirit and teamwork. The development of mental powers such as: concentration, motivation, and mental toughness are also important components to be considered and planned for. These factors are achieved by infusing the qualities of morale, character, determination and will power into each drill.

ENVIRONMENTAL FACTORS: Practice design is of little importance if the necessary facilities, equipment and manpower for task performance and evaluation are inadequate or unavailable. The environment (facilities and equipment) includes the location in which volleyball activities are to take place and the apparatus needed to complete these activities efficiently and safely. Effective drill operation must account for the number of players that can be accommodated by the facilities, i.e. the amount of court space available, and how it can be utilized most efficiently. Sufficient equipment, e.g., balls, ball carts, coaches boxes, nets, and score boards etc., must be available and in good, safe working condition. Safety is also an important factor that must be considered and planned for if practice is to be successful. A safe practice area should be neat, clean, and well organized with no sharp or protruding walls or floor attachments.

MINIMUM FACILITIES AND EQUIPMENT FOR EFFECTIVE TRAINING

EQUIPMENT

- Two balls per player - properly inflated
- Two ball cart
- A minimum of two coaches boxes

- Adequate training equipment
- Floor inserted standards/nets
- Unbreakable antenna's that can be securely attached
- Whiteboard-overhead projector-screen-TV-DVD

FACILITIES

- One court for every six players
- Ceiling at 25' minimum
- Good lighting
- Distance around court not to exceed 30'
- No wall or protruding fixtures within 20' of court

SUMMARY

Success in coaching is not automatically guaranteed by the number and type of drills used or the amount of time spent in training. The law of readiness states that skill learning is complete when a player can execute the skills practiced both technical and tactically with a reasonable degree of effectiveness and accuracy. To be most effective, training must be commensurate with a player's ability level, maturity and mental ability. By controlling the difficulty, complexity and intensity required when executing a drill, the demands of performance can be increased or decreased to meet the requirements found in various stages of learning, levels of expected competition and in relation to player ability. Strength of application and resistance as well as adjusting the height and length of movement will aid in controlling speed of execution and drill difficulty while providing variety in practice routine.

Coaches must remember that practice, although important, is not a major determiner for success. Practice is a process of installing new motor programs in addition to reinforcing or changing existing motor programs. The success or failure of any team in a contest is determined by genetics, motivation, in combination with the quality and content of its practice time. Practice is not just for conducting drills but the development of overall a team mind-set. The major objectives of a practice drill is: 1) to develop appropriate behavioral patterns such as cooperation, commitment, discipline and motivation and 2) to develop competitive behavior, intensity, and the concentration required for optimal competitive effort. In addition, practice drills provide experiences where by the individual and team can discover and achieve their maximum performance potential. For this to happen, each player and the coaching staff must come to practice with a positive supportive attitude and the desire to excel. Each player must understand and appreciate the need for quality production in training by making every contact on the ball to the best of his/her ability. A coachable player is one who works hard, assist and encourages their teammates, hustles on every play, helps maintain a proper gym atmosphere and follows instructions closely without argument.

Drills are an organized scheme designed to change player behavior patterns through a planned program (practice) that results in the desired terminal behavior. The main purpose of a drill or a series of drills is to assist the athlete in developing optimal physical, mental, technical, and tactical capability that efficiently leads to habits of correct skill execution. Effective drill design enhances learning of new skills and tactics while reinforcing previously learned skills by providing continual review and consistent repetitions. Trial and error learning is not a desirable alternative in the preparation and selection of drills.

Drills are most efficient when simply constructed to meet the desired objectives and goals. Creating new drills or modifying old drills to fit each player's specific learning needs that approximate the demands of performance and relate to the task to be taught may be the most efficient method of developing effective training procedures. Likewise, drills must be developed that meet the individual technical and tactical demands needed to accomplish team expectations and develop behaviors that mirror game situations. In short, players learn to perform best in situations that are routine and the training environment is relatively constant. Too much valuable training time is wasted when, performance is hindered and learning hampered by the constant need to explain and teach new drills and routines. In addition, horseplay, lack of attention and other non-productive behaviors must be eliminated.

Coaches should experiment, modify, and adapt to create a variety in drill selection. Modification of existing drills, while maintaining flexibility and similarity, may be the most efficient method of developing new drills and in maintaining drill approximation to a required performance task. By controlling the difficulty, complexity and intensity of execution, the demands of performance can be increased or decreased to meet the requirements found in various stages of competition and in relation to player ability. Strength of application, resistance, and adjustment of the height and length of the movement required can be altered to include frequent recovery periods which will aid in controlling the physical demands of execution. Remember, its players make the practice session meaningful and drill execution a success or failure.

DRILLS

The following set of drills encompasses the stages of motor development and drill classification. The objective is to provide all the information needed to run a drill effectively and cover each technical and tactical situation that could occur during a volleyball match. It has been suggested throughout this project that if a coach takes the various principles presented here and uses those which are relevant to their needs and coaching style performance and success will occur. Each type of drill deals with the various skills and tactics of serving, passing, setting, attacking, blocking and floor defense required in the game of volleyball. In addition there are drills dealing with transition, game situations, and motivation and behavior etc.

There are several factors that must be taken into account for a drill to provide effective and efficient motor program development and skill learning. For example, in every the stage of motor learning and skill execution the ability to execute efficiently will vary within each individual player and between players on the team. Therefore, an individual player may be able to execute parts of a serial skill better than the other aspects of the skill. Take for instance the forearm pass, when executing this skill a player may show the ability to move effectively to the point of contact and assume a good body position but may have trouble getting the arms into position in time to pass the ball to the target area. There are several situations in which a blocked practice will create a better learning environment than one which consist of discrete and serial skill training. Perhaps, a better learning situation for an inexperienced player would occur if the player practices the skill of moving to point of contact and catching the ball before practicing the hand and arm positioning of linear and non-linear passing.

Each set of drills are organized in a logical frame work that begins with simple individual skills that need to be learned in order to execute more difficult skills. Examples of the objectives, coaching points and concentration keys, est. have been provided that can be used in conducting a specific drill. However, the same drill can be easily adjusted to conform to other factors desired by the coach.

Introductory/Cognative Drills

**The following drills are classified as Introductory and are
Appropriate to the Cognitive Stage of Motor Learning**

The majority of early practice should consist of this type of skill learning and takes place in a Constant Practice format in which a single skill is executed, a Part practice in which a complex skill in broken down into part and practiced individually and a Blocked practice where there are many consecutive trails of a single skill. The type of skills used is as listed below:

- Closed skills- A single skill executed in a closed environment
- Simple skills- Skills involving limited joint movement

In the INTENSITY and SKILL SECTION of each DRILL, LVL stands for Level

DRILL: SHORT SERVICE Pr 1

TYPE OF DRILL: Coach centered-teaching

INTENSITY LVL: Low   **SKILL LVL:** 1

EQUIPMENT
1. 10+ Balls
2. Ball Cart

PERSONNEL: 10+

OBJECTIVE
1. Introduce basic serve mechanics
2. Develop confidence within serve technique
3. Reduce physical strength requirements
4. Provide multiple serve repetitions

COACHING POINTS-TECHNICAL EMPHASIS
1. Step in direction of target
2. Weight transfer from rear to front foot
3. Shoulders square to net
4. Hit flat though the ball (floater)
5. Eliminate excess body movement

CONCENTRATION KEYS
1. Step-Toss-Hit
2. Controlled toss
3. Quick arm swing
4. No get-tee-up (NO knee bend on toss)

ROTATION
1. Server-rotates to back of serving line after each serve
2. Players serve until performance goal is achieved

PERFORMANCE GOAL-SCORING
1. Timed repetitions: 5 min. stop and review serving technique
2. Number of repetitions (25 in row)

SEQUENCE OF ACTION
1. Coach explains skill/drill - experienced player models skill
2. Players line up in 3 or 4 lines on opposite sides of net about mid-court
3. Drill begins with one player serving across the net to a partner

DRILL VARIATIONS/PROGRESSION

Weak servers start inside the base line and gradually moves toward base line as strength/accuracy improve

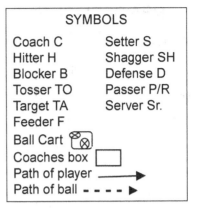

SYMBOLS

Coach C	Setter S
Hitter H	Shagger SH
Blocker B	Defense D
Tosser TO	Passer P/R
Target TA	Server Sr.
Feeder F	
Ball Cart	
Coaches box	
Path of player	
Path of ball	

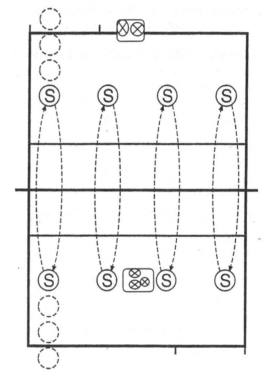

DRILL: AREA SERVICE Pr. 2

TYPE OF DRILL: Coach centered-teaching

INTENSITY LVL: Low   **SKILL LVL:** 1

EQUIPMENT
1. 10+ Balls
2. 2-Ball Carts

PERSONNEL: 10+

OBJECTIVE
1. Practice basic serve mechanics
2. Develop confidence in serve technique
3. Provide multiple serve repetitions

COACHING POINTS-TECHNICAL EMPHASIS
1. Step in direction of target
2. Weight transfer from rear to front foot
3. Shoulders square to net
4. Eliminate excess body movement

CONCENTRATION KEYS
1. Step-Toss-Hit
2. Controlled toss
3. Quick arm swing
4. No get-tee-up (Bent knee on toss)

ROTATION
1. Server Rotate to end of Server line after 5 serves

PERFORMANCE GOAL-SCORING
1. Timed repetitions (15 minutes maximum)
2. Number of repetitions (25 in row) into court to designated area

SEQUENCE OF ACTION
1. Coach explains skill — experienced player models skill
2. Players line up on opposite sides of court at base line
3. Players serve designated area of the court
4. Targets randomly move to various areas of court
5. Players continue to serve until performance goal achieved

DRILL VARIATIONS/PROGRESSION: Servers vary serve locations along base line

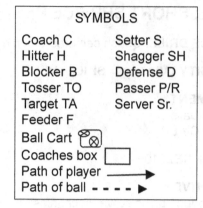

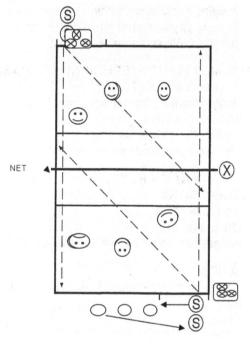

DRILL: FOREARM LINE PASS-pr 1

TYPE OF DRILL: Player centered/teaching

INTENSITY LVL: Medium   **SKILL LVL:** 1

EQUIPMENT
1. 1 Ball each line
2. 1 Ball Cart

PERSONNEL: 6+

OBJECTIVE-DESIRED BEHAVIOR
1. Practice forearm passing technique
2. Pass with control to a stationary target
3. Provide multiple repetitions

COACHING POINTS-TECHNICAL EMPHASIS
1. Get to contact point with split step before ball
2. Arms away from body
3. Keep hips lower than ball
4. Contact ball just above wrists
5. Focal point between contact point and target

CONCENTRATION KEYS
1. Thumbs together
2. Arms away from body
3. Elbows locked
4. Right foot steps to target

ROTATION: Pass and rotate to end of line

PERFORMANCE GOAL-SCORING
1. Number of repetitions (10 A moves to B)

SEQUENCE OF ACTION
1. Three passing lines (**B**) and tossers (**A**) at net equal distance apart
2. Player line **A** starts drill with toss to opposite player in line **B**
3. Player line **B** returns pass to player **A** and rotates to end of line
4. A players replace a B player when performance goal achieved

DRILL VARIATIONS/PROGRESSION: B
moves back toward base line as skill progresses

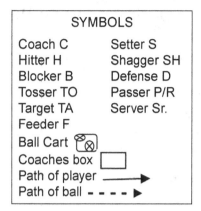

SYMBOLS

Coach C	Setter S
Hitter H	Shagger SH
Blocker B	Defense D
Tosser TO	Passer P/R
Target TA	Server Sr.
Feeder F	
Ball Cart	
Coaches box	
Path of player	
Path of ball - - - - ▶	

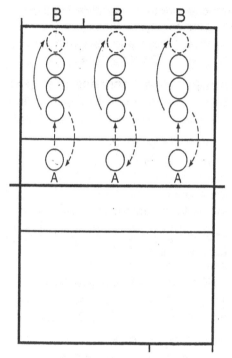

DRILL: FOREARM OVER THE NET PASS—Pr2

TYPE OF DRILL: Player centered Practice

INTENSITY LVL: Low   **SKILL LVL:** 1

EQUIPMENT
1. 1 Ball each line
2. 1 Ball cart

PERSONNEL: 10+

OBJECTIVE
1. improve forearm passing technique
2. Practice communication skills
3. Develop forearm passing control
4. Provide multiple repetitions

COACHING POINTS-TECHNICAL EMPHASIS
1. Move quickly to point of contact 10' line
2. Split step on approach to contact point

CONCENTRATION KEYS
1. Thumbs together
2. Step to target
3. Elbows locked
4. Square to target arm away from body

ROTATION: Pass 5 balls and rotate to end of line at baseline

PERFORMANCE GOAL-SCORING
1. Timed repetitions (15 minutes maximum)
2. Number of repetitions (25 in a row)

SEQUENCE OF ACTION
1. Drill started with toss over net
2. Ball passed back and forth over net between players at 10' line
3. Drill repeated until performance time limit reached

DRILL VARIATIONS/PROGRESSIONS
1. Overhead pass (See overhead line pass)

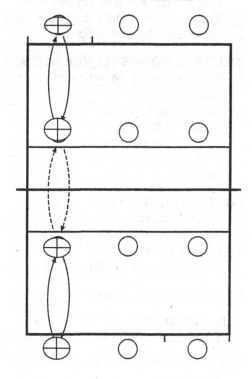

SYMBOLS

Coach C	Setter S
Hitter H	Shagger SH
Blocker B	Defense D
Tosser TO	Passer P/R
Target TA	Server Sr.
Feeder F	
Ball Cart	
Coaches box	
Path of player	
Path of ball	

NET

DRILL: ROTATION PASS Pr3

TYPE OF DRILL: Player centered/teaching

INTENSITY LVL: Low   **SKILL LVL:** 1

EQUIPMENT
1. 4+ Balls
2. 1 Ball Cart

PERSONNEL: 8+

OBJECTIVE
1. Train forearm passing technique
2. Improve movement skills
3. Provide multiple repetitions

COACHING POINTS-TECHNICAL EMPHASIS
1. Move quickly to next position with slide step
2. Arms away from body and elbow's locked
3. Extend wrist down to open/flatten forearms
4. Right foot forward and step to target

CONCENTRATION KEYS
1. Thumbs together
2. Beat the ball
3. Step to target
4. Platform out
5. Midline the pass

ROTATION
1. Passers rotate one position after each pass
2. Tosser to Passer on achievement of performance goal

PERFORMANCE GOAL-SCORING
1. Timed repetitions: 5 minutes max
2. Number of correct repetitions (20)

SEQUENCE OF ACTION
1. Coach or experienced player models skill
2. 4 players line up 3' apart at each 10'
3. One line consists of **T**ossing players
4. Opposite line consist of **P**assers
5. Passer return ball tossed with underhand pass and slide steps one place side way to (**T-2-T3-T4**) and returns to (**T1**) passing line
6. Upon achieving performance goal (**T**'s) replaces a passers
7. Drill repeated until performance goal achieved

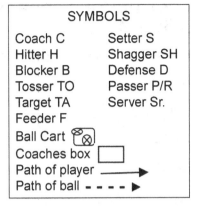

SYMBOLS

Coach C	Setter S
Hitter H	Shagger SH
Blocker B	Defense D
Tosser TO	Passer P/R
Target TA	Server Sr.
Feeder F	
Ball Cart	
Coaches box	
Path of player	
Path of ball	

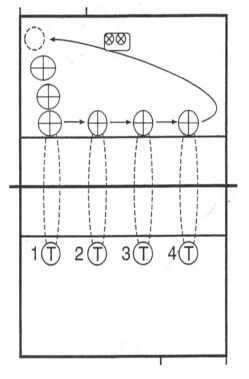

DRILL: CONTINUOUS FOREARM LINE PASS Pr.4

TYPE OF DRILL: Coach centered/Training

INTENSITY LVL: Medium   **SKILL LVL:** 1

EQUIPMENT: 2 balls

PERSONNEL: 8+

OBJECTIVES
1. Warm up
2. Improve technical passing accuracy
3. Teach/Practice linear-non linear passing
4. Provide multiple passing repetitions

COACHING POINTS-TECHNICAL
1. High controlled pass
2. Maintain proper passing technique on each attempt
3. Follow through to the target
4. Pass should be linear or non-linear
5. Call mine before each pass

CONCENTRATION KEYS
1. Right foot forward
2. Elbows locked
3. Non linear: arm raised on ball side of body
4. Step with platform in direction of target
5. Wrist flex downward

ROTATION: A to B/B to D//D to C/C to A after each pass

PERFORMANCE GOAL-SCORING
1. 10 passes without error
2. Re-start at 1 after each error

SEQUENCE OF ACTION
1. **A**-tosses ball to line **C** and rotates to **B** /**C** return pass A rotates to **A**
2. **D**-tosses ball to line **B** and rotates **C/B** returns pass **D** and rotates **D**
3. Drill repeated until performance goal achieved

VARIATION: Alternate linear and non-linear

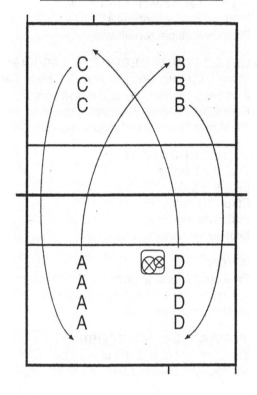

SYMBOLS

Coach C	Setter S
Hitter H	Shagger SH
Blocker B	Defense D
Tosser TO	Passer P/R
Target TA	Server Sr.
Feeder F	

Ball Cart

Coaches box

Path of player ────▶

Path of ball ‑ ‑ ‑ ‑ ▶

DRILL: GROOVE PASS- Pr. 5

TYPE OF DRILL: Player centered/training

INTENSITY LVL: Medium   **SKILL LVL:** 1-2

EQUIPMENT
1. 6 balls for each server
2. Tape to divide court

PERSONNEL: 8+

OBJECTIVE-DESIRED BEHAVIOR
1. Improve forearm passing technique/accuracy
2. Practice linear and rotational passing
3. Enhance body-court-ball spatial orientation
4. Provide multiple pass/serve repetitions

COACHING POINTS-TECHNICAL EMPHASIS
1. Assume proper body and court position
2. Focus on servers ball toss and hand contact
3. Make step toward ball on contact by server
4. Call out "mine" prior to ball crossing the net
5. Eyes focus between ball and contact point
6. Hold platform for 2 seconds after contact

CONCENTRATION KEYS
1. Ready position
2. Early communication
3. Beat the ball
4. Thumbs together/point to floor
5. Elbows away/locked

ROTATION: Sr to TA to P to Sr upon goal achievement

PERFORMANCE GOAL-SCORING
1. 8 out of 10 to target area
2. Passing Game
   a. 1 point for each pass to target
   b. Winner: least amount of passes needed to reach 5 points or first to 15 Pts

SEQUENCE OF ACTION
1. Divide court lengthwise down the middle
2. Both haves courts used for drill
3. Play begins with lob serve from service area
4. Ball passed to target area
5. 1 step to allowed receive ball
6. Target returns ball to server
7. Drill repeated until performance goal achieved

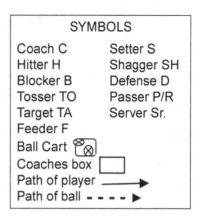

SYMBOLS	
Coach C	Setter S
Hitter H	Shagger SH
Blocker B	Defense D
Tosser TO	Passer P/R
Target TA	Server Sr.
Feeder F	
Ball Cart	
Coaches box	
Path of player ⟶	
Path of ball - - - ▶	

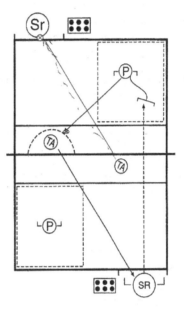

DRILL: 4 PERSON TEAM PASS Pr. 6

TYPE OF DRILL: Player centered/training

INTENSITY LVL: Medium   **SKILL LVL:** 1-2

EQUIPMENT: 10+ Balls and 1 Ball cart

PERSONNEL: 12+

OBJECTIVE-DESIRED BEHAVIOR
1. Practice 4 person reception positions
2. Develop spatial orientation with Ct and ball
3. Enhance team serve receive communication
4. Learn to read the server
5. Improve team passing technique
6. Provide multiple pass repetitions

COACHING POINTS-TACTICAL EMPHASIS
1. Read server's body position prior to ball contact
2. Eyes focus on ball toss and hand contact
3. Follow flight of ball using net as reference
4. Slow the flight of ball by "framing ball"
5. Communicate possible passer- before ball crosses the net
6. Non-passers turn toward passer/calls his/her name

CONCENTRATION KEYS
1. Pre-reception routine
2. Read server
3. Early communication
4. Be decisive and commit to pass

ROTATION
1. Passing team rotates 1position counter clockwise every 5 points
2. Serving team S/SH/S
3. Passing and serving teams alternate after goal achievement

PERFORMANCE GOAL-SCORING
1. Rally scoring to 15 points.
2. 1 pt. for each pass to target

SEQUENCE OF ACTION
1. Drill begins with **S**erve to receiving team
2. **P**ass must be to **T**arget area -**S**etter allowed 1 step and reach ball
3. **SH** returns ball to **S**erver
4. Repeat until performance goal achieved

DRILL VARIATION/PROGRESSION: Add set and attack

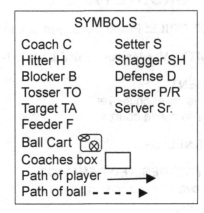

SYMBOLS
Coach C	Setter S
Hitter H	Shagger SH
Blocker B	Defense D
Tosser TO	Passer P/R
Target TA	Server Sr.
Feeder F	

Ball Cart
Coaches box
Path of player ⟶
Path of ball - - - - ▶

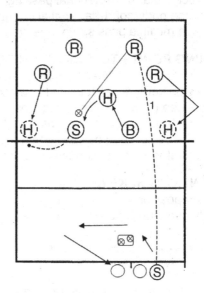

DRILL: OVERHEAD LINE PASS
Per 1

TYPE OF DRILL: Coach centered/training

INTENSITY LVL: Medium   **SKILL LVL:** 1

EQUIPMENT
1. 1 Ball each line
2. 1 Ball Cart

PERSONNEL: 6+

OBJECTIVE-DESIRED BEHAVIOR
1. Practice overhead passing technique
2. Pass OH with control to a stationary target
3. Develop movement skills
4. Provide multiple repetitions

COACHING POINTS-TECHNICAL EMPHASIS
1. Get to contact point before ball
2. Elbows away from body at 45 degree angle
3. Focal point between "V" made by thumbs and index fingers
4. Leg push as body extends to target

CONCENTRATION KEYS
1. Right foot forward
2. Hands above forehead
3. Fingers spread-relaxed
4. Forward weight transfer

ROTATION: Pass and rotate to end of line at baseline

PERFORMANCE GOAL-SCORING
1. Number of repetitions (25± in row) restart over at 1 on passing error

SEQUENCE OF ACTION
1. 3-4 passing lines each court with players at 10' line equal distance apart
2. Players line **A** starts drill with OH pass over the net to line **B** and rotates to end of line at base line
3. Player line **B** returns pass to player **A** and rotates to end of line at base line
4. Repeat drill until performance goal achieved

DRILL VARIATIONS/PROGRESSION
1. Move back toward base line as hand strength, ability and accuracy improve
2. Could also be used as forearm line pass

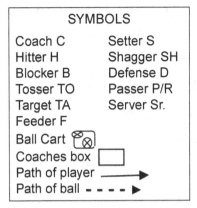

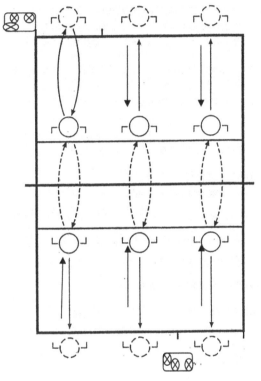

DRILL: CONTINUOUS OVERHEAD PASS Pr.2

TYPE OF DRILL: Player centered/training

INTENSITY LVL: Low   **SKILL LVL:** I

EQUIPMENT: 1 ball

PERSONNEL: 12+

OBJECTIVES
1. Warm up
2. Achieve OH passing accuracy
3. Develop technical mastery
4. Improve fitness and movement skills
5. Provide multiple passing repetitions

COACHING POINTS-TECHNICAL EMPHASIS
1. Place hands above head with thumbs pointing to forehead
2. Right foot slightly forward
3. Body relaxed with knees slightly bent
4. Face ball-target prior to contact

CONCENTRATION KEYS
1. Hands shape of ball
2. Springboard effect as ball is contacted by hands
3. Body - arms extend toward target
4. Thumbs to target

ROTATION: See sequence

PERFORMANCE GOAL-SCORING
1. 25 passes without error–restart at 1 after error
2. Time repetitions

SEQUENCE
1. **A** passes to **C** rotates to **B**
2. **C** passes to **A** and rotates to **A**
3. **D** passes to **B** and rotates to **C**
4. **B**. passes to **D** and rotates to **D**
5. Drill continues until performance goal achieved

DRILL VARIATIONS/PROGRESSIONS
1. Underhand pass
2. Alternate over head pass with forearm pass on every other attempt

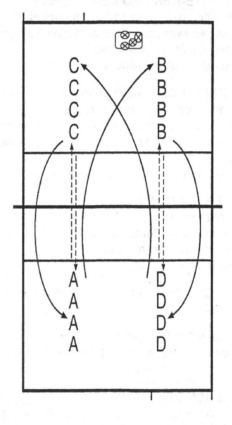

SYMBOLS	
Coach C	Setter S
Hitter H	Shagger SH
Blocker B	Defense D
Tosser TO	Passer P/R
Target TA	Server Sr.
Feeder F	
Ball Cart	
Coaches box	
Path of player	
Path of ball	

DRILL: OVERHEAD ROTATION PASS-Pr.3

TYPE OF DRILL: Player centered

INTENSITY LVL: Low   **SKILL LVL:** 1

EQUIPMENT: 1 Ball each line

PERSONNEL: 10+

OBJECTIVE
1. Improve overhead passing technique
2. Practice communication skills
3. Develop overhead passing control
4. Provide multiple repetitions

COACHING POINTS-TECHNICAL EMPHASIS
1. Move quickly to contact point
2. Face target
3. Communicate mine on each contact

CONCENTRATION KEYS
1. Hands to forehand
2. Step to target
3. Arms extend to target

ROTATION
1. When a player reach 15 correct passes they move to a T player position

PERFORMANCE GOAL-SCORING
1. Timed repetitions (3-5 minutes)
2. Number of repetitions (15 in a row)

SEQUENCE OF ACTION
1. **T**ossers and **P**assers line up on opposite 10'
2. Tossing line (**T**) serves or tosses ball to opposite passer
3. Opposite passer returns ball with overhead pass and slide steps one place sideways to **T-2-T3-T4**) etc. and returns to (**T1**) passing line
4. Drill repeated until performance goal achieved

DRILL VARATIONS

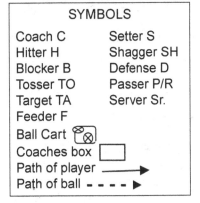

SYMBOLS

Coach C	Setter S
Hitter H	Shagger SH
Blocker B	Defense D
Tosser TO	Passer P/R
Target TA	Server Sr.
Feeder F	
Ball Cart	
Coaches box	
Path of player	⟶
Path of ball	- - - - ▶

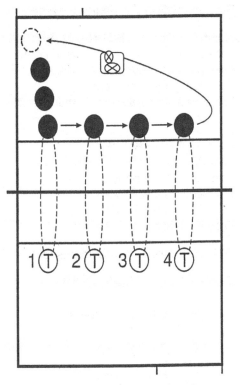

DRILL: TOSS-PASS-SET: Pr.4

TYPE OF DRILL: Player centered/teaching

INTENSITY LVL: Medium   SKILL:2

EQUIPMENT: 2 Balls per server

PERSONNEL: 3+

OBJECTIVE-DESIRED BEHAVIOR
1. Improve pass-set technique/accuracy
2. Introduce game-like ball movement
3. Develop court-player spatial orientation
4. Provide multiple passing/serve repetitions

COACHING POINTS-TECHNICAL EMPHASIS
1. Passers focus on ball toss-hand contact
2. Communicate before ball crosses net
3. Face ball prior to contact
4. Lower inside shoulder in direction of Setter on pass

CONCENTRATION KEYS
1. Beat the ball
2. Arms away from body
3. Thumbs together
4. Early communication
5. Pass to Setter

ROTATION: Passer to target to passer

PERFORMANCE GOAL-SCORING
1. Scoring:
   a. 1 pt each pass in setter
   b. 15 points and rotate
2. To score points setter allowed only one step and arms reach

SEQUENCE OF ACTION
1. Court divided in half lengthwise-Two teams of 3 on each half **CT**.
2. Ball tossed with lob toss at mid-court to **P** (**1**)
3. Passer passes ball to **S** (**2**) **S** sets ball to **TA** (**3**)
4. Target returns ball to **TO** and keeps score
5. Repeat drill until performance goal achieved

DRILL VARIATIONS/PROGRESSIONS
1. Change lob toss to high looping overhead serve as skill progresses
2. Gradually retreats toward base line as strength and accuracy improve

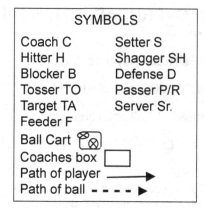

SYMBOLS	
Coach C	Setter S
Hitter H	Shagger SH
Blocker B	Defense D
Tosser TO	Passer P/R
Target TA	Server Sr.
Feeder F	
Ball Cart	
Coaches box	
Path of player	
Path of ball	

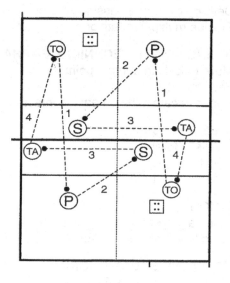

DRILL: OVERHEAD PASS AND MOVE P r. 5

TYPE OF DRILL: Player centered/teaching

INTENSITY LVL: Low   **SKILL LVL:** 1-2

EQUIPMENT: 1 Ball for each drill

PERSONNEL: 2+

OBJECTIVE
1. Teach overhead passing technique
2. Improve OH passing accuracy
3. Practice movement to the ball
4. Provide multiple passing repetitions

COACHING POINTS-TECHNICAL EMPHASIS
1. Slide step quickly to contact point
2. Pass ball at forehead and extend to target

CONCENTRATION KEYS
1. Front the pass
2. Feet to ball
3. Face target
4. Elbows extended

ROTATION: T to P on completion of performance goal

PERFORMANCE GOAL-SCORING
1. 25 passes without error

SEQUENCE
1. Drill at bottom of court: Player simply moves side to side to pass ball from **T**oss or **S**pike as skill progresses
2. Top drill: Ball **T**ossed or Hit to either side and back and forth
3. Ball pass back to **T**arget

DRILL VARIATIONS/PROGRESSIONS
1. Lower toss to increase speed
2. Lengthen distance of toss to increase movement demands
3. Replace toss with medium speed spike

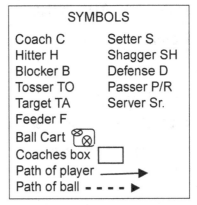

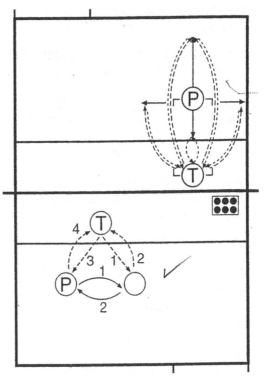

DRILL: SETTER TRAINING

TYPE OF DRILL: Coach centered/training

INTENSITY LVL: Medium   SKILL:1-2-3

EQUIPMENT: 6 balls and cart

PERSONNEL: 2+ setters, target/coach/tosser

OBJECTIVE-DESIRED BEHAVIOR
1. Perfect overhead set technique
2. Improve setter movement
3. Practice approach footwork
4. Train speed/set location
5. Provide multiple repetitions

COACHING POINTS-TECHNICAL EMPHASIS
1. Quick movement to target area-point of contact
2. Pursue bad pass from target area
3. Make eye contact with target before setting ball
4. Accuracy first-deception second
5. Communicate
    a. On approach- "I'm up"
    b. "Here" upon reaching target area
6. Add Jump set as skill progresses

CONCENTRATION KEYS
1. Last three steps on approach –R-L-R
2. Right foot must end up forward
3. Hands up early
4. Feet and hips under ball
5. Face and extend to target

ROTATION
1. Change setters on goal achievement

PERFORMANCE GOAL-SCORING
1. 20 consecutive sets at correct height-trajectory-speed-distance off net as shown in each of the four drill locations

SEQUENCE OF ACTION
1. Drill begins with **T** toss to target area or to various setting areas
2. **S**etter alternates approach from areas 1-4 court zones
3. **S**etter sets designated set to pre-determined setting zone
4. Repeat drill until performance goal achieved

DRILL VARIATIONS: Same sequence of drills with middle and back set

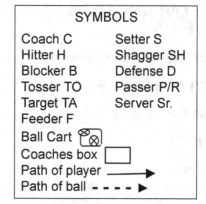

SYMBOLS

Coach C	Setter S
Hitter H	Shagger SH
Blocker B	Defense D
Tosser TO	Passer P/R
Target TA	Server Sr.
Feeder F	
Ball Cart	
Coaches box	
Path of player	⟶
Path of ball	- - - ▸

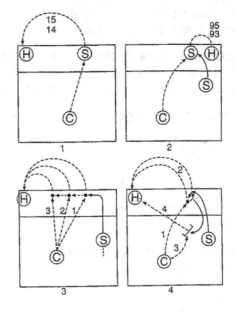

DRILL: 3 STEP APPROACH Pr 1

TYPE OF DRILL: Coach centered/teaching

INTENSITY LVL: Medium **SKILL LVL:** 1

EQUIPMENT

PERSONNEL: 1+

OBJECTIVE
1. Practice approach and retreat footwork efficiency and timing
2. Provide multiple repetitions

COACHING POINTS-TECHNICAL EMPHASIS
(3 step)
1. Introduce- practice 3-4 step approach footwork
2. Instill approach foot work before attempting retreat
3. Practice retreat footwork
4. Combine two skills to develop single motor program

CONCENTRATION KEYS
1. Right foot forward-Pendulum arm swing
2. Left-Right-Left
3. Right foot heel/toe on contact with floor

ROTATION: Rotate to end of line after 3 attempts

PERFORMANCE GOAL-SCORING
1. 15 perfect approaches

SEQUENCE OF ACTION
1. Divide players into 3 lines
2. Each group assumes an evenly spaced approach position at 10' line
3. Approach: Right foot forward with body forward of base big first step with left foot- short second step with right foot for closed step at net with left foot- Quick pendulum arm swing with full extension or arms-last two steps must be right/left together
4. Retreat: Pivot on landing and retreat to attack position
5. (see progression #2 PRP drill)
6. Repeat until performance goal achieved

DRILL VARIATIONS/PROGRESSIONS: 4
STEP APPROACH
1. 4 step approach same body movement only approach starts with left foot forward
2. Last two steps must be with right/left closed and heel/toe movement with right foot

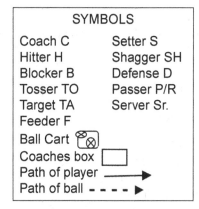

SYMBOLS

Coach C	Setter S
Hitter H	Shagger SH
Blocker B	Defense D
Tosser TO	Passer P/R
Target TA	Server Sr.
Feeder F	

Ball Cart

Coaches box

Path of player ⟶

Path of ball - - - ▶

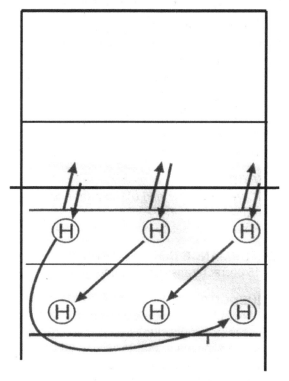

DRILL: PIVOT/RETREAT/PIVOT-Pr#2

TYPE OF DRILL: Players centered/Teaching

INTENSITY LVL: Medium   SKILL:1

EQUIPMENT

PERSONNEL: 3+

OBJECTIVE
1. Train efficient transition movement skills
2. Review approach skills
3. Teach retreat footwork
4. Provide multiple correct repetitions

COACHING POINTS-TECHNICAL EMPHASIS
1. On retreat keep shoulder/eyes toward opposite court
2. Foot work opposite for left handed hitters

CONCENTRATION KEYS-RETREAT
1. Wide pivot
2. Quick slide steps
3. Three step on approach to net after retreat

ROTATION
1. Players rotate to end of line after each retreat
2. Rotate after set number of repetitions

PERFORMANCE GOAL-SCORING
1. 15 correct transitions retreats

SEQUENCE OF ACTION
1. Three players assume curt position at net left-middle-right side
2. Players initiate retreat to 10' line and prepare for approach to net
   a. On landing after an attack place weight on left foot (right hander's)
   b. Pivot toward 10" line at 180° angle to net
   c. Slide 2 steps toward 10' placing weight on right foot
   d. Pivot off right foot 180 degrees for 3 step approach to net
3. Begin 3 step approach to the net with Right foot forward
4. Approach starts with long step by the left foot followed by a right-left heal toe closing step
5. Retreat and approach repeatedly until performance goal achieved

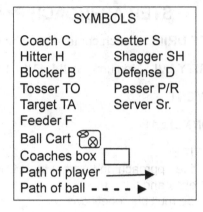

SYMBOLS

Coach C	Setter S
Hitter H	Shagger SH
Blocker B	Defense D
Tosser TO	Passer P/R
Target TA	Server Sr.
Feeder F	
Ball Cart	
Coaches box	
Path of player	⟶
Path of ball	- - - ▶

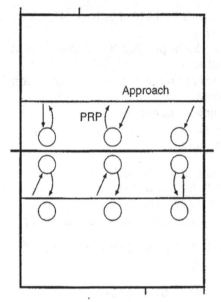

DRILL: INTRODUCTORY SPIKE-Pr. 3

TYPE OF DRILL: Coach centered/Training

INTENSITY LVL: Medium   **SKILL LVL:** 1

EQUIPMENT
1. 10+ Balls per station
2. 1 Ball carts

PERSONNEL: 3+ per station

OBJECTIVE
1. Introduce spiking techniques
2. Improve approach and jump timing
3. Provide skill progression
4. Provide multiple repetitions

COACHING POINTS-TECHNICAL EMPHASIS
1. Assume attack position at 45 degree angle to net
2. Last step of approach must be right/left
3. Point non-hitting hand at ball
4. Swing hard with quick arm on all sets

CONCENTRATION KEYS
1. Right/left
2. Pendulum arm swing
3. Force in force out on floor contact
4. High arm extension
5. Finger spread

ROTATION: Alternate attackers after goal achievement

PERFORMANCE GOAL-SCORING
1. Number of repetitions (5 in row at each position)

SEQUENCE OF ACTION
1. Drill begins with attacker and coach at net
2. 1st sequence-player stands at net jumps and hits ball tossed by Coach
3. 2nd sequence-Player starts 1 step off net with right/left (closed step) approach jump and hits ball
4. 3rd sequence-Player starts **2** steps off net and right foot forward with long approach step with left foot followed by a right- left closing step
5. Add a fourth step for 4 step approach
6. Start with left foot forward for left handed attackers
7. Drill continues until performance goal achieved

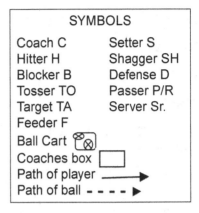

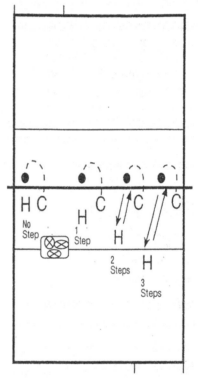

DRILL: WALL HIT – Pr. #4

TYPE OF DRILL: Player centered/training

INTENSITY LVL: Medium/high   **SKILL LVL:** 2

EQUIPMENT: 1 ball per player

PERSONNEL: 1+

OBJECTIVE-DESIRED BEHAVIOR
1. Improve arm swing-ball contact
2. Improve arm-hand acceleration
3. Learn to impart top spin with wrist snap
4. Coordinate arm swing with jump
5. Provide multiple correct repetitions

COACHING POINTS-TECHNICAL EMPHASIS
1. Foot non- hand hitting forward
2. Two hand toss followed by full arm swing
3. Non-hitting hand points at ball
4. Heel of hitting hand contacts ball first
5. Contact ball slightly below center-snap wrist
6. Non-hitting hand drops quickly to hip with bent elbow as hitting hand moves forward

CONCENTRATION KEYS
1. High two hand toss
2. Locate to ball
3. Pendulum arm swing
4. High contact point
5. Reach and snap
6. Fingers spread
7. Quick arm swing

PERFORMANCE GOAL-SCORING
1. 5 min.-25 consecutive balls hit with correct arm swing

SEQUENCE OF ACTION
1. Drill begins with high two hand toss with player facing a wall
2. Ball hit down onto the floor and off the wall
3. Hitter makes second contact after ball bounces off wall into the air
4. Ball again hit down onto floor and off the wall
5. Repeat without stopping
6. Drill repeated until performance goal achieved

DRILL VARIATIONS/PROGRESSIONS
1. Add jump and hit

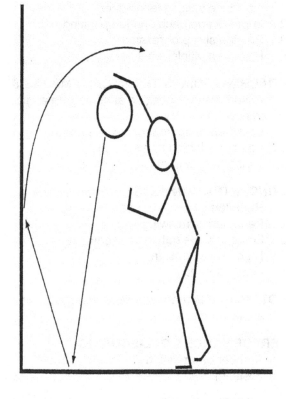

```
SYMBOLS
Coach C            Setter S
Hitter H           Shagger SH
Blocker B          Defense D
Tosser TO          Passer P/R
Target TA          Server Sr.
Feeder F
Ball Cart
Coaches box
Path of player ──────▶
Path of ball  - - - ▶
```

DRILL: SELF TOSS AND HIT Pr. 5

TYPE OF DRILL: Player centered/teaching

INTENSITY LVL: Medium   **SKILL:**1-2

EQUIPMENT: 1 ball for every two player

PERSONNEL: 2+

OBJECTIVE-DESIRED BEHAVIOR
1. Learn to locate to the ball
2. Train top spin for ball control
3. Practice deep court attack technique
4. Improve attack accuracy
5. Provide multiple repetitions

COACHING POINTS-TECHNICAL EMPHASIS
1. High two hand toss
2. Keep ball out in front of body
3. Point non-hitting hand at ball
4. Reach for ball with high arm extension
5. Contact ball with heel of hand first
6. Roll fingers over top with wrist snap
7. Non-hitting elbow drops to waist on follow through

CONCENTRATION KEYS
1. Feet to ball
2. Pendulum arm swing
3. Guide arm up
4. Quick arm swing
5. High contact point
6. Wrist snap
7. Hit through ball

ROTATION

PERFORMANCE GOAL-SCORING
1. 10 consecutive hits to designated player or area
2. Partner keeps accuracy score

SEQUENCE OF ACTION
1. Hitters starts with attack mid-court
2. Drill begins with high two handed self-toss
3. Tosser attacks ball to designated partner in opposite court
4. Partner digs/catches ball and returns attack
5. Repeat drill until performance goal achieved

DRILL VARIATIONS: Move back from net as technique improves

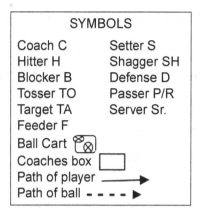

SYMBOLS

Coach C	Setter S
Hitter H	Shagger SH
Blocker B	Defense D
Tosser TO	Passer P/R
Target TA	Server Sr.
Feeder F	
Ball Cart	
Coaches box	
Path of player	
Path of ball	

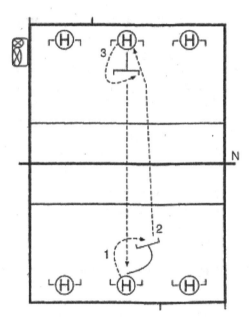

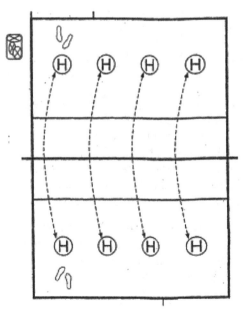

DRILL: OFF SPEED ATTACK –Pr. 6

TYPE OF DRILL: Coach centered/teaching

INTENSITY LVL: Medium   **SKILL LVL:** 1-2-3

EQUIPMENT: 10+ Balls

PERSONNEL: 4+

OBJECTIVE-DESIRED BEHAVIOR
1. Develop off speed attack techniques
2. Improve attack deception/accuracy
3. Provide multiple repetitions

COACHING POINTS-TECHNICAL EMPHASIS
1. Attack with full approach-jump and arm swing to disguise attack
2. Roll shot: hit behind/under ball, roll finger through and over top of ball
3. Tip shot: push ball with firm wrist and fingers
4. Reverse tip with right hand I
5. Tip ball to center of court or deep corners
6. Tip ball just before peak of jump

CONCENTRATION KEYS
1. Deception with full arm swing
2. Attack open areas
3. Firm wrist

ROTATION: Hitter shags ball-rotates to end of hitting line

PERFORMANCE GOAL-SCORING
1. Game scoring: 15 points—1.point for each attack to designated area

SEQUENCE OF ACTION
1. Areas open to tip marked on court marked with **X**
2. Drill begins with toss **C** to **S** (**1**) who sets predetermined set (**2**)
3. **H**itter attacks set with off speed hit to marked areas of court (**3**) or deep court (**4**)
4. **S**etter and next **H** practice covering **H**
5. Drill continues until performance goal achieved

DRILL VARIATIONS/PROGRESSIONS
1. Coach calls area to be attacked after set
2. Alternate hit-tip-hit-roll
3. Move drill to middle and left side

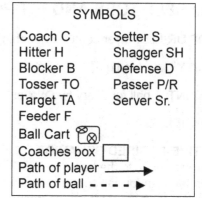

SYMBOLS

Coach C	Setter S
Hitter H	Shagger SH
Blocker B	Defense D
Tosser TO	Passer P/R
Target TA	Server Sr.
Feeder F	
Ball Cart	
Coaches box	
Path of player	
Path of ball	

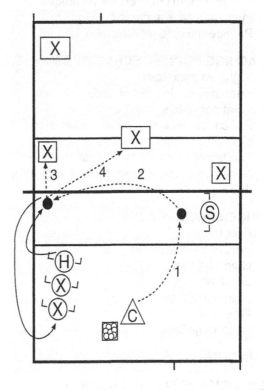

DRILL: CONTINUOUS DINK

TYPE OF DRILL: Player centered/training

INTENSITY LVL: Medium   **SKILL LVL:** 1-2-3

EQUIPMENT
1. 1 Ball per 1/2 court
2. Tape/antennae

PERSONNEL: 2/3 players per 1/2 court Team

OBJECTIVE-DESIRED BEHAVIOR
1. Practice off speed attack technique/accuracy
2. Improve team work
3. Practice communication skills
4. Develop ball control
5. Provide skill drill warm up
6. Have fun
7. Provide multiple repetitions

COACHING POINTS-TECHNICAL EMPHASIS
1. Visually check defense prior to approach
2. Full approach and arm swing
3. Slow tip: place spread finger slightly under ball with soft wrist action
4. Hard tip: with fingers on top of ball push down on ball with firm, abrupt arm action

CONCENTRATION KEYS
1. Read defense
2. Normal arm swing
3. Tip at peak of jump
4. Tip to open areas
5. Control and placement

ROTATION: Game rotation after each point

PERFORMANCE GOAL-SCORING
1. Rally score game to 15 point
2. 5 minute time limit for warm-up

SEQUENCE OF ACTION
1. Tape line lengthwise at mid court and antennae on net at mid-court to divide
2. Play begins with toss (**1**) to any one of 3 players in opposite court half court
3. Player passes ball to setter who set hitter (2) Hitter attacks ball (**3-4-5**)
4. Play must include 3 contacts per side
5. Exception: setter may use left hand tip on Second contact
6. All entering adjacent court cannot be played
7. Drill continues until performance goal achieved

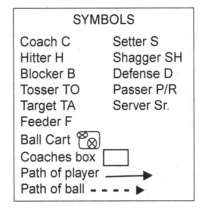

SYMBOLS

Coach C	Setter S
Hitter H	Shagger SH
Blocker B	Defense D
Tosser TO	Passer P/R
Target TA	Server Sr.
Feeder F	

Ball Cart
Coaches box
Path of player ——▶
Path of ball - - - ▶

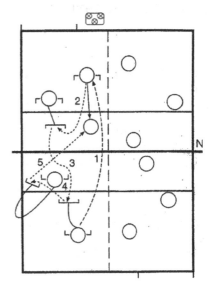

DRILL: CONTINUOUS BLOCK Pr.1

TYPE OF DRILL: Player centered-teaching

INTENSITY LVL: Medium   **SKILL:**1

EQUIPMENT

PERSONNEL: 6+

OBJECTIVE
1. Train block movement/jump timing
2. Practice blocking technique
3. Improve anaerobic conditioning
4. Provide multiple correct repetitions

COACHING POINTS-TECHNICAL EMPHASIS
1. Alternate slide and crossover step
2. Reach over net and push on opposite blockers hands
3. Communicate jump timing with opposite blocker
4. Max effort on each block attempt

CONCENTRATION KEYS
1. Hands up just above head with elbows bent
2. Thumbs up
3. Penetrate
4. Spread fingers with stiff wrists

ROTATION: Move to end of opposite line

PERFORMANCE GOAL-SCORING
1. Timed intervals: (15 minutes activity-)
2. Number of repetitions: 25

SEQUENCE OF ACTION
1. Three players line up on each side of net in blocking positions (lf-mf-rf)
2. Players jump together and block in starting position
3. Drill starts with a block jump and push on opposite players hands
4. Both players move to block middle followed by a right side block
5. Objective: to time jump, penetrate net and push on opposing blockers hands
6. Middle blocker pair up with opposite middles
7. Repeat drill until performance goal achieved

DRILL VARIATIONS/PROGRESSIONS

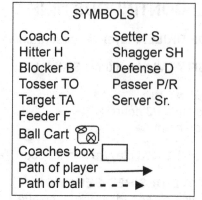

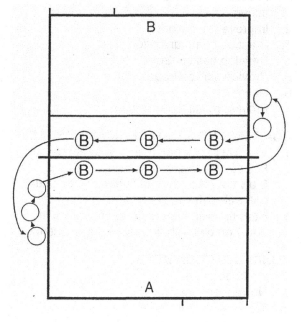

DRILL: SIMPLE BLOCK Per.2

TYPE OF DRILL: Coach centered/teaching

INTENSITY LVL: High   **SKILL LVL:** I

EQUIPMENT
1. 10+ Balls
2. 1 Cart-1 coaches box

PERSONNEL: 10+

OBJECTIVE
1. Develop blocking technique
2. Improve block jump timing-
3. Teach (PSC) penetration-seal the net-close the block technique
4. Provide multiple repetitions

COACHING POINTS-TECHNICAL EMPHASIS
1. Elbows at shoulder heights-hands a head
2. Reach over net place hand on ball
3. Slight pike at height of jump
4. Time block so ball blocked on way up or peak of jump

CONCENTRATION KEYS
1. Firm wrists
2. Shrug shoulders on reach over net
3. Head up
4. Eyes on ball
5. PCS (penetrate/closes seams/seal the net)

ROTATION
1. SH/B – H/SH every 12 blocks
2. Offensive to Defense goal achievement

PERFORMANCE GOAL-SCORING
1. Goal achievement 24 blocks-5 minutes

SEQUENCE OF ACTION
1. Drill begins with **H** on box holding ball 1 foot from net and above net
2. **B**lockers make repeated jump attempts to place hands on ball and push
3. Drill repeated until performance goal achieved

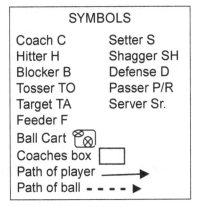

SYMBOLS
Coach C	Setter S
Hitter H	Shagger SH
Blocker B	Defense D
Tosser TO	Passer P/R
Target TA	Server Sr.
Feeder F	
Ball Cart	
Coaches box	
Path of player	
Path of ball	

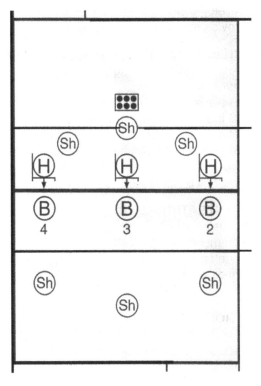

DRILL: 2 PLAYER BLOCK BOX Pr. 3

TYPE OF DRILL: Player-centered/training

INTENSITY LVL: High   SKILL:1- 2

EQUIPMENT: 10 balls-1 cart

PERSONNEL: 8+

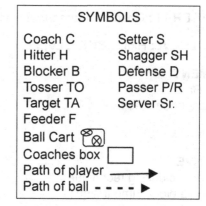

SYMBOLS

Coach C	Setter S
Hitter H	Shagger SH
Blocker B	Defense D
Tosser TO	Passer P/R
Target TA	Server Sr.
Feeder F	
Ball Cart	
Coaches box	
Path of player	
Path of ball	

OBJECTIVE-DESIRED BEHAVIOR
1. Practice block footwork and jump timing
2. Improve team blocking technique
3. Coordinate middle and outside block
4. Develop blocking communication
5. Provide multiple block repetitions

COACHING POINTS-TECHNICAL EMPHASIS
1. Front the hitter by lining up in angle of attack
2. OB places inside hand on ball
3. MB lines up with nose on hitting hand
4. OB sets block/communicates timing of jump
5. MB moves to block outside with crossover step
6. Divert all blocked balls to center court

CONCENTRATION KEYS
1. Focus on attackers hitting hand
2. Communicate attack information
3. Penetrate-Close block-Seal net
4. Hands on ball
5. Close to center court

ROTATION
1. Outside SH/F/SH/B rotate after 5 attempts
2. Middle B to end of line after 5 block attempts

PERFORMANCE GOAL-SCORING
1. 5 blocks each position (70 total)

SEQUENCE OF ACTION
1. Blockers assume blocking position at the net Hitter assume attack position on bench/box
2. Drill begins with slap of the ball and a high two hand toss and hit by **H**
3. Hitter alternates hitting ball cross court/line/middle
4. Middle **B** transition to block on slap of ball (middle blocker out of position)
5. Repeat drill until performance goal achieved

DRILL VARIATIONS/PROGRESSIONS
1. Move block middle-left side

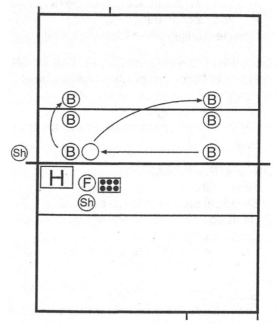

DRILL: BLOCK RETREAT TO ATTACK: Pr. #3

TYPE OF DRILL: Players centered/Teaching

INTENSITY LVL: Medium   **SKILL LVL:** 1- 2

EQUIPMENT
1. 3+ balls
2. 3 Ball Carts

PERSONNEL: 4-12

OBJECTIVE
1. Train transition from block to attack
2. Develop transition efficiency
3. Improve movement skills
4. Provide multiple correct repetitions

COACHING POINTS-TECHNICAL EMPHASIS
1. Blocker prepare to turn prior to landing pivot) foot
2. Blockers land with weight on outside and turn into court upon landing
3. Upon landing pivot and turn into court and retreat in direction of attack position 10' line

CONCENTRATION KEYS
1. Weight pivot foot
2. Pivot-Retreat-Retreat-Pivot
3. Three step approach

ROTATION
1. Offense: SH/H/F/H-F/F/H on goal achievement
2. Defense: Shaggers to Block

PERFORMANCE GOAL-SCORING
1. 60 seconds of continuous movement
2. 15 correct transitions

SEQUENCE OF ACTION
1. Divide players into 4 groups of 3
2. 3 Players assume attack position on coaches box
3. 3 players assume blocking position at net
4. Player on box slaps ball and hits into block
5. Blocker jumps/blocks and retreats to attack position at 10' line and approaches net and blocks next hit
6. Drill repeated until performance goal achieved

DRILL VARIATIONS/PROGRESSIONS
1. Add setter and attack after transition.

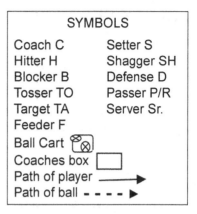

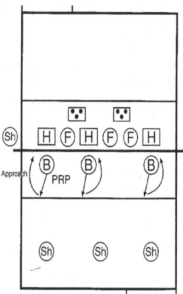

DRILL: BLOCK RECOVERY

TYPE OF DRILL: Coach centered/teaching

INTENSITY LVL: Medium   **SKILL LVL:** 1-2

EQUIPMENT
1. 10+ BALLS
2. Ball Carts-1 Coaching boxes

PERSONNEL 10+

OBJECTIVE
1. Introduce proper coverage body position
2. Learn attack coverage court positions
3. Train "watch the block" principle
4. Provide multiple repetitions

COACHING POINTS-TECHNICAL EMPHASIS
1. Read Keys-Attacker/Ball/Block/Ball
2. Be stopped and assume low body position prior to ball contact by attacker
3. Play ball up to center court
4. If in doubt find a hole in coverage and fill it

CONCENTRATION KEYS
1. Watch the block
2. Low platform
3. "J" stroke

ROTATION: SH/TO to coverage to B/B/SH

PERFORMANCE GOAL-SCORING
1. Number of balls dug by coverage team
2. Game scoring to 15-1 pt. each ball dug

SEQUENCE OF ACTION
1. Review positioning and technique coverage prior to start of drill
2. Attacking team assume attack coverage positions
3. Blockers assume block position on coaches boxes
4. Drill begin with toss or hit by stationary attacker directly into blockers on boxes at net
5. Blockers block ball to different areas of court
6. Coverage player assume coverage positions and retrieve ball up to mid-court
7. Drill continues until performance goal achieved

DRILL VARIATIONS/PROGRESSIONS
1. Live attack off toss to setter-ball hit into block
2. Move coverage to middle-right side of court

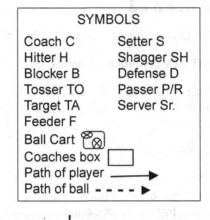

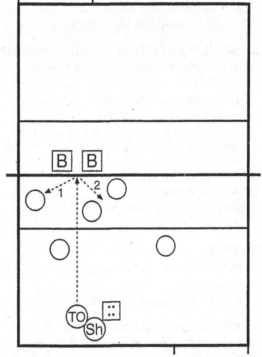

DRILL: NO BLOCK DIG THE BOX

INTENSITY LVL: High   **SKILL LVL:** 1- 2-3

EQUIPMENT: 10+ balls and cart

PERSONNEL: 8+

OBJECTIVE-DESIRED BEHAVIOR
1. Learn defensive positioning
2. Practice floor defensive technique
3. Develop player-ball-court spatial orientation
4. Improve the ability to read attack angle
5. Provide multiple repetitions

COACHING POINTS-TECHNICAL EMPHASIS
1. Assume on help court position
2. Offside blocker responsible for middle tip
3. Use parallel movement on balls hit between defenders
4. Read attackers arm and hand position

CONCENTRATION KEYS
1. Read attacker
2. Stay deep
3. Forward body position
4. Run through
5. Parallel movement

ROTATION: SH/F/TA/B/DSH after goal achievement

PERFORMANCE GOAL-SCORING
1. 10 balls dug to target

SEQUENCE OF ACTION
1. Drill begins by alternating hits to defensive player's or open spaces **forcing** parallel movement and run troughs
2. Defensive players start in base position and transition to reaction position or slap of ball
3. Hitter slaps ball-self tosses- hits ball
4. Repeat drill until performance goal achieved

DRILL VARIATIONS/PROGRESSIONS: Move attack to middle/right side

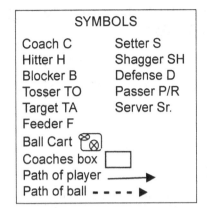

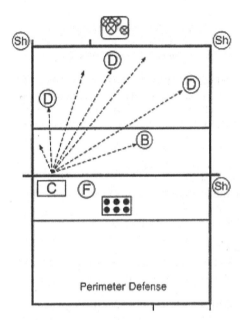
Perimeter Defense

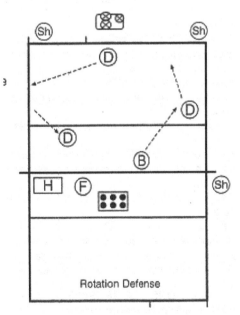
Rotation Defense

DRILL: SINGLE BLOCK THE BOX FLOOR DEF

TYPE OF DRILL: Coach Centered/Training

INTENSITY LVL: Medium   **SKILL LVL:** 2-3

EQUIPMENT: 20 Balls
1. Ball cart-
2. Coaches Box

PERSONNEL: 10+

OBJECTIVE-DESIRED BEHAVIOR
1. Improve ability of defense to read attack in relation to a single block
2. Practice transition/defensive movement
3. Improve blocking/floor defensive technique
4. Provide multiple dig repetitions

COACHING POINTS-TECHNICAL EMPHASIS
1. Read attackers arm/hand movement position
2. Transition to perimeter defense position
3. Defense assumes on-help position outside blocks shadow

CONCENTRATION KEYS
1. Parallel movement
2. Base to recognition
3. Quick retreat
4. On help court position

ROTATION
1. Block-feeders to defense-shagger every 10 hits
2. Offense to defense on goal achievement

PERFORMANCE GOAL-SCORING
1. Game scoring to 25 points 1 point for each dig

SEQUENCE OF ACTION
1. Player/coach on box alternates hitting to(D) defensive player (1-2) or court area
2. Ball can be hit to open areas of court between players forcing parallel movement
3. Stationary single block placed at the point of attack
4. Blocker reads angle of attack and attempts to block the attack
5. Back court Defensive player's starts in base position and retreats to recognition position on ball slap
6. Defense reacts to ball after reading angle of attack
7. Defense pursues any ball dug out of court area
8. Shagger at net critiques block technique/ defensive Shagger critique defense play
9. Drill repeated until performance goal achieved

DRILL VARIATIONS/PROGRESSIONS: Move block/attack to middle-right side

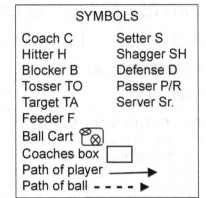

SYMBOLS

Coach C	Setter S
Hitter H	Shagger SH
Blocker B	Defense D
Tosser TO	Passer P/R
Target TA	Server Sr.
Feeder F	
Ball Cart	
Coaches box	
Path of player	
Path of ball	

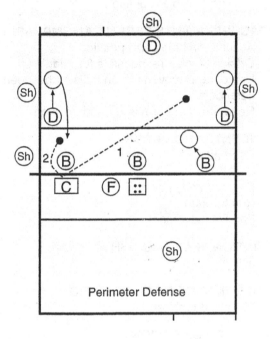

Perimeter Defense

DRILL: DIG AND MOVE

INTENSITY LVL: Medium-high   **SKILL LVL:** 2-3

EQUIPMENT
1. 15 balls
2. 2 Ball carts and coaches boxes

OBJECTIVE
1. Improve dig technique
2. Practice defensive movement
3. Physical conditioning
4. Provide multiple repetitions

COACHING POINTS-TECHNICAL EMPHASIS
1. Maintain a low body position
2. Linear and non-linear passing technique
3. Go to floor only as last resort

CONCENTRATION KEYS
1. Read attackers body position-arm swing
2. Beat ball to spot
3. Split step prior to ball contact
4. Get arms between ball and floor

ROTATION: D/TA/\SH/F/SH/D on goal achievement

PERFORMANCE G the net OAL –SCORING
1. Number of repetitions 5
2. Number of passes to target 5

SEQUENCE OF ACTION
1. Attacker on box hits ball to D A (1) D A passes ball to TA (2) and runs parallel to side line and back to original position
2. Attacker hits ball to D B (3) who passes ball to target (4) and runs to parallel side line and back to original position
3. Sequence of attack-action repeated with defenders passing ball to TA and running forward at an angle to the 10' line and back to original position
4. Repeat until performance goal achieved

DRILL VARIATION/PROGRESSION
1. Players side steps to back corners of court and return to original position
2. Players run backward to back line and return to original position

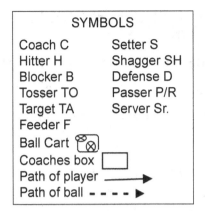

SYMBOLS

Coach C	Setter S
Hitter H	Shagger SH
Blocker B	Defense D
Tosser TO	Passer P/R
Target TA	Server Sr.
Feeder F	

Ball Cart

Coaches box

Path of player ——▶

Path of ball - - - - ▶

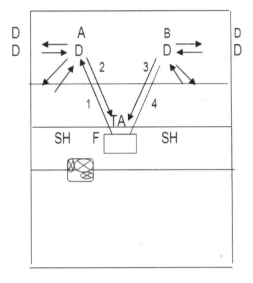

DRILL: DOUBLE BLOCK FLOOR DEFENSE:Pr.#3

TYPE OF DRILL: Coach Centered/Teaching

INTENSITY LVL: High **SKILL LVL:** 2-3

EQUIPMENT: 20 Balls and Ball Cart

PERSONNEL: 10+

OBJECTIVE-DESIRED BEHAVIOR
1. Improve ability of defense to read attack in relation to a double block
2. Practice transition/defensive movement
3. Improve blocking/floor defensive technique
4. Provide multiple block/floor defense repetitions

COACHING POINTS-TECHNICAL EMPHASIS
1. Read angle of attack and point of contact
2. Line defender responsible for tip over block
3. Move the rotation defense position on attack read
4. Block must cover a area of the court from attack

CONCENTRATION KEYS
1. Read attacker arm position
2. Close hole in block
3. On balance

ROTATION
1. D/B//F/ SH/ on goal achievement

PERFORMANCE GOAL-SCORING
1. 7 out of 10 ball must be blocked or settable digs
2. Game scoring to 20 points—1 point each dig

SEQUENCE OF ACTION
1. **C** on box slaps ball and alternates hitting to a defensive player or position
2. Stationary block placed at the point of attack
3. Ball can be hit to open areas of court between players forcing parallel movement
4. Blocker reads angle of attack and attempts to block the attack
5. Defensive players start in base position and transition to recognition position after ball slap
6. Defense react to ball after reading angle of attack
7. Defense pursues ball dug out of court area
8. Drill repeated until performance goal achieved

DRILL VARIATIONS
9. Move to middle and right side attack

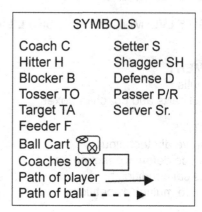

SYMBOLS

Coach C	Setter S
Hitter H	Shagger SH
Blocker B	Defense D
Tosser TO	Passer P/R
Target TA	Server Sr.
Feeder F	
Ball Cart	
Coaches box	
Path of player	
Path of ball	

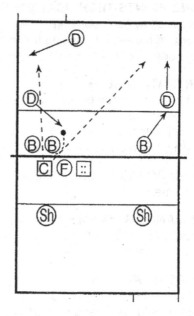

DRILL: NET RETRIEVAL

TYPE OF DRILL: Player centered/teaching

INTENSITY LVL: Low **SKILL LVL:** 1-2

EQUIPMENT
1. Progression #1-1   ball cart with 10 balls
2. Progression #2-1   ball cart with 10 balls

PERSONNEL: 2+

OBJECTIVE-DESIRED BEHAVIOR
1. Learn to play ball hit or passed into net
2. Develop efficient movement to contact point
3. Learn to achieve correct body position
4. Provide multiple repetitions

COACHING POINTS-TECHNICAL EMPHASIS
1. Ball that hits high on net drops down
2. Ball that hits middle and bottom of net pops out
3. Assume body position with shoulder to net
4. Foot nearest net should be forward
5. Play ball as close to floor as possible
6. Play ball up and away from net to mid-court

CONCENTRATION KEYS
1. Turn shoulder to net
2. Low body position
3. Arms lower than ball
4. "J" pass

ROTATION: D/TO/SH/D/D on goal achievement

PERFORMANCE GOAL-SCORING
1. 5 successful digs out of net to SH or S

SEQUENCE OF ACTION
1. Drill #1D/H assume position at 10' line
   a. **TO** tosser/s underhand's tosses ball into net at various angles-speeds, (**1**)
   b. **D** plays ball up to **SH** at mid court (2)
2. Drill #2 **D** assume position at 10' line
   a. **TO** tosser underhand's ball into net at various angles and speeds (**1**)
   b. **D** plays ball out of net high to **S** setter at midcourt (**2**)
   c. **S**etter sets outside **H** (**3**) **H** attacks ball (**4**)
3. Drills repeated until performance goal achieved

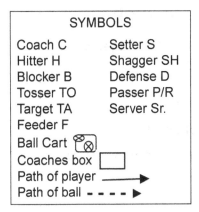

SYMBOLS

Coach C	Setter S
Hitter H	Shagger SH
Blocker B	Defense D
Tosser TO	Passer P/R
Target TA	Server Sr.
Feeder F	

Ball Cart
Coaches box
Path of player
Path of ball - - - - ▶

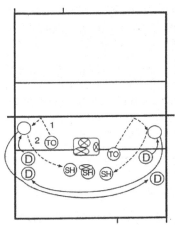

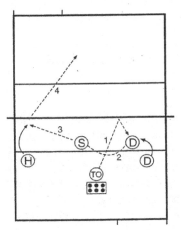

DRILL: SUICIDE DIG

TYPE OF DRILL: Player centered/training

INTENSITY LVL: Medium   **SKILL LVL:** 2

EQUIPMENT: 4 Balls

PERSONNEL: 5+)

OBJECTIVE-DESIRED BEHAVIOR
1. Fun
2. Warm Up
3. Dig accuracy
4. Reaction training
5. To develop digging rhythm and control
6. To provide multiple dig repetitions

COACHING POINTS-TECHNICAL EMPHASIS
1. Read hitters body position and arm swing
2. Touch hands to floor to lower body position
3. Arms away from body prior to ball contact
4. Maintain balanced floor position

CONCENTRATION KEYS
1. Speed step
2. Stay low
3. Weight on toes
4. Platform out

ROTATION: Hitter rotate to hit positions 1-2-3-4 on goal achievement

PERFORMANCE GOAL-SCORING
1. 4 accurate digs back to each attacker

SEQUENCE OF ACTION
1. Each of the 4 **H** hitters hits a ball at defensive player in the hitting order **1-2-3-4**
2. **H**itters self-toss and attack ball at **D**efensive player who passes ball back to **H**itter
3. Hitters 2-3-4 in order rotate to position 1ball on goal achievement
4. **D**iggers rotate to hitting positions 4-3-2-1 on goal achievement
5. **H**itters may hit-tip-or overhead pass ball
6. Outside players shag balls
7. Drill repeated until performance goal achieved

DRILL VARIATIONS/PROGRESSIONS
1. Decrease/increase distance between hitter/ digger depending on skill level

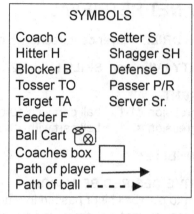

SYMBOLS

Coach C	Setter S
Hitter H	Shagger SH
Blocker B	Defense D
Tosser TO	Passer P/R
Target TA	Server Sr.
Feeder F	
Ball Cart	
Coaches box	
Path of player	
Path of ball	

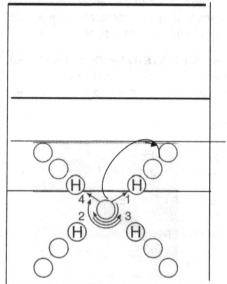

DRILL: DIG/SET/HIT

TYPE OF DRILL: Coach centered/Training

INTENSITY LVL: Medium **SKILL LVL:** 2

EQUIPMENT
1. 10+ BALLS
2. 1 Ball cart- 1 Coaches box

PERSONNEL: 7+

OBJECTIVE
1. Practice defense/set/attack technique
2. Train "on help" and "on balance" body position
3. Provide multiple repetitions

COACHING POINTS-TECHNICAL EMPHASIS
1. Maintain perimeter defensive position
2. Pass dig to target or mid-court
3. Set high outside set on dig off the net
4. Vary hitting angle on each attack

CONCENTRATION KEYS
1. On help court position
2. Balanced body position
3. Read attacker

ROTATION
1. D/H upon completion of performance goal
2. F/SH/H to D on goal achievement

PERFORMANCE GOAL-SCORING
1. Number of consecutive individual digs/ attacks

SEQUENCE OF ACTION
1. Drill begins with attack by **C**oach/player at 10' line or on coach's box at net to **H** player, (**1**)
2. **H** offensive player digs ball to **S** or to center court at 10' line (**2**)
3. **S**etter set predetermine set to **H** (**3**)
4. Hitter attacks randomly selected areas of court (**4**)
5. Upon completion of attack the next ball is hit at the next offensive player
6. Drill repeated until performance goal achieved

DRILL VARIATIONS/PROGRESSION
1. Move location of defensive player
2. Move location of attack player on box to middle/right side

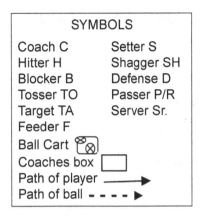

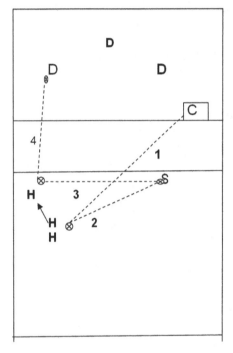

DRILL: LINE/WALL TOUCH

TYPE OF DRILL: Coach centered/conditioning

INTENSITY LVL: High   **SKILL LVL:** Stage 1-3

EQUIPMENT
1. 15+ Balls
2. 1 Cart/1 Coaches box

PERSONNEL: 8+

OBJECTIVE
1. Improve anaerobic conditioning with skill set number of repetitions
2. Practice forearm/overhead passing technique
3. Instill mental toughness
4. Provide positive reinforcement
5. Provide multiple repetitions

COACHING POINTS-TECHNICAL EMPHASIS
1. Maintain low balanced body position
2. Active rest between sets
3. Sprint to line/wall should be at near max effort

CONCENTRATION KEYS
1. Focus attention on pass to target
2. On balance

ROTATION: Rotate out upon goal achievement

PERFORMANCE GOAL-SCORING
1. Timed interval repetitions
2. Number of repetition (3 sets of 10 number of reps)

SEQUENCE OF ACTION
1. 3 Players assume court position lined up at mid Ct. about 3 ft apart
2. Drill begins with **C** on box who alternates hitting ball to **P**layers (1-2-3-)
3. Upon passing ball to **TA, P**ayers run to pre-determined spot or rear wall
4. After touching wall or line player return quickly to previous **Ct**. position
5. Player alternate running forward, backward and side step
6. Repeat drill until performance goal achieved

DRILL VARIATIONS/PROGRESSIONS
1. Toss over net instead of hit from **C** box
2. Begin with serve at mid-court in place of hit to duplicate serve receive

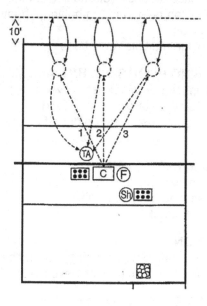

SYMBOLS

Coach C	Setter S
Hitter H	Shagger SH
Blocker B	Defense D
Tosser TO	Passer P/R
Target TA	Server Sr.
Feeder F	

Ball Cart

Coaches box

Path of player

Path of ball - - - - ▶

Perfection/Advanced/Combined Drills

The following consist of drills that that are designed to prefect skills and motor learning consistent with the Advanced/Combined drill classifications.

The majority of practice in the perfection stage of motor learning should concentrate drills that consist of skill learning that takes place in a Constant and Variable Practice in which only variation of a single skill is executed that has no beginning or end. A Progressive Part Practice where single skills are slowly integrated in a whole skill and Retrieval Practice in which a random practice is used to retrieve motor programs from long- term memory can be used in later stage

- Cognitive skills- Are skills in which decision making and intellectual processing are the major determinants for success
- Complex skills- Skills that require a coordination of many body parts over time to produce movement
- Discrete skills- Brief skill action which has no beginning or end
- Serial Skills- Are skills composed of several discrete skills strung together in which the order of execution is critical to success

In the INTENSITY and SKILL SECTION of each DRILL, LVL stands for Level

DRILL: SERVING THE LANES OR SEEMS

TYPE OF DRILL: Player centered/training

INTENSITY LVL: Low   **SKILL LVL:** 2-3

EQUIPMENT
1. 12 Balls and cart per service area
2. Elastic-hula hoops-tape

PERSONNEL: 1-6 per service area

OBJECTIVE-DESIRED BEHAVIOR
1. Practice service technique
2. Improve service accuracy-control-placement
3. Train for low trajectory/high velocity
4. Provide multiple serving repetitions

COACHING POINTS-TECHNICAL EMPHASIS
1. Practice pre-service routine
2. Square shoulders to target
3. Step in direction of target
4. Consistent toss location
5. Quick arm swing to provide power

CONCENTRATION KEYS
1. Stride for power
2. Stiff wrist float serve
3. Hit ball in middle
4. Hit flat through ball
5. Line the serve

ROTATION
1. After each serve
2. After 5 consecutive successful serves

PERFORMANCE GOAL-SCORING
1. 10 in row into court
2. 8 out of 10 to designated target
3. Game scoring to 15-1 point each serve to a target

SEQUENCE OF ACTION
1. Diagram #1 Sr. serves to of the 8 passing zones
2. Diagram# 2 Sr. serves open area between passers

DRILL VARIATIONS/PROGRESSIONS
1. Horse/21

SYMBOLS

Coach C	Setter S
Hitter H	Shagger SH
Blocker B	Defense D
Tosser TO	Passer P/R
Target TA	Server Sr.
Feeder F	

Ball Cart
Coaches box
Path of player →

Perimeter lanes

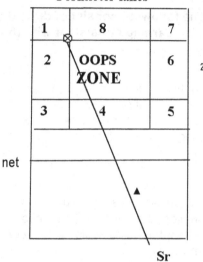

Interior Seems

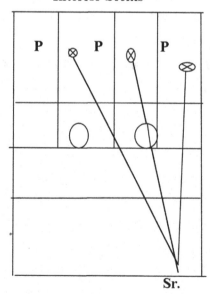

DRILL: TARGET SERVE

TYPE OF DRILL: Coach centered/training

INTENSITY LVL: Low   **SKILL LVL:** 2-3

EQUIPMENT
1. 20 Balls 2 carts
2. Elastic-hula hoops-tape

PERSONNEL: 12+

OBJECTIVE-DESIRED BEHAVIOR
1. Practice service technique
2. Improve service accuracy-control-placement
3. Train for low trajectory/high velocity
4. Provide multiple serving repetitions

COACHING POINTS-TECHNICAL EMPHASIS
1. Square shoulders to target
2. Step in direction of target
3. Consistent toss location
4. Practice pre-service routine REMOVE BOTTOM DIAGRAM

CONCENTRATION KEYS
1. Stride for power
2. Finer spread
3. Hit ball in middle
4. Hit with flat hand through ball
5. Line the serve

ROTATION: After 5 serves Sr./SH/SH/ser

PERFORMANCE GOAL-SCORING
1. 8 out of 10 to designated target
2. Game scoring to 15-1 point each serve to target

SEQUENCE OF ACTION

Serve 1: Attach elastic to antennas/serve between elastic and net

Serve 2: Hold hula hoops at and above net/ serve through hoops

Serve 3: Serve into hula hoops placed on court in strategic service areas or to numbered targets taped on court

DRILL VARIATIONS/PROGRESSIONS

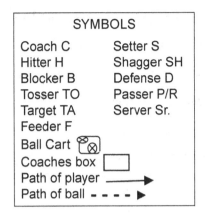

SYMBOLS

Coach C	Setter S
Hitter H	Shagger SH
Blocker B	Defense D
Tosser TO	Passer P/R
Target TA	Server Sr.
Feeder F	

Ball Cart

Coaches box

Path of player ⟶

Path of ball - - - ▶

Path of ball

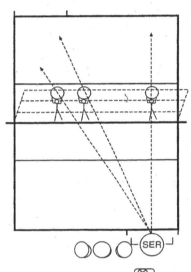

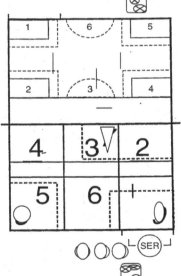

DRILL: 4 PERSON TEAM PASS

TYPE OF DRILL: Player centered/training

INTENSITY LVL: Medium   **SKILL LVL:** 1-2

EQUIPMENT: 10+ Balls and 1 Ball cart

PERSONNEL: 8+

OBJECTIVE-DESIRED BEHAVIOR: Ball Cart
1. Practice 4 person reception position, player movement, spatial relationship
2. Enhance team serve receive communication
3. Learn to read the server
4. Improve team passing technique
5. Provide multiple game like pass repetitions

COACHING POINTS-TECHNICAL EMPHASIS
1. Read the server's body position prior to contact with ball
2. Eyes focus on ball toss and hand contact
3. Follow flight of ball using net as reference
4. Slow the flight of ball by "framing ball"
5. Communicate possible passer, before ball crosses the net
6. Non-passers turn toward passer/calls his/her name

CONCENTRATION KEYS
1. Pre-reception routine
2. Read server
3. Early communication
4. Be decisive and commit

ROTATION
1. Passers rotate every 3 serves
2. Passing and serving teams alternate after goal achievement

PERFORMANCE GOAL-SCORING
1. Game/rally scoring/ to 18 points.- 1 pt. for each pass to target
2. 7 min. time limit

SEQUENCE OF ACTION
1. Drill begins with **S**erve to **R** receiving team (**1**)
2. **R** passes to **S**etter - 1 step allowed server
3. **S**etter sets ball to **R** who becomes a **H** hitter
4. Shaggers returns ball to server
5. Repeat until performance goal achieved

DRILL VARIATION/PROGRESSION

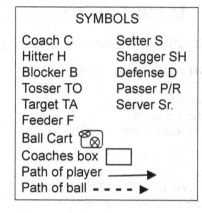

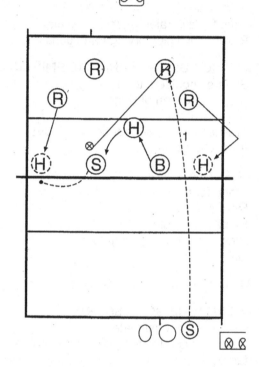

DRILL: NARROW COURT PASS

TYPE OF DRILL: Player centered/training

INTENSITY LVL: Medium/high   **SKILL LVL:** 2

EQUIPMENT
1. 1 Ball per 1/2 court
2. Tape/antennae

PERSONNEL: 2/3 players per 1/2 court Team

OBJECTIVE-DESIRED BEHAVIOR
1. Warm up with skills specific to volleyball
2. Combine correct body posture with passing movement
3. Establish required passing angles
4. Develop team work and competitive attitude
5. Provide multiple repetitions

COACHING POINTS-TECHNICAL EMPHASIS
1. Call for ball early
2. Pass ball high and close to net
3. Attack open areas of court

CONCENTRATION KEYS
1. Anticipation
2. Communication
3. Beat ball to spot
4. Control pass

ROTATION: Game rotation after each point

PERFORMANCE GOAL-SCORING
1. Timed 5-minutes
2. Game scoring to 15 points

SEQUENCE OF ACTION
1. Court divided into haft by antennae at net/ tape on floor
2. Teams consist of 2-3 players per side
3. Play starts; with toss across net (**1**)
4. Play must consist of 3 touches per side before ball crosses net
5. Last contact must be forearm or two hand passed across net
6. Attacking players must retreated behind 10' line after ball crosses net into opponents court
7. Ball volleyed across net until one team misses
8. Blocking is not allowed
9. Drill repeated until performance goal achieved

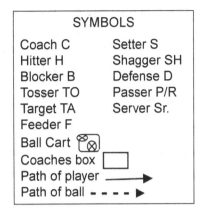

```
SYMBOLS
Coach C            Setter S
Hitter H           Shagger SH
Blocker B          Defense D
Tosser TO          Passer P/R
Target TA          Server Sr.
Feeder F
Ball Cart
Coaches box
Path of player ———▶
Path of ball - - - -▶
```

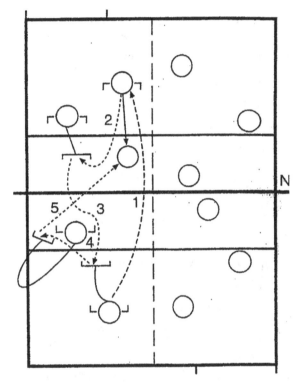

DRILL: RIGHT SIDE SET

TYPE OF DRILL: Coach centered/training

INTENSITY LVL: Medium   **SKILL LVL:** 1-2

EQUIPMENT: 10 Balls

PERSONNEL: 8+

OBJECTIVE-DESIRED BEHAVIOR
1. Develop right front hitter set technique
2. Improve overhead pass accuracy
3. Provide multiple repetitions

COACHING POINTS-TECHNICAL EMPHASIS
1. All balls passed overhead to target
2. Setter calls out right front hitter to set if he/she passes ball or is unable to set
3. RF sets ball high set inside court off net to left side attacker

CONCENTRATION KEYS
1. Square to target
2. Leg extension
3. High sets to left side hitter

ROTATION
1. SH/T/SH/R/H on goal achievement
2. 5 tosses to R-5 tosses to S rotate

PERFORMANCE GOAL-SCORING
1. Game scoring to 25 points

SEQUENCE OF ACTION
1. Drill begins with high ball **T** toss to any **R** (**1**)
2. **R**eceiver passes ball to **S** (**2**) who sets left side hitter (**3**)
3. Ball tossed to **S** in back court position (**4**)
4. **S**etter passes ball to **RF** hitter (**5**) who sets high set to left side **H** (**6**)
5. Drill repeated until performance goal achieved

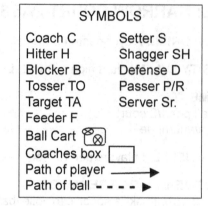

SYMBOLS

Coach C	Setter S
Hitter H	Shagger SH
Blocker B	Defense D
Tosser TO	Passer P/R
Target TA	Server Sr.
Feeder F	
Ball Cart	
Coaches box	
Path of player	
Path of ball	

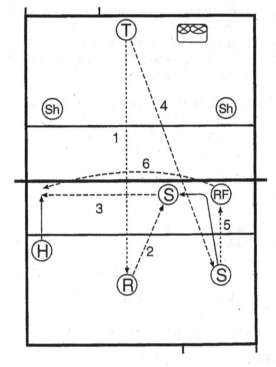

DRILL: OFF THE NET SET

TYPE OF DRILL: Player centered/training

INTENSITY LVL: Medium   **SKILL LVL:** 2-3

EQUIPMENT: 10 Balls and 1 Cart

PERSONNEL: 10+

OBJECTIVE-DESIRED BEHAVIOR
1. Practice setting ball passed off the net
2. Perfect 15-33-95 sets off deep pass
3. Teach hitters to adjust to balls set from varying angles and distances off the net
4. Simulate game conditions
5. Provide multiple repetitions

COACHING POINTS-TECHNICAL EMPHASIS
1. Back sets should be made off the right shoulder
2. Additional leg drive needed on deep front set
3. Use collapse set on low passes
4. Maintain 45 degree angle between setter and hitter on passes off the net
5. Attackers communicate desired set/location

CONCENTRATION KEYS
1. Face target
2. Zone set
3. Set ball inside court/off the net
4. Set best set option

ROTATION: Offense to defense/SH on goal achievement

PERFORMANCE GOAL-SCORING
1. Game score to 15 points
2. 1 pt. for each correct set/successful attack

SEQUENCE OF ACTION
1. Area of attack determined by quality and location of pass
2. Drill begins with toss by **C** to various positions on/off the net (**1**)
3. **S**etter transition off net to set **H** (**2**) who hit ball down line (**3**)
4. A second ball is tossed to **S** (**4**) who sets **H** (**5**) who hits ball cross court (**6**)
5. Coach tosses third ball to **S** (**7**) who sets **H** (**8**) who hits line (**9**)
6. Drill repeated until performance goal achieved

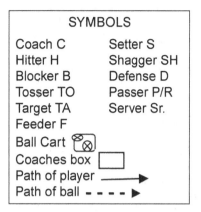

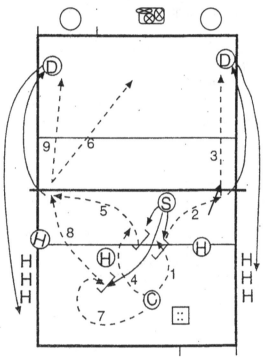

DRILL: SETTING GAME

TYPE OF DRILL: Player centered/training

INTENSITY LVL: Medium   SKILL:1-2

EQUIPMENT: 1 Ball

PERSONNEL: 2-5

OBJECTIVE-DESIRED BEHAVIOR
1.   Have Fun warm
2.   Perfect overhand passing accuracy
3.   Improve underhand passing accuracy
4.   Instill movement to the ball concepts
5.   Provide multiple random repetitions

COACHING POINTS-TECHNICAL EMPHASIS
1.   Anticipate angle of ball off rim/backboard
2.   Move quickly to point of contact
3.   Sight target with peripheral vision
4.   Aim just over front of rim

CONCENTRATION KEYS
1.   Locate to the ball
2.   Square shoulders to basket
3.   Right foot forward
4.   Sight ball and basket

PERFORMANCE GOAL-SCORING
1.   15 points wins
2.   1 pt. for each basket made from free throw line-
3.   2 pts. for basket made from top of key
4.   1 pt. for basket made after missed shoot that touches rim/backboard

SEQUENCE OF ACTION
1.   First player starts game with self toss and overhead set at basket from free throw line (**1**)
2.   If basket is made, player continues to overhead set from free throw line
3.   A missed shot that touches backboard or rim and bounces forward is played by the next player inline (**2**)
4.   The ball may be played in the air with an overhead pass or after one bounce off the floor with an forearm pass at the basket (**3**)
5.   If player makes a basket they replace the player at free throw line
6.   If a shot from the free throw line misses the rim or back board, the next player restarts play with a set from the free throw line
7.   A ball hitting the backboard or rim must come forward to be playable
8.   Repeat drill until performance goal achieved

DRILL VARIATION/PROGRESSIONS: Two point for setting at ball from back of key

SYMBOLS

Coach C	Setter S
Hitter H	Shagger SH
Blocker B	Defense D
Tosser TO	Passer P/R
Target TA	Server Sr.
Feeder F	
Ball Cart	
Coaches box	
Path of player	
Path of ball - - - - ▸	

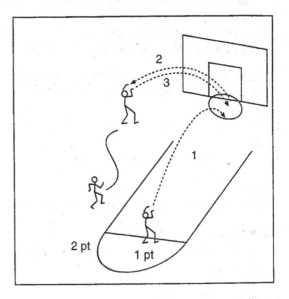

DRILL: SETTER READ

TYPE OF DRILL: Coach centered/training

INTENSITY LVL: Medium   **SKILL LVL:** 2-3

EQUIPMENT: 5+ balls and Cart

PERSONNEL: 8 +

OBJECTIVE-DESIRED BEHAVIOR
1. Train setter to read attacker in relation to block
2. Improve setter eye/attention focus
3. Practice setting technique
4. Provide multiple set attempts

COACHING POINTS-TECHNICAL EMPHASIS
1. Broad to narrow attention focus
2. Attention focus pass broad/ block narrow/ attacker broad
3. Maintain block in peripheral vision in preparation o set
4. Set opposite blocker movement or overload

CONCENTRATION KEYS
1. Jump set if possible
2. Communicate number of blockers
3. Set hittable ball

ROTATION
1. Offense to defense on goal achievement

PERFORMANCE GOAL-SCORING
1. 1 point for each Setter accurate reads of block
2. Game scoring to 15 points
3. 1 point for each kill can also be used

SEQUENCE OF ACTION
1. Drill begins with TO toss to Setter
2. Setter approaches target area from zone **1** or **4** sets best option see **(4)** below
3. Middle blocker remain stationary or moves left or right just before ball is set
4. Setter must read movement of block and sets opposite to blocker movement
5. Drill repeat until performance goal achieved

DRILL VARIATIONS/PROGRESSIONS

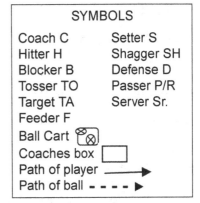

SYMBOLS

Coach C   Setter S
Hitter H   Shagger SH
Blocker B   Defense D
Tosser TO   Passer P/R
Target TA   Server Sr.
Feeder F
Ball Cart
Coaches box
Path of player
Path of ball

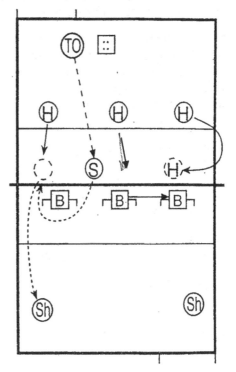

DRILL: SETTER ATTACK

TYPE OF DRILL: Coach centered/training

INTENSITY LVL: Medium   **SKILL LVL:** 2

EQUIPMENT: 10+ Balls and 1 Ball cart

PERSONNEL: 4+

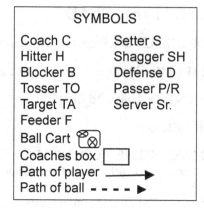

SYMBOLS

Coach C	Setter S
Hitter H	Shagger SH
Blocker B	Defense D
Tosser TO	Passer P/R
Target TA	Server Sr.
Feeder F	
Ball Cart	
Coaches box	
Path of player	
Path of ball	

OBJECTIVE
1. Develop setter as an attack force
2. Improve setter attack techniques
3. Teach the ability to make good decisions
4. Provide multiple set/block repetitions

COACHING POINTS-TECHNICAL EMPHASIS
1. Use left hand to attack or spike ball
2. Ball must be tipped at an angle to block/net
3. Tip ball off fake jump set
4. Tip must be quick and deceptive
5. Use right hand to attack ball behind setter

CONCENTRATION KEYS
1. Read defense
2. Slam dunk
3. Tip the angle
4. Attack off jump

ROTATION
1. Rotate setters on goal achievement 10 kills
2. Defense to attack every 10 attempts
3. Blocker every 10 attacks

PERFORMANCE GOAL-SCORING
1. Number repetitions (10 to each area of court)

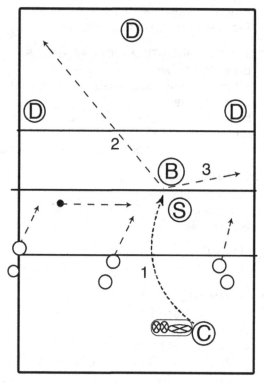

SEQUENCE OF ACTION
1. Drill begins with toss (**C**) to **S** (**1**)
2. Setter jumps and either sets to **H** or attacks ball (**2-3**) with tip or hit
3. Alternate angle and type of attack on each attempt
4. **H**itters must approach for attack on each set attempt
5. Blocker attempts to block randomly
6. Drill continues until performance goal achieved

DRILL VARIATIONS/PROGRESSION
1. Add block, floor defense as technique improves

DRILL: SET AND STEP

INTENSITY LVL: Low   **SKILL LVL:** 1-2

TYPE OF DRILL: Player centered/training

EQUIPMENT: 1 Ball

PERSONNEL: 2+

OBJECTIVE
1. Develop overhead passing technique
2. Improve overhead passing control
3. Improve movement/positioning to ball
4. Provide multiple repetitions

COACHING POINTS-TECHNICAL EMPHASIS
1. Weight forward extend through ball
2. Hands in shape of the ball
3. Push with legs to improve force
4. Arms follow through to target

CONCENTRATION KEYS
1. Feet to ball
2. Right foot forward
3. Thumbs to forehead

PERFORMANCE GOAL-SCORING
1. Timed (3 minutes)
2. Number of correct repetitions 15

SEQUENCE OF ACTION
1. First setters assumes position near net
2. Second setter assumes position inside base line
3. Drill begins with two handed pass by passer **(1)**
4. Each setter takes one step forward each time they pass the ball
5. Ball passed back and forth until passers are 3' apart **(2-3-4)**
6. At this point they pass and take one step back until they reach original starting point
7. Drill repeated until performance goal achieved

DRILL VARIATIONS
1. Repeat drill with underhand pass

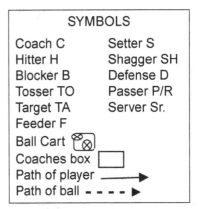

SYMBOLS

Coach C   Setter S
Hitter H   Shagger SH
Blocker B   Defense D
Tosser TO   Passer P/R
Target TA   Server Sr.
Feeder F
Ball Cart
Coaches box
Path of player ⟶
Path of ball - - - ▶

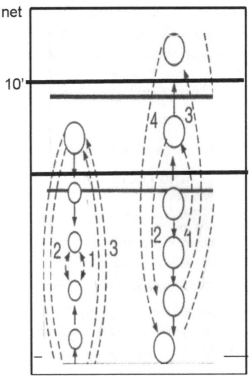

net

10'

DRILL: SERVE - PASS - SET

TYPE OF DRILL: Player centered/training

INTENSITY LVL: Medium   SKILL:1- 2

EQUIPMENT: 10 Ball per side

PERSONNEL: 3+

OBJECTIVE-DESIRED BEHAVIOR
1. Improve passing technique
2. Introduce game-like ball movement
3. Develop court-player spatial orientation
4. Improve pass-set accuracy
5. Provide multiple pass/set repetitions

COACHING POINTS-TACTICAL EMPHASIS
1. Focus on server ball toss and hand contact
2. Communicate passer before ball crosses net
3. Face ball prior to contact
4. Lower inside shoulder in direction of target
5. First option is over head pass

CONCENTRATION KEYS
1. Beat the ball
2. Arms away from body
3. Thumbs together
4. Early communication
5. Pass to target

ROTATION: TO/TA/P/S Every 5 passes

PERFORMANCE GOAL-SCORING
1. Scoring: 1 pt for each serve/pass/set to target
2. Performance goal 25 points

SEQUENCE OF ACTION
1. Court divided in half lengthwise-two teams of **4** on each half court
2. **TO** tosses ball with lob toss at mid-court to **P (1)**
3. **P**asser passes ball to **S**-**(2)**
4. **S**etter set ball to **TA** **(3)**
5. **TA** returns ball to **TO** **(4)** and keeps score
6. Repeat drill until performance goal achieved

DRILL VARIATIONS/PROGRESSIONS
1. Change lob toss to high looping overhead serve as skill progresses
2. Server gradually retreats toward base line as strength and accuracy improve

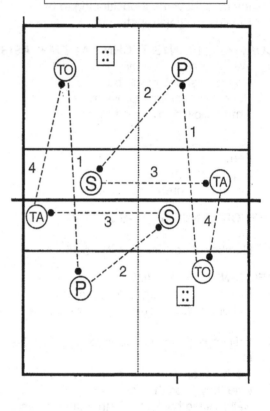

SYMBOLS

Coach C	Setter S
Hitter H	Shagger SH
Blocker B	Defense D
Tosser TO	Passer P/R
Target TA	Server Sr.
Feeder F	

Ball Cart

Coaches box

Path of player ——————▶

Path of ball - - - - ▶

DRILL: NARROW COURT ATTACK

TYPE OF DRILL: Player centered/training

INTENSITY LVL: Med./high   **SKILL LVL:** -3

EQUIPMENT
1. 1 Ball per 1/2 court
2. Tape floor/attach antennae at net mid-court

PERSONNEL: Team of 2/3 players per 1/2 court

OBJECTIVE-DESIRED BEHAVIOR
1. Warm up with skills specific to volleyball
2. Learn to attack open areas of court
3. Develop team work and competitive attitude
4. Provide multiple repetitions

COACHING POINTS-TACTICAL EMPHASIS
1. Call for ball early
2. Pass ball high and close to net
3. Attack open areas of court

CONCENTRATION KEYS
1. Anticipation
2. Communication
3. Beat ball to spot
4. Control pass

ROTATION: Game rotation after each point

PERFORMANCE GOAL-SCORING
1. Game scoring to 15 points
2. As warm-up drill play 5 min.

SEQUENCE OF ACTION
1. Court divided into haft by antennae at net/ tape on floor
2. Teams consist of 3 players per each of 4 court sections
3. Play starts; with toss across net to a passer (**1**)
4. Ball passed to (**2**) who sets (**3**) who attacks to (**4**)
5. Ball is hit back and forth across net until one team kills the ball
6. Last pass must be an attack or tip-no overhand or forearm passes
7. Ball must be touched 3 time before crossing net
8. Blocking is not allowed or enter adjacent court
9. Drill repeated until performance goal achieved

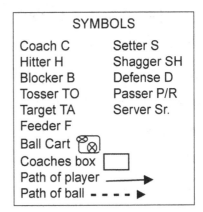

SYMBOLS

Coach C	Setter S
Hitter H	Shagger SH
Blocker B	Defense D
Tosser TO	Passer P/R
Target TA	Server Sr.
Feeder F	
Ball Cart	
Coaches box	
Path of player	
Path of ball	

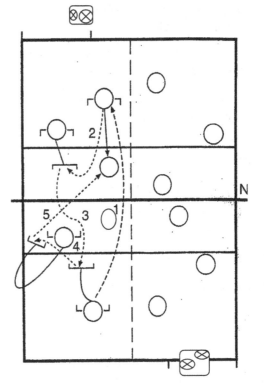

DRILL: DEEP COURT ATTACK

TYPE OF DRILL: Player centered/training

INTENSITY LVL: Medium   **SKILL LVL:** 2-3

EQUIPMENT: 10+ Balls

PERSONNEL: 6 each half court

OBJECTIVE-DESIRED BEHAVIOR
1. Increase attack alternatives
2. Practice deep court set and attack techniques
3. Improve hitting and setting accuracy
4. Provide multiple repetitions

COACHING POINTS-TACTICAL EMPHASIS
1. Set ball just in front of 10' line
2. Hitter takes off behind 10' line with slight broad jump
3. Set left side set lower than right side
4. Attack ball with top spin to deep court

CONCENTRATION KEYS
1. Stay behind ball
2. Full arm extension
3. Open hand-fingers spread
4. Top spin-heel first-wrist snap -fellow through
5. Deep set/deep hit

ROTATION: TO/ H/SH/TO after each attack

PERFORMANCE GOAL-SCORING
1. 1 point for correct attack from each area A-B-C
2. Attacker receives point only for a correct hit
3. Game scoring 25 points

SEQUENCE OF ACTION
1. Drill begins with **TO** toss to **S** (**1**)
2. **S**etter sets ball to designated attack area slightly front of 10" line (**2**)
3. **H**itter attacks ball randomly into court (**3**) lands over 10' line
4. **H**itter Transition to areas from area **A** to areas **B-C** replace **TO** after attack
5. Drill repeated until performance goal achieved

DRILL VARIATIONS/PROGRESSIONS
1. Progression Add blockers
2. Progression Add floor defense

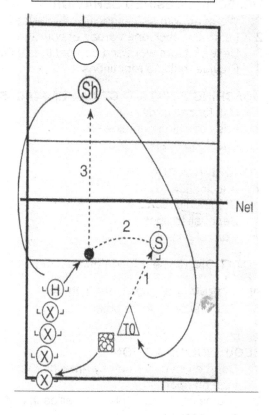

SYMBOLS

Coach C	Setter S
Hitter H	Shagger SH
Blocker B	Defense D
Tosser TO	Passer P/R
Target TA	Server Sr.
Feeder F	
Ball Cart	
Coaches box	
Path of player	
Path of ball	

DRILL: WIPE OFF

TYPE OF DRILL: Player centered/training

INTENSITY LVL: High   **SKILL LVL:** 1-2

EQUIPMENT: 20+ balls––2 ball carts

PERSONNEL: 9+

OBJECTIVE-DESIRED BEHAVIOR
1. Perfect wipe-off attack technique
2. Develop the ability to adjust the attack to change in defensive situations
3. Provide multiple repetitions

COACHING POINTS-TACTICAL EMPHASIS
1. Adjust timing and body position relative to the location of ball.
2. Rotate shoulders in direction of attack after take off
3. On an outside wipe off, hit or push ball of the blocker outside hand
4. On inside wipe-off, hit or push the ball off blockers hand inside the CT,

CONCENTRATION KEYS
1. Read block location
2. Shoulder rotation
3. Aim for outside of hands
4. High contact point

ROTATION
1. Offense SH/TO/H/SH every attack
2. Defense Blockers to SH every 5 blocks

PERFORMANCE GOAL-SCORING
1. Game scoring to 25 points
2. 1 point for each successful hit off block
3. Ball must be touched by blocker to score
4. 2 points to block for stuff block

SEQUENCE OF ACTION
1. Drill begins with **TO** toss to **S**etter
2. **S**etter sets 14/15 set to leftside-93/95 to right side
3. **H**itter hit-pushes ball off blockers outside or inside hand
4. Repeat drill until performance goal achieved

DRILL VARIATIONS: Move attack to middle and right side/vary set accordingly

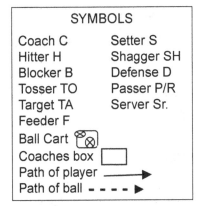

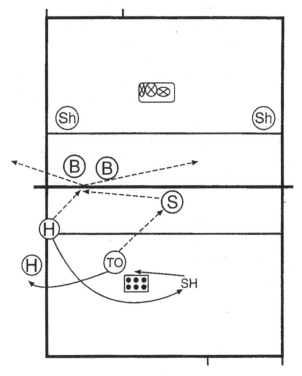

DRILL: 3 POSITION ATTACK

INTENSITY LVL: Medium   **SKILL LVL:** 1-2

TYPE OF DRILL: Coach centered/Training

EQUIPMENT
1. 10 + Balls
2. 1 Cart

PERSONNEL: 10+

OBJECTIVE-DESIRED BEHAVIOR
1. Introduce attack from 3 positions
2. Improve offense transition movement
3. Coordinate timing of hitter and setter
4. Develop attack consistency
5. Practice floor defense technique
6. Provide multiple attack repetitions

COACHING POINTS-TACTICAL EMPHASIS
1. Attacker controls timing on high sets
2. Setter controls timing on low or quick sets
3. Left side hitter approach outside in angle
4. Right side hitter approach inside out angle
5. Adjust body position and timing in relation to set

CONCENTRATION KEYS
1. Delay approach
2. Quick approach and arm swing
3. Jump quick/swing hard
4. Control and placement

ROTATION
1. H to D to H on goal achievement
2. Alternate setters on 5 hit series

PERFORMANCE GOAL-SCORING: Players keep own score
1. 8 out of 10 hits to assigned attack zone
2. 10 consecutive hits to randomly selected areas
3. 25 point game: 1 point each attack success

SEQUENCE OF ACTION
1. Divide players into groups of 3 attackers - 3 defenders- 3 shaggers
2. Drill begins with ball tossed **C** to **S**
3. Setter sets **H** in position (**1-2-3**)
4. Hitter attacks ball to designated area of court (line-x court-etc.)
5. Drill repeated until performance goal achieved

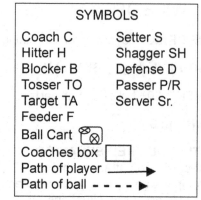

SYMBOLS

Coach C	Setter S
Hitter H	Shagger SH
Blocker B	Defense D
Tosser TO	Passer P/R
Target TA	Server Sr.
Feeder F	
Ball Cart	
Coaches box	
Path of player	
Path of ball	

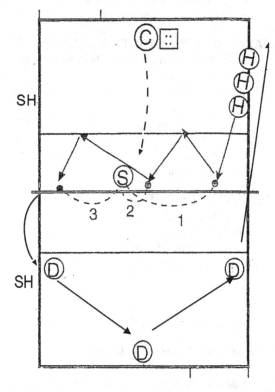

DRILL: MIDDLE ATTACK

TYPE OF DRILL: Coach centered/training

INTENSITY LVL: High   **SKILL LVL:** 2-3

EQUIPMENT: 10+ balls and 1 cart

PERSONNEL: 8+

OBJECTIVE-DESIRED BEHAVIOR
1. Develop the ability to read the set in relation to the block
2. Learn to attack at an angle to the block
3. Introduce tactical attack skills
4. Provide multiple repetitions

COACHING POINTS-TECHNICAL EMPHASIS
1. Read the location/timing of block and attack open areas at angle to block
2. Ball set to left of hitting shoulder/across the mid-line of body
   a. Rotate shoulders and hit cutback angle
   b. Thumb of hitting hand points up on completion of arm Swing and wrist snap
3. Ball set to right of hitting shoulder
   a. Hit at right angle to block
   b. Thumb of hitting hand point down

CONCENTRATION KEYS
1. Quick approach and jump
2. Shoulder rotation
3. Thumb up/thump down
4. Must hit angle on low sets

ROTATION
1. R /R/H/D/B/TO//D every 5 points
2. Offense to defense on achievement of goal

PERFORMANCE GOAL-SCORING
1. Game to 15 points-1 point each successful attack

SEQUENCE OF ACTION
1. Drill begins with **TO** toss or lob serve to **R** (**1**)
2. **R** passes ball to **S** (**2**) S sets quick or medium tempo set to middle **H**itter (**3**)
3. **H**itter hits ball at appropriate angle in relation to block (**4-5**)
4. **B**lock fronts **H**
5. Repeat drill until performance goal achieved.

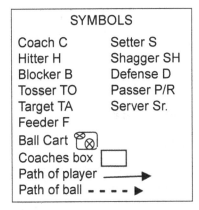

SYMBOLS

Coach C	Setter S
Hitter H	Shagger SH
Blocker B	Defense D
Tosser TO	Passer P/R
Target TA	Server Sr.
Feeder F	
Ball Cart	
Coaches box	
Path of player ⟶	
Path of ball ⁃ ⁃ ⁃ ▶	

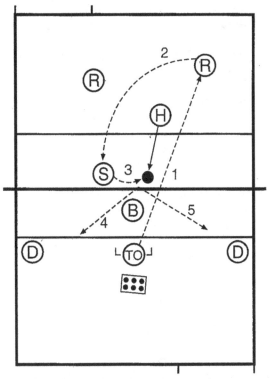

DRILL: REPETITIOUS HIT

TYPE OF DRILL: Player centered/skill repetition

INTENSITY LVL: Medium   **SKILL LVL:** 2-3

EQUIPMENT: 10+ Balls and cart

PERSONNEL: 6+

OBJECTIVE-DESIRED BEHAVIOR
1. Teach various approach angles/footwork
2. Improve approach-jump-arm swing timing
3. Improve setter/hitter timing
4. Provide multiple pass/set/attack repetitions

COACHING POINTS-TACTICAL EMPHASIS
1. Approach 45 degree angle to net
2. Delay start of approach to stay behind ball
3. Accelerate to take off
4. Force in-force out of floor on jump
5. Quick jump and arm swing
6. Left hand points to ball
7. High elbow as hitting arms lead to ball

CONCENTRATION KEYS
1. Feet to ball
2. Heal-toe take off
3. Grunt on contact with ball
4. Toe-heal landing

ROTATION
1. H/SH/TO/P/H after each attack

PERFORMANCE GOAL-SCORING
1. 10 consecutive) attacks to predetermined area (blocked drill)
2. 8 out of 10 attacks to alternate target area (random-variable drill)
3. 15 pt. game: 1 point each successful attack

SEQUENCE OF ACTION
1. Drill begins with **T** toss to **R** (**1**) **R** passes to **S**etter (**2**)
2. **S**etter sets play action (**3**) as called by coach to setter prior to approach
3. **H**itter attacks ball to predetermine or random area of court (**4-5-6**)
4. Drill continues until performance goal is achieved

DRILL VARIATIONS/PROGRESSIONS
1. Move attack middle/left attack zones

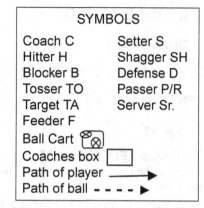

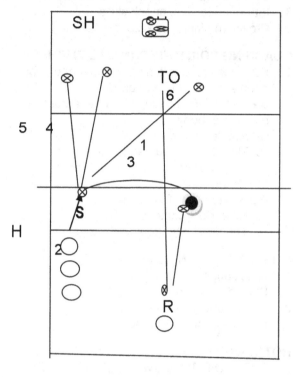

DRILL: LINE ATTACK

TYPE OF DRILL: Coach centered/Training

INTENSITY LVL: High   **SKILL LVL:** 2-3

EQUIPMENT: 10+ Balls and ball cart

PERSONNEL: 10+

OBJECTIVE-DESIRED BEHAVIOR
1. Develop ability to read block
2. Practice line attack techniques
3. Improve attack movement
4. Provide multiple attack repetitions

COACHING POINTS-TECHNICAL EMPHASIS
1. Approach for down line attack
2. Attack ball off blockers outside hand
3. Tip just over block down line or deep to back CT.

CONCENTRATION KEYS
1. Read location of block in relation to court
2. Thumbs up on left side/down or right side hit
3. Aim to hit ball off outside hand

ROTATION
1. Defense rotates B/D/Sh/TA every 5 points
2. Passer replace hitter every 5 points
3. Offensive changes with defensive on goal achievement

PERFORMANCE GOAL-SCORING
1. Rally scoring to 15 points
2. 1 point for dig to target-1 pt each kill down line

SEQUENCE OF ACTION
1. Drill begins with **C** toss or mid court serve to **P** (**1**) who passes to **S** (**2**)
2. **S**etter sets 14-15 left side or 95-93 if hitting from right (**3**)
3. **D**efense starts in base position/transitions to line assume "on help position"
4. **B**locker must give line and set up for cross court hit
5. **H**itter must hit ball down line (**4**) **D** digs attack to **TA/S** area (**5**)
6. Repeat drill until performance goal achieved

DRILL VARIATIONS/PROGRESSION
1. Move attack to right side
2. Line Attack Drill can be used in conjunction with Line Defense Drill

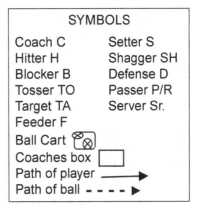

SYMBOLS

Coach C	Setter S
Hitter H	Shagger SH
Blocker B	Defense D
Tosser TO	Passer P/R
Target TA	Server Sr.
Feeder F	

Ball Cart

Coaches box

Path of player ———▶

Path of ball - - - - ▶

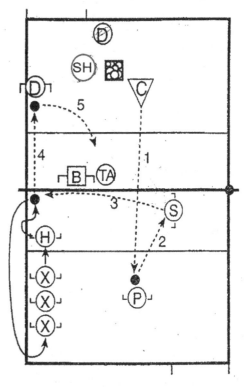

DRILL: OFF SPEED ATTACK –Pr. 6

TYPE OF DRILL: Coach centered/teaching

INTENSITY LVL: Medium   **SKILL:**2-3

EQUIPMENT: 10+ Balls

PERSONNEL: 4+

OBJECTIVE-DESIRED BEHAVIOR
1. Develop off speed attack techniques
2. Improve attack deception/accuracy
3. Provide multiple repetitions

COACHING POINTS-TACTICAL EMPHASIS
1. Attack with full approach-jump and arm swing to disguise attack
2. Roll shot: hit behind/under ball, roll finger through and over-loop just top of ball
3. Tip push ball with firm wrist and fingers - thumb down on ball
4. Tip ball to center of court or deep corners
5. Tip ball just before peak of jump

CONCENTRATION KEYS
1. Deception with full arm swing
2. Attack open areas
3. Firm wrist

ROTATION: H/SH/SH -rotates to end of hitting line

PERFORMANCE GOAL-SCORING
1. Game scoring: 15 points— point for each attack to designated area

SEQUENCE OF ACTION
1. Areas open to tip marked on court marked with X
2. Drill begins with toss C to **S** (**1**) who sets predetermined set (**2**)
3. **H**itter attacks set with off speed hit to open areas of court (**3-4**) or deep court
4. **S**etter and alternating **H**itter must cover attacker
5. Drill continues until performance goal achieved

DRILL VARIATIONS/PROGRESSIONS
1. Coach calls area to be attacked after set
2. Alternate hit-tip-hit-roll

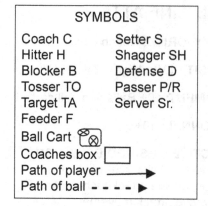

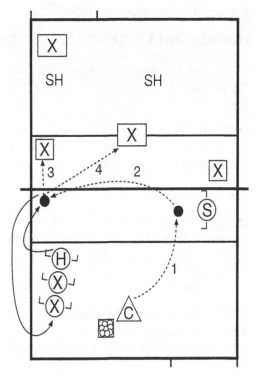

DRILL: LINE DEFENSE

TYPE OF DRILL: Coach centered/Training

INTENSITY LVL: High   **SKILL LVL:** 2-3

EQUIPMENT: 10+ Balls and ball cart

PERSONNEL: 9+

OBJECTIVE-DESIRED BEHAVIOR
1. Develop ability of defender to read attacker
2. Practice line transition and dig techniques
3. Improve block movement and technique
4. Practice line attack
5. Provide multiple attack repetitions

COACHING POINTS-TECHNICAL EMPHASIS
1. Block must not reach outside for ball
2. Line defender assumes "on help" body position
3. Floor defense assumes base court position

CONCENTRATION KEYS
1. Read attacker
2. On balance
3. Dig ball to target

ROTATION
1. Defense rotates H/B/D/SH/TA/P/H every 5 points
2. Passer replace hitter every 5 attacks
3. Offensive changes with defensive on goal achievement

PERFORMANCE GOAL-SCORING
1. Rally scoring to 15 points
2. 1 point for dig to target

SEQUENCE OF ACTION
1. Drill begins with **C** toss to mid-court to **P** (**1**) who passes to **S** (**2**)
2. **S**etter sets 14-15 left side or 95-93 if hitting from right (**3**)
3. **De**fense starts in base position/transitions to line "on help position"
4. **B**locker must give line and set up for cross court hit
5. **H**itter must hit ball down line (**4**) **D** digs ball to **TA** area (**5**)
6. Repeat drill until performance goal achieved

DRILL VARIATIONS/PROGRESSION
1. Move attack to right side

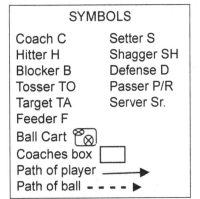
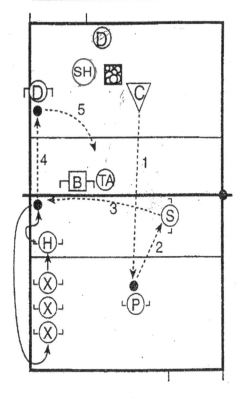

DRILL: JOUSTING

TYPE OF DRILL: Coach centered/teaching

INTENSITY LVL: Medium   **SKILL LVL:** 2-3

EQUIPMENT
1. 2+balls and cart
2. Referee's stand or coaches box

PERSONNEL: 8+

OBJECTIVE-DESIRED BEHAVIOR
1. Develop proficiency at penetrating net
2. Execute ball recovery off block
3. Improve block communication
4. Enhance block jump timing
5. Provide multiple block repetitions

COACHING POINTS-SKILL EMPHASIS
1. Penetrate net by extending shoulders to ears
2. Place hands on ball and push
3. Play ball blocked on your side of net up high to center court

CONCENTRATION KEYS
1. Head up-eyes open
2. Extend shoulders
3. Hands on ball finger spread
4. Stiffen wrists and push

ROTATION: B/SH on completion of performance goal

PERFORMANCE GOAL-SCORING
1. 10 successful blocks
2. Start over if either player touches net

SEQUENCE OF ACTION
1. Two teams of two players assume blocking position on opposite sides of net
2. Drill begins with ball tossed over center of net by coach (**1**) from referee's stand or coach's box
3. **B**lockers attempt to penetrate and stuff ball into the opponents court
4. Side ball stuffed on plays ball up to center court for an attack
5. Drill repeated until performance goal achieved

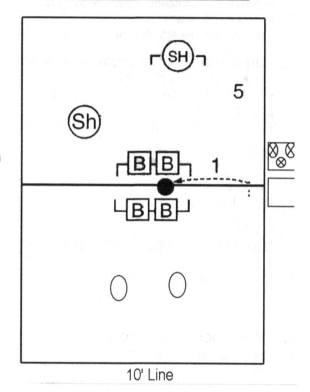

SYMBOLS

Coach C	Setter S
Hitter H	Shagger SH
Blocker B	Defense D
Tosser TO	Passer P/R
Target TA	Server Sr.
Feeder F	
Ball Cart	
Coaches box	
Path of player	
Path of ball	

10' Line

DRILL: BLOCK/ATTACK OVER PASS/SET

TYPE OF DRILL: Coach centered/teaching

INTENSITY LVL: Medium   **SKILL LVL:** 2-3

EQUIPMENT: 10+ balls and cart

PERSONNEL: 6+

OBJECTIVE-DESIRED BEHAVIOR
1. Teach locating to the ball/fronting the hitter on an over pass/set
2. Learn to attack the over pass/set
3. Develop visual blocking/attacking cues
4. Provide multiple block repetitions

COACHING POINTS-TECHNICAL EMPHASIS
1. Quick read of the balls trajectory toward the net
2. Beat the opponent to the ball
3. Place both hands on ball and push to open court
4. Attack with quick jump and arm swing if possible

CONCENTRATION KEYS
1. Read and front hitter
2. Block an area
3. Penetrate with firm ball contact

ROTATION
1. Option 1 H/B/TO/SH on goal achievement
2. Option 2 SH/H/B/SH on goal achievement

PERFORMANCE GOAL-SCORING
1. Attackers must get 15 points before blockers get 6 points
2. Block gets 2 points each successful block
3. Attack gets 1 point each successful attack

SEQUENCE OF ACTION
1. Option 1 and Drill begins with ball **TO** toss or set over but close to top of net
   a. **B**locker locates to ball and blocks or attacks over pass/set at the point of contact
   b. **H**itter locates to point of contact and hits/blocks over pass/set
2. Repeat drill until performance goal e achieved

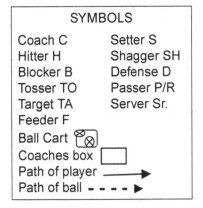

SYMBOLS

Coach C	Setter S
Hitter H	Shagger SH
Blocker B	Defense D
Tosser TO	Passer P/R
Target TA	Server Sr.
Feeder F	
Ball Cart	
Coaches box	
Path of player	
Path of ball - - - - ▶	

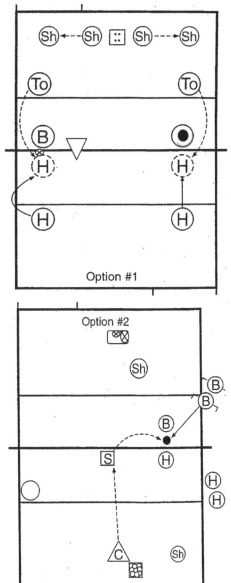

Option #1

Option #2

DRILL: DEFENDING THE SETTER ATTACK

TYPE OF DRILL: Coach centered/training

INTENSITY LVL: Medium   **SKILL LVL:** 2

EQUIPMENT: 20 Balls and 1

PERSONNEL: 9+

OBJECTIVE
1. Develop the ability to read setter
2. Practice defending the setter attack
3. Provide multiple attack repetitions

COACHING POINTS-TECHNICAL EMPHASIS
1. Determine if setter is in front or back court
2. Floor defenders maintain base position
3. Left side blocker lines up opposite setter
4. L/S blocker's first responsibility stop setter attack
5. Setter will tip to right side of court with left hand
6. Setter will reverse tip with right hand to left side court

CONCENTRATION KEYS
1. Locate setter
2. High hand position
3. Read setter arm and hand
4. Read angle of attack

ROTATION
1. Defending team front to back on every 5 attempts
2. Defense to offense after 15 pt rally score

PERFORMANCE GOAL-SCORING
1. 12 out of 15 successful defense of setter attack in rally score game

SEQUENCE OF ACTION
1. Drill begins with **T** toss to **S**etter
2. **S**etter jump on all sets and randomly varies the attack from setter to hitter
3. **B**lockers attempt to read **S** and attempts to **B**lock **S**etter attack
4. **D**efenders dig balls not blocked
5. Repeat drill until performance goal achieved

DRILL VARIATIONS

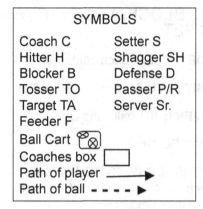

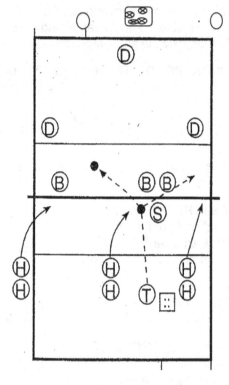

DRILL: THE MIDDLE ATTACK DEFENSE

TYPE OF DRILL: Coach centered/training

INTENSITY LVL: High   **SKILL LVL:** 2-3

EQUIPMENT: 10+ Balls and cart

PERSONNEL: 9+

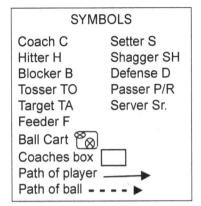

OBJECTIVE-DESIRED BEHAVIOR
1. Defend the middle attack
2. Instill a base position mentality on middle attack defense
3. Improve block timing-coordination
4. Practice middle attack defensive tactics
5. Provide multiple repetitions

COACHING POINTS-TECHNICAL EMPHASIS
1. Defense maintains base position
2. Left side blocker lines up opposite setter
3. Blockers must block middle of court
4. Middle Blocker must jump with middle attacker on quick set

CONCENTRATION KEYS
1. Read attack angle
2. Maintain base position
3. Read point of contact - angle of attack
4. Middle blockers must penetrate net

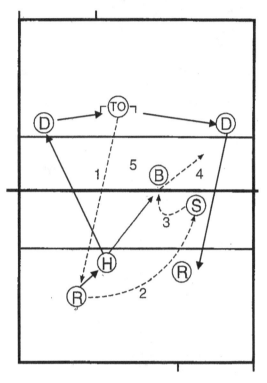

ROTATION
1. R/ R/H/D/TO/B/D/R after each attack
2. Offensive to defense on goal achievement

PERFORMANCE GOAL-SCORING
1. 1 Point for each successful hit
2. 2 points for every successful block
3. Game scoring to 15 points

SEQUENCE OF ACTION
1. Drill begins with 1/2 court **T** toss to **S**
2. Ball passed to **S** area
3. **S**etter sets any of the 3 **H** attack positions
4. Ball attacked/tipped to left or right of block
5. Defense blocks or digs ball
6. Repeat drill until performance goal achieved

DRILL VARIATIONS/PROGRESSION
1. Can be used in conjunction with Middle Attack Drill

DRILL: PURSUIT

TYPE OF DRILL: Coach centered/training

INTENSITY LVL: Medium   **SKILL LVL:** 2-3

EQUIPMENT
1. 10+ Balls and cart
2. Coaches Box

PERSONNEL: 6+

OBJECTIVE-DESIRED BEHAVIOR
1. Learn to play ball hit out of court area
2. Develop team work
3. Instill idea of relentless pursuit
4. Provide multiple repetitions

COACHING POINTS-TECHNICAL EMPHASIS
1. All players except off side hitter must move to play the ball
2. Player with best angle plays ball up to mid-court if possible
3. Following players must communicate heir location to player making contact with ball play
4. Ball passed-set-hit if possible
5. Last play on ball should be an attack

CONCENTRATION KEYS
1. Team pursuit
2. Communication
3. "J" stroke
4. Up on 2 over on 3

PERFORMANCE GOAL-SCORING
1. Game situation: vary starting score
2. Game scoring to 15 points

ROTATION: Game rotation after successful retrieval

SEQUENCE OF ACTION
1. Drill begins with **P** hitting ball from box out of bounds or at a designated digger who hits ball deep out of court in any direction
2. All players **D-B** pursuit ball except offside attacker who moves to center court
3. Ball played by **D** up on first hit into pursuit mid-court is set to the offside **H**itter for attack
4. Ball played into court on second touch is played deep into opponent's court
5. Repeat drill until performance goal achieved:

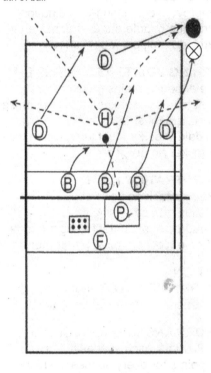

SYMBOLS	
Coach C	Setter S
Hitter H	Shagger SH
Blocker B	Defense D
Tosser TO	Passer P/R
Target TA	Server Sr.
Feeder F	
Ball Cart	
Coaches box	
Path of player	
Path of ball	

Path of ball

DRILL: RUN THROUGHS

TYPE OF DRILL: Coach centered/training

INTENSITY LVL: High   **SKILL LVL:** 2-3

EQUIPMENT
1. 10 Balls and Ball Cart
2. 1 Coaching Box

PERSONNEL: 6+

OBJECTIVE-DESIRED BEHAVIOR
1. Learn and practice run throughs
2. Learn to play ball without going to floor
3. Perfect emergency procedures
4. Instill the concept of relentless pursuit
5. Provide multiple repetitions

COACHING POINTS-TECHNICAL EMPHASIS
1. Run through ball and pass with two arms up to mid-court
2. Use body momentum to produce passing force
3. Pass should be controlled toward target area
4. Use overhead "J" stroke when past target area
5. Execute run through with parallel movement

CONCENTRATION KEYS
1. Stay on feet
2. Extend arms
3. Pass to target

ROTATION
1. TA/D/D/D/F after goal achievement

PERFORMANCE GOAL-SCORING
1. 5 Tosses to and passes to TA by each defender

SEQUENCE OF ACTION
1. Players assume base defensive positions
2. Drill begins with toss to or hit **C** deep left **CT** for middle **D**efender (**1**)
3. Second toss short to for right side **D**efender (**2**)
4. Third toss to mid-court to left side **D**efender (**3**)
5. Fourth toss deep right back to middle **D**efender (**4**)
6. Repeat drill until performance goal achieved

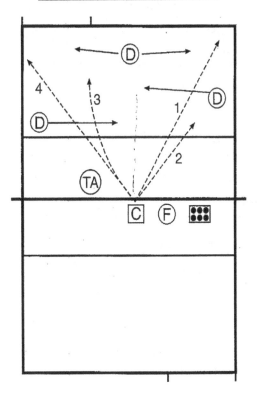

DRILL: DOUBLE D QUICK: pr1

TYPE OF DRILL: Player centered/training

INTENSITY LVL: High   **SKILL LVL:** 2-3

EQUIPMENT
1. 15 Balls
2. Ball cart and coaches boxes

OBJECTIVE-DESIRED BEHAVIOR
1. To improve dig technique
2. To practice reading attackers arm motion
3. To provide multiple dig repetitions

COACHING POINTS-TECHNICAL EMPHASIS
1. Maintain a low body position
2. Assume proper body position in relation to ball
3. Focus on attacker shoulder-arm-hand motion

CONCENTRATION KEYS-QUEUES
1. Place arms between ball and floor
2. Cushion ball to reduce force of attack

ROTATION
1. SH/D/D/SH/A/F/F/A performance goal

PERFORMANCE GOAL-SCORING
1. Number of repetitions 10 passes to each D
2. Number of passes to target 10 in a row

SEQUENCE OF ACTION
1. Two **D**efensive players- one **T**arget - two Attackers on box- two-**F**eeders
2. **A**ttacker 1 **A** hits ball crosscourt to a **D** (**1**) who passes ball to **T**
3. **A**ttacker 2 **A** hits ball cross court to **D** (**2**) who passes ball to **T**
4. **A**ttacker 1A hits ball down line to **D** (**3**) who passes ball to **T**
5. **A**ttacker 2A hits ball down the line to **D** (**4**) who passes ball **T**
6. **R**epeat drill sequence until performance goal achieved

DRILL VARIATION/PROGRESSION

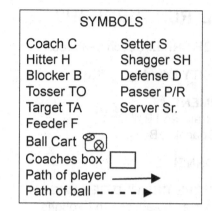

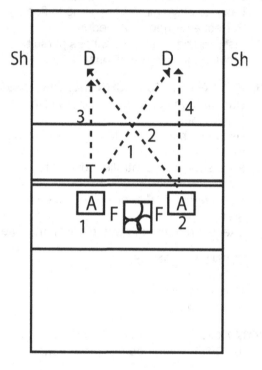

DRILL: BARRELL ROLL

TYPE OF DRILL: Coach centered/teaching

INTENSITY LVL: High   **SKILL LVL:** 2-3

EQUIPMENT
1. 10+ Balls and 2 Ball Cart
2. 2 Coaches Box

PERSONNEL: 8+

OBJECTIVE-DESIRED BEHAVIOR
1. Develop safe method of floor contact
2. Learn emergency procedures
3. Practice-perfect barrel roll technique
4. Provide multiple repetitions

COACHING POINTS-TECHNICAL EMPHASIS
1. Maintain upright position and run through if possible
2. Assume low body position prior to extension
3. Full arm and body extension before roll to distribute weight of fall over length of body
4. Flex lead leg and extend (drive through)
5. Extend rear leg - whip bottom leg over lead leg

CONCENTRATION KEYS
1. Run through- only go to floor as last resort
2. Step to ball
3. Full extension
4. Quick return to feet.

ROTATION: F/TA/D/SH/SH/ D upon goal achievement

PERFORMANCE GOAL-SCORING
1. 10 correct rolls per defender-5 each side

SEQUENCE OF ACTION
1. Right and left back defender assumes base position
2. Drill begins with deep hit to right, side **Defender (1)**
3. Second toss or hit (**2**) short for left side **Defender**
4. Hit should be at a distance to extend defender
5. Hit alternates Right-Left **D**efenders
6. Repeat drill until performance goal achieved

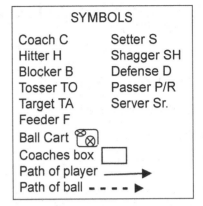

SYMBOLS

Coach C	Setter S
Hitter H	Shagger SH
Blocker B	Defense D
Tosser TO	Passer P/R
Target TA	Server Sr.
Feeder F	
Ball Cart	
Coaches box	
Path of player ——▶	
Path of ball - - - ▶	

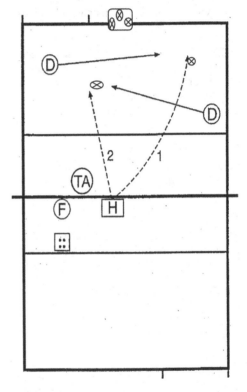

DRILL: DOUBLE BLOCK FLOOR DEFENSE: Pr. #3

TYPE OF DRILL: Coach Centered/Teaching

INTENSITY LVL: High   **SKILL LVL:** 2-3

EQUIPMENT: 20 Balls and Ball Cart

PERSONNEL: 10+

OBJECTIVE-DESIRED BEHAVIOR
1. Improve ability of defense to read attack in relation to a double block
2. Practice transition/defensive movement
3. Improve blocking/floor defensive technique
4. Provide multiple repetitions

COACHING POINTS-TECHNICAL EMPHASIS
1. Read angle of attack and point of contact
2. Line defender responsible for tip over block
3. Maintain perimeter defense position
4. Back row player move parallel behind front row player

CONCENTRATION KEYS
1. Parallel movement
2. Base to recognition
3. On balance

ROTATION
1. Offense to defense on goal achievement
2. Blocking team front to back every 15 hits
3. Blocking team rotate on position after every hit

PERFORMANCE GOAL-SCORING
1. 7 out of 10 balls must be settable digs
2. Game scoring to 15 points––1 point each settable dig

SEQUENCE OF ACTION
1. Coach/player on box slaps ball and alternates hitting to a defensive player or court position
2. Ball can be hit to open areas of court between players forcing parallel movement
3. Stationary block placed at the point of attack
4. Blocker reads angle of attack and attempts to block the attack
5. Defense reacts to ball after reading angle of attack
6. Defense pursues ball dug out of court area
7. Drill repeated until performance goal achieved

DRILL VARIATIONS: Move attack to middle and right side block

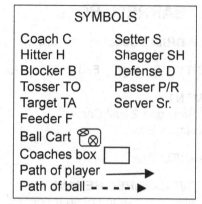

SYMBOLS

Coach C	Setter S
Hitter H	Shagger SH
Blocker B	Defense D
Tosser TO	Passer P/R
Target TA	Server Sr.
Feeder F	
Ball Cart	
Coaches box	
Path of player	
Path of ball	

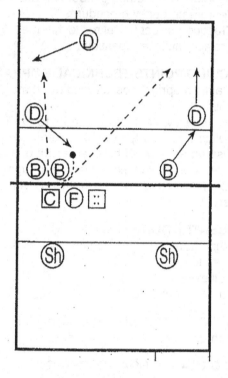

Automonous/Automatic/Competitive

**The following drills are consistent with the autonomous stage of motor
learning and the competitive/automatic drill classification**

The majority of Autonomous practice consists of serial, discrete, complex, and cognitive skills training
that takes In a Random, Continuous, and Variable Practice:

In the INTENSITY and SKILL SECTION of each DRILL, LVL stands for Level

DRILL: 3 PASSER SERVE

TYPE OF DRILL: Player centered/Tactics

INTENSITY LVL: Medium   **SKILL LVL:** 2-3

EQUIPMENT: 10+ Balls and cart

PERSONNEL: 8+

OBJECTIVE-DESIRED BEHAVIOR
1. Develop service tactics
2. Practice service technique
3. Improve individual serving accuracy
4. Establish game like serving conditions
5. Provide multiple service repetitions

COACHING POINTS-TACTICAL EMPHASIS
1. Read the reception formation
2. Serve the open area-seams-weaknesses
3. Vary trajectory-speed-location of serve
4. First serve in court

CONCENTRATION KEYS
1. Pre-service routine
2. Serve tough but keep serve in court
3. Vary the location of serve along base line

ROTATION
1. Passing team rotates clock wise every 6 points scored by serving team from SH//P/ P/P/TA
2. Serving team to passing team on goal achievement
3. Serving team every three serves

PERFORMANCE GOAL-SCORING
1. Game scoring: 25 point rally scoring
2. Point scoring by serving team:
   a. 2 point each ace
   b. 1 point each un-settable pass
   c. 1 point for passing team for each good pass to target

SEQUENCE OF ACTION
1. Server performs pre-service routine
2. Drill begins with random serve to open area/ seam/weaknesses in passing formation
3. Target keeps score of passing and serving accuracy-returns ball to servers
4. Repeat until performance goal achieved

SYMBOLS

Coach C	Setter S
Hitter H	Shagger SH
Blocker B	Defense D
Tosser TO	Passer P/R
Target TA	Server Sr.
Feeder F	

Ball Cart

Coaches box

Path of player

Path of ball - - - - ▶

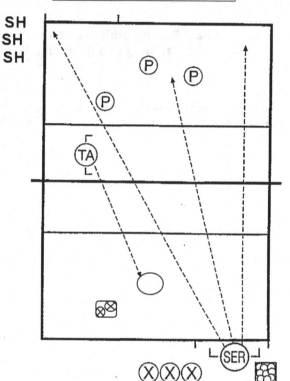

DRILL: THREE PLAYER PASS

TYPE OF DRILL: Player centered/training

INTENSITY LVL: Medium   **SKILL LVL:** 3

EQUIPMENT
1. 15 balls
2. 2-Ball cart

OBJECTIVE
1. Improve individual-team passing-serving technique- accuracy
2. Provide multiple game like repetitions

COACHING POINTS-TECHNICAL EMPHASIS
1. Practice pre-service and passing routines
2. Focus on server's body and court position
3. Establish spatial-temporal relationship with serve/court
4. Communicate location of serve before crossing net

CONCENTRATION KEYS-QUES
1. Thumbs together
2. Arms away from body
3. Elbows locked
4. Step to target

ROTATION: TA- SH-P-P—P-SH-SR-SH on goal achievement

PERFORMANCE GOAL-SCORING
1. 2 points for each serve target if target does not have to move
2. Set a number of passes to TA-Target only allowed 1 step to set ball
3. Game scoring: 15 passes in row to target wins

SEQUENCE OF ACTION
1. Passers-servers perform pre-service routine
2. Drill begins with random serve to **P** (**1-2-3**) who pass ball to **TA** (setter) (4)
3. **TA** returns ball to **SH**
4. Setter allowed one step to receive a point
5. Repeat serving until performance goal achieved

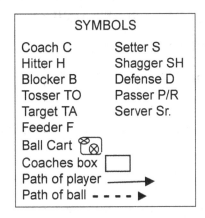

SYMBOLS

Coach C	Setter S
Hitter H	Shagger SH
Blocker B	Defense D
Tosser TO	Passer P/R
Target TA	Server Sr.
Feeder F	

Ball Cart
Coaches box
Path of player ⟶
Path of ball - - - - ▶

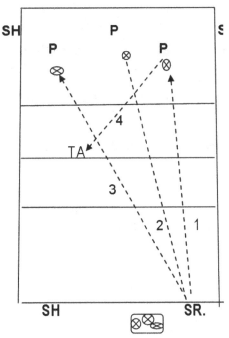

DRILL: SETTER TRAINING

TYPE OF DRILL: Coach centered/training

INTENSITY LVL: Medium   **SKILL LVL:** 1-2-3

EQUIPMENT: 10balls and ball cart

PERSONNEL: 2+ setters, target-coach (TO)

OBJECTIVE-DESIRED BEHAVIOR
1. Perfect overhead set technique
2. Improve setter movement
3. Practice approach footwork
4. Train various types/speed/location of sets
5. Provide multiple repetitions

COACHING POINTS-TECHNICAL EMPHASIS
1. Quick movement to target area or point of contact
2. Last two steps on right side approach to target area are left- right
3. Pursue bad pass from target area
4. Make eye contact with target before setting ball
5. Communicate
   a. On approach- "I'm up"
   b. "Here" upon reaching target area
6. Left side approach last step weight on right foot pivot for right/left position
7. Jump set to speed up attack

CONCENTRATION KEYS
1. Right foot forward
2. Hands up early
3. Feet and hips under ball
4. Face and extend to target
5. Thumbs extend toward ball after release
6. Accuracy first-deception second

ROTATION
1. Change setters on goal achievement

PERFORMANCE GOAL-SCORING
1. 20 consecutive sets at correct height-trajectory-speed-distance off net

SEQUENCE OF ACTION
1. Drills begins with toss **C** off the net to various setting areas
2. Setter alternates approach from areas 1-4 court zones
3. Setter sets designated set to pre-determined hitting zone
4. Repeat drill until performance goal achieved

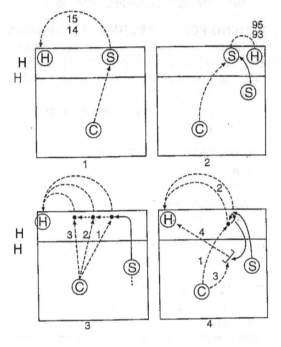

SYMBOLS

Coach C	Setter S
Hitter H	Shagger SH
Blocker B	Defense D
Tosser TO	Passer P/R
Target TA	Server Sr.
Feeder F	

Ball Cart
Coaches box
Path of player ———▶
Path of ball - - - - ▶

DRILL: READING THE BLOCK - Pr.1setter

TYPE OF DRILL: Coach centered/teaching

INTENSITY LVL: High   **SKILL LVL:** 3

EQUIPMENT: 10+ balls and cart

PERSONNEL: 10+

OBJECTIVE-DESIRED BEHAVIOR
1. Develop the ability read block location, movement and set aspirate attacker
2. Reinforce set/attack technique/tactics
3. Practice blocking technique
4. Provide multiple repetitions

COACHING POINTS-TECHNICAL EMPHASIS
1. Recognize and communicate number/ location of weak/strong blockers prior to serve
2. Pick up block with peripheral vision
3. Set to the best location in relation to attacker/block/floor defense
4. Coverage players call seams in block

ROTATION
1. SH/SH/B/B and SH/SH/TO/H every 5 attempts
2. Attack to Defense upon goal achievement

PERFORMANCE GOAL-SCORING
1. Game scoring to 15 point
    a. 1 Point for successful attack
    b. 2 Points for a kill

SEQUENCE OF ACTION
1. Block assumes stationary position at the net
2. Drill begins with **TO** toss to **S** (**1**)
3. Setter sets predetermined set in relation to block (**2**)
4. Block varies position from line/hole/cross court
5. Attacker reads block position and attacks open areas (**3**)
6. Drill repeated until performance goal achieved

DRILL VARIATION
1. Move attack to middle-right side

SYMBOLS

Coach C	Setter S
Hitter H	Shagger SH
Blocker B	Defense D
Tosser TO	Passer P/R
Target TA	Server Sr.
Feeder F	

Ball Cart
Coaches box
Path of player ⟶
Path of ball - - - - ▶

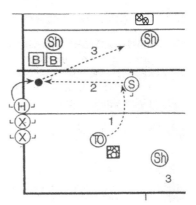

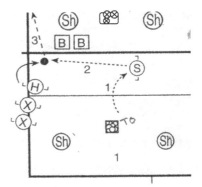

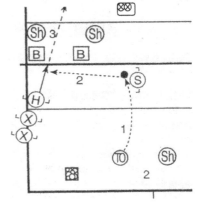

DRILL: READ THE BLOCK: Pr#2 attacker

TYPE OF DRILL: Player centered/ tactical training

INTENSITY LVL: Medium   **SKILL LVL:** 3

EQUIPMENT
1. 15 balls
2. Ball cart and coaches boxes

OBJECTIVE
1. Reinforce individual attack technique-accuracy
2. Develop the ability to read the block
3. Improve team communication-coverage skills
4. Provide multiple game like repetitions

COACHING POINTS-TACTICAL EMPHASIS
1. Take quick look at block on approach to attack
2. Keep block in peripheral vision as ball is set
3. Listen to communication keys from teammates
4. Attack the open areas of block

CONCENTRATION KEYS-QUES - on coaches signal
1. 1 finger end blockers block
2. 2 fingers line blocker blocks
3. 3 fingers two middle blockers block
4. 4 fingers all blockers block

ROTATION
1. Upon achieving performance goal
2. H to B––B to SH––SH to TO/H after 5 repetitions

PERFORMANCE GOALS-SCORING
1. Number of repetitions 5 each hitter
2. Number of hits past the block-
3. Timed interval-5 min
4. Game scoring: first team to 15 min.

SEQUENCE OF ATCTION
1. Four blockers placed in blocking position
2. Drill begins with toss to S (**1**) who sets to **H** (**2**) who attacks ball past block (3)
3. Prior to toss to setter **C**oach signals number of blockers **1-2-3-4**
4. Repeat sequence until performance goal achieved

DRILL VARIATION/PROGRESSION
1. Rotate to middle and right side block
2. Two player block-Coach signal block location and number of blockers
   a. Left hand block line
   b. Two hands up leave hole in block
   c. Right hand up gives line
3. Attacker reads block position and attacks open area in block

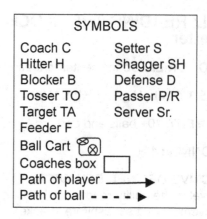

SYMBOLS

Coach C	Setter S
Hitter H	Shagger SH
Blocker B	Defense D
Tosser TO	Passer P/R
Target TA	Server Sr.
Feeder F	

Ball Cart
Coaches box
Path of player ———▶
Path of ball - - - - ▶

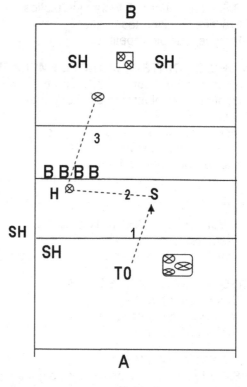

DRILL: 3 POSITION ATTACK

INTENSITY LVL: High   **SKILL LVL:** 1-2-3

TYPE OF DRILL: Coach centered/Training

EQUIPMENT
1. 10 + Balls
2. 1 Cart

PERSONNEL: 5+

OBJECTIVE-DESIRED BEHAVIOR
1. Perform attack from 3 positions
2. Reinforce transition skills
3. Coordinate timing of hitter and setter
4. Develop attack consistency
5. Practice floor defense techniques
6. Provide multiple attack repetitions

COACHING POINTS-TECH.TACTICAL EMPHASIS
1. Attacker controls timing on high sets
2. Setter controls timing on low or quick sets
3. Left side hitter approach outside in angle
4. Right side hitter approach inside out angle

CONCENTRATION KEYS
1. Delay approach
2. Quick approach and arm swing
3. Jump quick/swing hard
4. Control and placement

ROTATION
1. H to D to H on goal achievement
2. Alternate setters on 15 hit series

PERFORMANCE GOAL-SCORING
1. Players keep own score 8 out of 10 hits to assigned attack zone
2. 10 consecutive hits to randomly selected areas

SEQUENCE OF ACTION
1. Divide players into groups of 3 attackers - 3 defenders - 2 shaggers
2. Drill begins with ball **C** tossed to **S**
3. Setter sets hitter in position 1-2-3
4. Hitter hits ball to designated area of court (line-x court-etc.)
5. Drill repeated until performance goal achieved

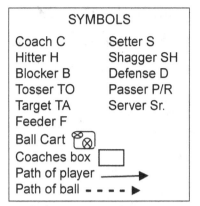

SYMBOLS

Coach C	Setter S
Hitter H	Shagger SH
Blocker B	Defense D
Tosser TO	Passer P/R
Target TA	Server Sr.
Feeder F	
Ball Cart	
Coaches box	
Path of player	
Path of ball	

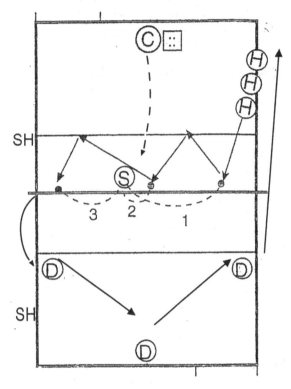

DRILL: SIDEOUT ATTACK

TYPE OF DRILL: Player centered-tactics

INTENSITY LVL: Medium   **SKILL LVL:** 3

EQUIPMENT
1. 10+ Balls
2. 2 Ball Carts

PERSONNEL: 10+

OBJECTIVE
1. Instill automatic side out attack concepts
2. Improve transition technical skills
3. Reinforce team concepts
4. Provide game like repetitions

COACHING POINTS-TACTICAL EMPHASIS
1. Run aggressive sideout offense
2. Setter checks with coach/opponent before calling play
3. First option set to primary attacker
4. 2nd option set might be a medium tempo set

CONCENTRATION KEYS
1. Communicate location of weak blockers
2. Attack open seems block-open areas of Ct.
3. Be aggressive

ROTATION
1. Serve/receiving team rotates 1 position clockwise on every side out
2. Serving team becomes receiving team on achievement of performance goal

PERFORMANCE GOAL-SCORING
1. Game score to 15 points
2. Game situation scoring 8-10 11-7 to 15 points

SEQUENCE OF ACTION
1. Players divided into 2 teams of 6
2. Drill begins with **Sr.** serve to **R** (**1**) **R** passes to **S** (**2**) **S**etter sets **H** (**3**)
3. **H**itter attacks ball cross court (**4**) or open areas of court.
4. Play is continuous until ball is dead— Winning team serves next ball
5. Serving team serves until performance goal is achieved

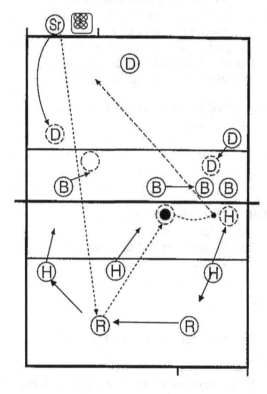

SYMBOLS

Coach C	Setter S
Hitter H	Shagger SH
Blocker B	Defense D
Tosser TO	Passer P/R
Target TA	Server Sr.
Feeder F	

Ball Cart
Coaches box
Path of player
Path of ball - - - ▶

DRILL: COMBO TIP-DEEP COURT-NET ATTACK

TYPE OF DRILL: Player centered/training

INTENSITY LVL: High   **SKILL LVL:** 3

PERSONNEL: 12

OBJECTIVE-DESIRED BEHAVIOR
1. Reinforce ability to read the defense
2. Improve individual tip, hit at net and deep court attack technique/tactics
3. Instill a team concept mentality
4. Provide multiple game-like repetitions

COACHING POINTS-TACTICAL EMPHASIS
1. Check defense to determine open areas
2. Defender releases for tip coverage if block covers ball
3. Full approach and arm swing on off speed attack

CONCENTRATION KEYS
1. Read defense
2. Disguise attack
3. Anticipate type of attack based on quality of set
4. Attack the open areas of Ct.

ROTATION: Both teams rotate 1 position after 3 points

PERFORMANCE GOAL-SCORING
1. Rally scoring: to 25 points
2. Timed execution: 20 minutes
3. 1 point reward to attacking team upon achieving 3 attacks in a row

SEQUENCE OF ACTION
1. Drill begins with Serve to **R (1) R** passes to **S (2) S** sets **H (3)**
2. Team receiving serve may attack with either a tip-deep court or net attack
3. After each successful attack a ball is tossed by **C (4)** to winning team who passes to **S (5)** for set to **H**
4. Second ball must be attacked with 1 of the remaining 2 attack options
5. Third ball must be attacked with remaining attack option
6. Second and all succeeding balls tossed by coach until set point is won
7. Play continues until all three option have been achieved by either team
8. First team to complete hit-tip-deep court attack is awarded a point and the serve
9. New play action begins with serve by the team completing goal of 3 consecutive attacks
10. Repeat drill until performance goal achieved:

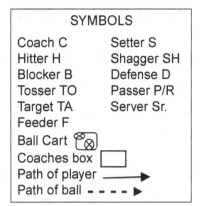

SYMBOLS

Coach C	Setter S
Hitter H	Shagger SH
Blocker B	Defense D
Tosser TO	Passer P/R
Target TA	Server Sr.
Feeder F	
Ball Cart	
Coaches box	
Path of player	
Path of ball	

net

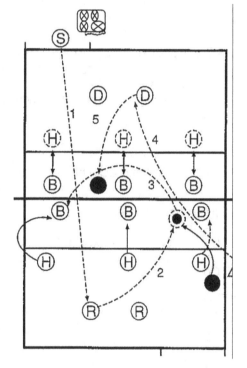

DRILL: MIDDLE TO LEFTSIDE TRANS

TYPE OF DRILL: Coach centered/training

INTENSITY LVL: High   **SKILL LVL:** 3

EQUIPMENT: 10 Balls and Cart

PERSONNEL: 10+

OBJECTIVE-DESIRED BEHAVIOR
1. Reinforce transition from middle attack to left side attack
2. Improve hitter/setter communication
3. Practice 14-15-33-53 sets
4. Provide multiple attack repetitions

COACHING POINTS-TECHNICAL EMPHASIS
1. Hitter focus on passer to determine speed and location of pass
2. Hitter maintain 45 degree angle between setter and point of contact
3. Middle hitter must approach at angle to block
4. Middle hitter cut back to left or hits sharp angle to right of double block on middle attack

CONCENTRATION KEYS
1. Read pass
2. Quick retreat and approach from middle to left side hit
3. Communicate desired set

ROTATION
1. Team B Ct.-B/SH/TO/SH/B after 5 blocks
2. Team A Ct.-R/TO/R/H after each attack
3. Defense to offense after 7 min.

PERFORMANCE GOAL-SCORING
1. Timed interval: 7 min. A—B exchange courts.

SEQUENCE OF ACTION
1. Players' divided into 2-teams of 6 players
2. Drill begins with toss from **TO** court **B** to **R** in court **A** (**1**).
3. Receiver in court **A** passes ball to **S** (**2**)
4. **S**etter sets middle attacker (**3**)
5. **M**iddle **H** hits set (**4**) and transition for left side attack
6. **S**etter **Ct**. **A** receives second toss from **TO** in court **A** (**5**)
7. **S**etters sets 4-14 set to left side **H** (**6**)
8. **H**itter attacks ball down line or seam in block (**7**)
9. Drill repeated until performance goal achieved

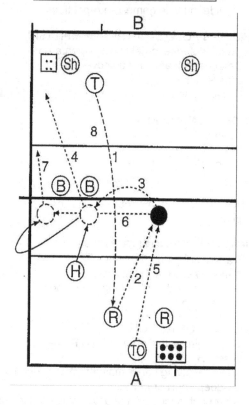

SYMBOLS

Coach C   Setter S
Hitter H   Shagger SH
Blocker B   Defense D
Tosser TO   Passer P/R
Target TA   Server Sr.
Feeder F
Ball Cart
Coaches box
Path of player
Path of ball - - - -

DRILL: LEFT TO MIDDLE TRANSITION - Pr. 2

TYPE OF DRILL: Coach Centered/training

INTENSITY LVL: High   **SKILL LVL:** 3

EQUIPMENT: 15+ Balls and 3 Ball cart

PERSONNEL: 12+

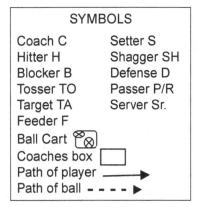

SYMBOLS

Coach C	Setter S
Hitter H	Shagger SH
Blocker B	Defense D
Tosser TO	Passer P/R
Target TA	Server Sr.
Feeder F	

Ball Cart

Coaches box

Path of player ——▶

Path of ball - - - - ▶

OBJECTIVE
1. Train left side defense positioning and movement to attack
2. Instill concept of transition from defense to attack–– attack to block- block to attack
3. Provide multiple tactical repetitions

COACHING POINTS-TECHNICAL EMPHASIS
1. Move quickly for outside in approach
2. Look over inside shoulder to pick up pass
3. Max jump and arm swing on hit and block

CONCENTRATION KEYS
1. Locate pass-set
2. Focus on area of attack
3. Quick transition to attack-block-attack

ROTATION
1. Ct. B H/F/SH/SH/F every 3 pt.
2. Ct. A H/B/D after each of attack transition
3. A to B after 7 min. or 15 points

PERFORMANCE GOAL-SCORING
1. Goal achievement to 15 points

SEQUENCE OF ACTION
1. Players divided into 2 teams of 6
2. Drill begins with attack cross Ct. from **Hitter** on box on left side **Ct. B** to **D/H CT. A (1)**
3. Left side **D/H** court **A** digs ball to **S (2)** and transition for left side attack
4. **Setter** sits ball to left side **H/D (3)** who hit ball deep to **SH Ct. B (4)**
5. **Hitter** transition to net to block **H** on Box right side **Ct. B** and transition off net to 10' line
6. **Hitter** on box left side **Ct. B** hits second ball to **D/H** at 10' line **(5)**
7. **Defender** passes ball to **S (6)** and transition for middle attack
8. **Setter** sets middle **H/D (7)** who hit ball to **SH** in **Ct. B (8)**
9. Drill repeated until performance.

DRILL VARIATIONS/PROGRESSIONS
1. Reproduce drill on right side of court

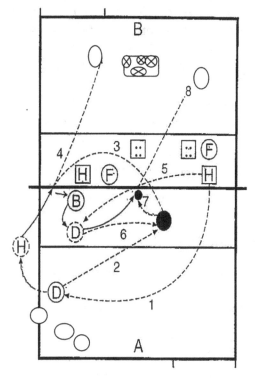

DRILL: 3/3 TRANSITION Pr. 3

TYPE OF DRILL: Player centered/tactics

INTENSITY LVL: High   **SKILL LVL:** 3

EQUIPMENT: 20 Balls and 2 Carts

PERSONNEL: 10+

OBJECTIVE-DESIRED BEHAVIOR
1. Practice attack to defense transition
2. Practice defense to attack transition
3. Improve transition movement/speed
4. Provide multiple transition repetitions

COACHING POINTS-TACTICAL EMPHASIS
1. Hitter communicates to setter if they are in position to attack and the desired set
2. Quick retreat from net to attack
3. Shorten the approach to attack

CONCENTRATION KEYS
1. Quick transition off the net to attack
2. Offensive read the block/floor defense
3. Communicate
4. Defense read the attack/block

PERFORMANCE GOAL-SCORING
1. Game scoring to 15 points

SEQUENCE OF ACTION
1. Players divided into 2 teams of 6
2. 3 players team CT B assume attack position at 10' line
3. 3 players team CT A assume block position at net
4. Out players toss or shag
5. Drill begins with toss **TO** to **S**etter in court **B (1)**
6. Setter **Ct. B** sets any of 3 front row **H** or pre-determined play action (**2**)
7. Hitter **Ct. B** attacks ball (**3**) and all **H** transitions to **Bl**ock
8. **B**lockers court **A B**lock and transitions to attack
9. **S**etter court **A** transitions from base position **1** to receive toss **TO** (**4**) at net
10. Setter **Ct A** sets any of 3 front row **H** or pre-determined play action (**5**)
11. Hitter **Ct. A** attacks ball (**6**) and transitions to block
12. Drill repeated until performance goal reached

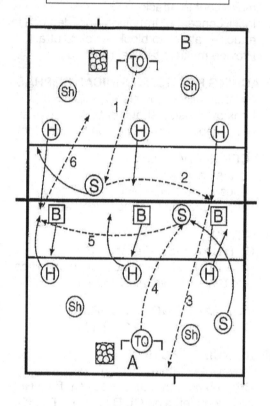

SYMBOLS

Coach C	Setter S
Hitter H	Shagger SH
Blocker B	Defense D
Tosser TO	Passer P/R
Target TA	Server Sr.
Feeder F	
Ball Cart	
Coaches box	
Path of player	
Path of ball - - - - ▶	

DRILL: OVER THE NET PEPPER

TYPE OF DRILL: Player centered/training

INTENSITY LVL: Med./high   **SKILL:** 2-3

EQUIPMENT
1. 1 ball per 1/2 court
2. Antenna/tape

PERSONNEL: 12+ players

OBJECTIVE DESIRED BEHAVIOR
1. Warm up with volleyball skill activity
2. Create practice enthusiasm
3. Develop team work
4. Improve ball control on off speed attack
5. Provide multiple repetitions

COACHING POINTS-TECHNICAL EMPHASIS
1. Attack weakness in the defense
2. Read the angle of attack
3. Hit off-speed to open areas
4. Wipe attack off block

CONCENTRATION KEYS
1. Communication
2. Emphasis on technical execution net

ROTATION: Game rotation on after every point scored

PERFORMANCE GOAL-SCORING
1. To warm up with a 5 minute time limit
2. Rally scoring to 15 points if used as practice drill

SEQUENCE OF ACTION
1. Players divided into 4 teams of 3 players
2. Place antennae on net at mid-court-Tape mid- line of court if possible
3. Drill begins with D tossing to **S Ct A (1)** who sets to **H (2)** who plays ball over net **(3)**
4. Ball must be contacted 3 times per side **(3-4-5)** before is it played over net **(6)**
5. Ball played over on 1st or 2nd touch losses **point**
6. Ball re-tossed by scoring team on termination of play
7. Drill repeated until performance goal achieved

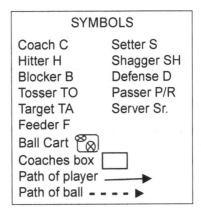

SYMBOLS

Coach C	Setter S
Hitter H	Shagger SH
Blocker B	Defense D
Tosser TO	Passer P/R
Target TA	Server Sr.
Feeder F	
Ball Cart	
Coaches box	
Path of player	
Path of ball	

net

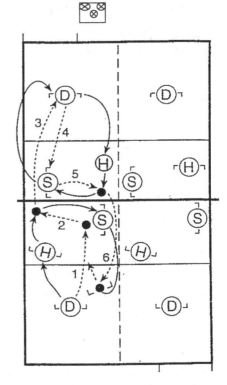

DRILL: DEEP COURT VOLLEY

TYPE OF DRILL: Coach Centered/training

INTENSITY LVL: High   **SKILL LVL:** 2-3

EQUIPMENT: 10+ balls

OBJECTIVE-DESIRED BEHAVIOR
1. Develop ball control-accuracy
2. Train deep court attack/defense techniques
3. Reinforce team concepts-team work
4. Enhance spatial orientation in relation to 10'
   line
5. Provide multiple attack repetitions.

COACHING POINTS-TECHNICAL EMPHASIS
1. Set ball slightly in front of 10' line
2. Slight broad jump on take of–land past 10'
   line
3. Diggers focus on hitters arm swing

CONCENTRATION KEYS
1. Read the hitters arm swing
2. Stay behind ball
3. Full arm swing
4. Full arm extension
5. Top spin
6. Think deep

ROTATION: Rotate opposite side hitting line
after each attack

PERFORMANCE GOAL-SCORING
1. 15 point rally score game
2. One point each successful attack

SEQUENCE OF ACTION
1. Players divided into two teams of six and a
   Setter on each court with 2 lines of **H/D**
2. Objective is to keep ball in play not to beat
   the opponent
3. Drill starts with cross court toss from **C (1)**
   Ball passed to **S (2)**
4. **S**etter sets deep court set **(3) H** must take
   off behind the 10' line
5. **H**itter attacks ball cross court or down line
   directly to **D (4)**
6. Defense digs ball to **S (5) S** sets deep court
   (6) to **H** who attacks ball **(7)**
7. If an error occurs re-started play with a toss
   from **C** to non-erroring team
8. Repeat drill until performance goal achieved

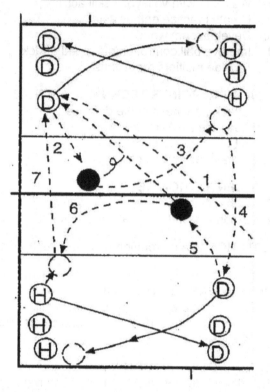

DRILL: LEFTSIDE BLOCK & REPLAY

TYPE OF DRILL: Coach centered/training

INTENSITY LVL: High   **SKILL LVL:** 3

EQUIPMENT
1. 20+ Balls
2. 2 Ball Carts

PERSONNEL: 10+

OBJECTIVE-DESIRED BEHAVIOR
1. Practice offense to defense transition
2. Practice recovery footwork-body position
3. Improve attack and blocking technique
4. Provide multiple transition repetitions

COACHING POINTS-TACTICAL EMPHASIS
1. Blockers quick pivot to receive ball if tossed by to
2. Quick retreat and transition to approach
3. Keep shoulders square to net on retreat

CONCENTRATION KEYS
1. Quick pivot off outside foot
2. Communicate to setter readiness for attack

ROTATION
1. Ct B -H/SH/TO/SH after each attack
2. Ct. A-SH/TO/B/B/SH after every 5 attempts
3. Court B to A on goal achievement

PERFORMANCE GOAL-SCORING
1. Game situation scoring to 15 points

SEQUENCE OF ACTION
1. Drill begins with ball tossed by **TO** to **S** court **B** (**1**)
2. **S**etter court **B** sets **H** (**2**) who hits ball (**3**) and transition to block position
3. **B**lockers in Ct. **A** block attack and pivot for transitions to attack position at 10" line
4. **TO** Ct **A** has two options
   a. Option 1: **TO** tosses ball at blockers as they pivot of net (**4**) who pass ball to setter at mid Ct.
   b. Option 2: **TO** tosses ball high to **S** at mid-court
5. **S**etter sets either outside or middle **B/H** (**6**) who have transition to attack (**7**)
6. Drill repeated until performance goal achieved

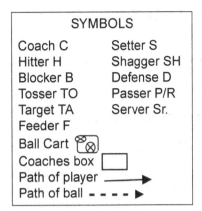

```
SYMBOLS
Coach C          Setter S
Hitter H         Shagger SH
Blocker B        Defense D
Tosser TO        Passer P/R
Target TA        Server Sr.
Feeder F
Ball Cart
Coaches box
Path of player  ──────▶
Path of ball   - - - - ▶
```

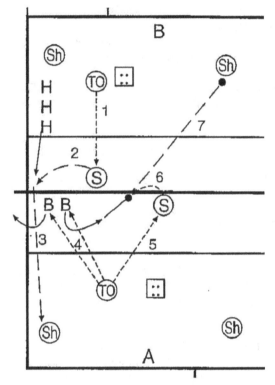

DRILL: RIGHT SIDE BLOCK - REPLAY Pr 1

TYPE OF DRILL: Coach centered/training

INTENSITY LVL: HIGH   **SKILL LVL:** 3

EQUIPMENT: 10+ Balls and cart

PERSONNEL: 12+

OBJECTIVE-DESIRED BEHAVIOR
1. Practice replay of ball hit past block-dug in back court
2. Improve defensive/offensive transition
3. Practice setter transition to target area
4. Improve right side blockers setting ability
5. Provide multiple repetitions

COACHING POINTS-TACTICAL EMPHASIS
1. Blockers feel or see side of the body ball is hit
2. Blockers land with weight on outside pivot foot and make wide pivot off outside foot

CONCENTRATION KEYS
1. Quick pivot
2. Low hand position
3. Pass ball to mid court

ROTATION
1. Ct. B- SH/R/H/SH after each hit
2. Ct. A- SH/T/B/B/H
3. Ct. A to Ct. B on achieving performance goal

PERFORMANCE GOAL-SCORING
1. Game scoring to 15 points-1 point for ball played up to mid court set and hit

SEQUENCE OF ACTION
1. Two teams of 6 players
2. Drill begins with toss over the net by **T** to **R** (**1**) in court **B**
3. Ball passed to **S** (**2**) who sets **H** (**3**) **H** attacks ball deep over block Ct A (**4**)
4. **B**lockers Ct. **A** block and on landing pivot and prepare for transition to attack
5. **T** Ct **A** has two options
   a. Option #1: **T** tosses ball low to pivoting blockers **B** (**5**) who pass ball high to mid-court for set
   b. Option # 2: **T** tosses ball to **S** (**6**) who has transition to net and sets ball to **H** (**7**)
6. Repeat drill until performance goal achieved

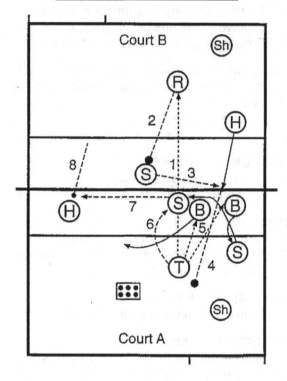

SYMBOLS

Coach C	Setter S
Hitter H	Shagger SH
Blocker B	Defense D
Tosser TO	Passer P/R
Target TA	Server Sr.
Feeder F	
Ball Cart	
Coaches box	
Path of player	
Path of ball	

DRILL: BLOCK VS ATTACK

TYPE OF DRILL: Coach center/training

INTENSITY LVL: High   **SKILL:**3

EQUIPMENT: 10 balls and cart

PERSONNEL: 12+

OBJECTIVE-DESIRED BEHAVIOR
1. Improve blocking technique
2. Practice middle block footwork/jump timing
3. Coordinate middle and outside block
4. Improve blocking communication
5. Provide multiple block repetitions

COACHING POINTS-TECHNICAL EMPHASIS
1. Locate hitters/setter by communicating number, location and by pointing to hitters
2. Read the location and tempo of pass/set
3. Focus on hitter's angle of approach/hitting arm
4. Outside blocker communicates jump timing
5. Middle blocker jumps with middle attacker

CONCENTRATION KEYS
1. Read the set
2. Read the hitter
3. Front the hitter
4. Penetrate, close the block and seal net
5. Hands on ball
6. Close to center court
7. Eyes open/ head up

ROTATION
1. B to SH on completion of performance goal
2. Blocking team to attack on goal achievement
3. Hitters rotate to opposite hitting line after every point

PERFORMANCE GOAL-SCORING
1. Game scoring offense: game to 15 points
2. 1 point for each successful block
3. 2 points for each stuff block

SEQUENCE OF ACTION
1. Drill begins with toss **C** to **S** attacking team **(1)**
2. **S**etter sets designated set or play action (**2-3-4**)
3. Middle blocker blocks middle and/or slides to block outside
4. Repeat drill until performance goal achieved

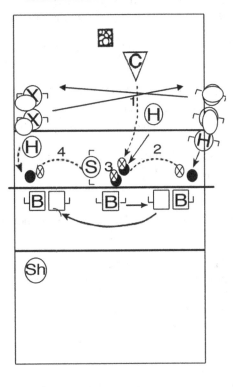

SYMBOLS	
Coach C	Setter S
Hitter H	Shagger SH
Blocker B	Defense D
Tosser TO	Passer P/R
Target TA	Server Sr.
Feeder F	
Ball Cart	
Coaches box	
Path of player	
Path of ball	

DRILL: READ THE ATTACK

TYPE OF DRILL: Player center/training

INTENSITY LVL: High   **SKILL LVL:** 2-3

EQUIPMENT: 10 + Balls

PERSONNEL: 12+

OBJECTIVE-DESIRED BEHAVIOR
1. Reinforce the ability to read location/ angle of attack
2. Improve team floor defensive technique
3. Develop ability to read location/angle of attack
4. Practice single/multiple player block
5. Provide multiple defensive read repetitions

COACHING POINTS-TACTICAL EMPHASIS
1. Floor defense assumes base position
2. Read/communicate direction of set-location-attack
3. Read block in relation to net-angle of attack
4. Keep ball and attackers arm/hand in view
5. Line diggers plays for dink if block covers ball
6. Crosscourt digger lines up outside blocker
7. Middle back lines up in hole in block

CONCENTRATION KEYS
1. Read sequence: Ball-Setter-Ball-Hitter-Ball
2. Stay deep
3. Read-communicate-transition
4. Be stopped on ball contact
5. Focus on attacker's wrist and hand

ROTATION
1. Defense front to back every 5 points
2. Defense to offense upon goal achievement

PERFORMANCE GOAL-SCORING
1. Game scoring to 15
2. Game situation scoring: vary starting score

SEQUENCE OF ACTION
1. 2 teams of 6 players
2. Drill begins with **TO** toss to **S (1)** who sets **H (2) H** attacks ball **(3)**
3. Block reads attack and moves to blocking position
4. Floor defense reads attack location and transitions contact point
5. Ball dug to target area
6. Defense plays dug balls to conclusion
7. Repeat drill until performance goal achieved

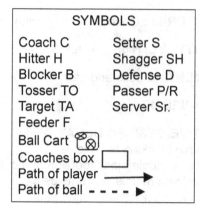

SYMBOLS

Coach C	Setter S
Hitter H	Shagger SH
Blocker B	Defense D
Tosser TO	Passer P/R
Target TA	Server Sr.
Feeder F	

Ball Cart

Coaches box

Path of player

Path of ball

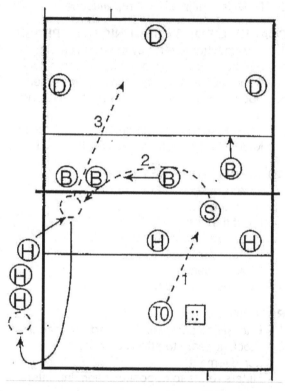

DRILL: TEAM ATTACK COVERAG

TYPE OF DRILL: Coach Centered/training

INTENSITY LVL: High **SKILL LVL:** 3

EQUIPMENT: 10+ Balls/1 Ball Cart

PERSONNEL: 10+

OBJECTIVE
1. Develop team attack coverage concepts
2. Practice transition to attack coverage
3. Reinforce attack coverage tactics
4. Provide multiple coverage repetitions

COACHING POINTS-TACTICAL EMPHASIS
1. Assume 3-2 attack coverage right/left/deep court attack
2. Deep court coverage takes place on the net at point of attack
3. Focus on attackers arm until ball is hit
4. Focus on block after ball is attacked

CONCENTRATION KEYS
1. Focus sequence-hitter-ball-block-ball
2. Follow the set
3. Stop on ball contact by attacker
4. Low body position
5. Arms out––J Stroke
6. If in doubt find a hole and cover it

ROTATION
1. Defense to coverage upon goal achievement
2. Game position rotation after each dig

PERFORMANCE GOAL-SCORING
1. 10 coverage digs to mid-court
2. Game scoring to 15 points-1 point for each dig

SEQUENCE OF ACTION
1. Players divided into two teams of 6 players
2. Drill begins with **TO** toss to **R** attacking team (**1**)
3. Ball passed to **S**etter (**2**)
4. Setter set anyone of three attack positions (**3**)
5. Hitter hit ball directly into block
6. Attacking team assume coverage position upon reading attack location
7. Repeat drill until performance goal achieved

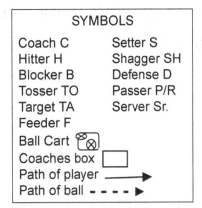

SYMBOLS
Coach C	Setter S
Hitter H	Shagger SH
Blocker B	Defense D
Tosser TO	Passer P/R
Target TA	Server Sr.
Feeder F	
Ball Cart	
Coaches box	
Path of player	
Path of ball	

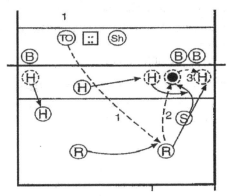

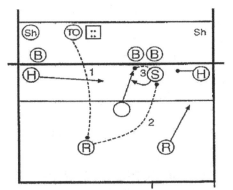

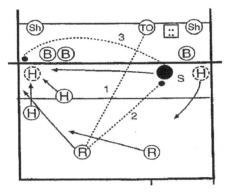

DRILL: BLOCK THE WIDE SET

TYPE OF DRILL: Player centered/Training

INTENSITY LVL: High   **SKILL LVL:** 2

EQUIPMENT
1. 10+ Balls
2. 1 Ball cart

PERSONNEL: 10+

OBJECTIVE
1. Practice hitting ball set outside antenna
2. Learn how to block wide attack
3. Learn floor defensive positioning on wide attack
4. Provide multiple repetitions

COACHING POINTS-TECHNICAL EMPHASIS
1. Ball cannot be attacked into shaded area
2. On wide sets block moves away from antennae
3. Hands position toward mid court
4. Backcourt rotates opposite direction of set
5. Right or left back moves to cover tip

CONCENTRATION KEYS
1. Block off the antenna
2. Cover off-speed attack
3. Rotate opposite set

ROTATION
1. Blocking team front to back on goal completion
2. Attacking team to defense on goal achievement

PERFORMANCE GOAL-SCORING
1. Number of successful attacks
2. Number of successful blocks

SEQUENCE OF ACTION
1. Drill begins with toss to S (**1**)
2. Setter alternates sets inside/outside antenna (**2**)
3. H hits ball into open area of court (**3**)
4. Defense reads set and moves to proper court and block position
5. Drill repeated until performance goal achieved

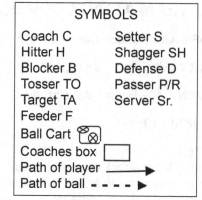

SYMBOLS

Coach C	Setter S
Hitter H	Shagger SH
Blocker B	Defense D
Tosser TO	Passer P/R
Target TA	Server Sr.
Feeder F	
Ball Cart	
Coaches box	
Path of player	
Path of ball	

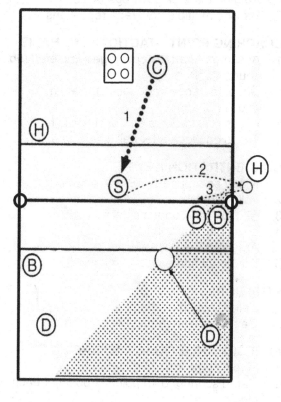

DRILL: SINGLE BLOCK ATTACK
DEFENSE: Pr #4

TYPE OF DRILL: Player centered/training

INTENSITY LVL: Medium   **SKILL LVL:** 2-3

EQUIPMENT
1. 20 Balls
2. 1 Ball cart-

PERSONNEL: 10+

OBJECTIVE-DESIRED BEHAVIOR
1. Improve ability of defense to read attack in relation to a single block
2. Practice transition/defensive movement
3. Improve blocking/floor defensive technique
4. Provide multiple block repetitions

COACHING POINTS-TECHNICAL EMPHASIS
1. Transition to assigned defense position
2. Read the angle of attack
3. Read attackers arm movement/hand position

CONCENTRATION KEYS
1. Base to recognition
2. Parallel movement
3. Assume on help defensive position

ROTATION
1. Blockers rotate front to back every 5 hits
2. Hitters rotate attack position after each attack
3. Offense to defense on goal achievement (15 points)

PERFORMANCE GOAL-SCORING
1. Dug ball must be settable to get a point
2. Game scoring to 15 points

SEQUENCE OF ACTION
1. Play starts with **TO** toss to **S** (**1**) who can set any of the 3 **H** positions (**2**)
2. Ball hit (**3**) to open areas of court between players forcing parallel movement
3. Stationary single **B** placed at the point of attack
4. **B**locker reads angle of attack and attempts to block the **H**
5. Defense reacts to ball after reading angle of attack
6. Drill repeated until performance goal achieved

DRILL VARIATIONS/PROGRESSIONS
1. Alternate perimeter/rotation defense

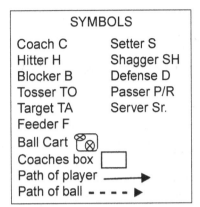

SYMBOLS

Coach C	Setter S
Hitter H	Shagger SH
Blocker B	Defense D
Tosser TO	Passer P/R
Target TA	Server Sr.
Feeder F	

Ball Cart

Coaches box

Path of player ⟶

Path of ball - - - - ▶

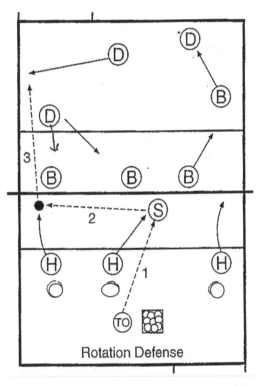

Rotation Defense

DRILL: ISOLATION DEFENSE Pr. #1

TYPE OF DRILL: Player centered

INTENSITY LVL: Med./high   **SKILL LVL:** 2-3

EQUIPMENT
1. 20 Balls
2. 2 Ball Carts 2 Coaches Boxes

PERSONNEL: 12+

OBJECTIVE-DESIRED BEHAVIOR
1. Practice defensive floor position/movement
2. Improve dig technique
3. Provide multiple block/dig repetitions

COACHING POINTS-TECHNICAL
1. Improve line block and dig technique
2. Assume a balanced "on help" court position
3. Blocker blocks line and closes to center court

CONCENTRATION KEYS
1. "On help"
2. Balanced floor position

ROTATION
1. SH/D/B//TA/F/SH on goal achievement

PERFORMANCE GOAL-SCORING
1. Rotate after 5 digs to target

SEQUENCE OF ACTION
1. Drill begins with defender in base position at side lines
2. **H**itter on box slaps ball signaling defender to prepare for attack
3. **H**itter hits or tips ball at defenders (**1-2-3**) ball dug to target area
4. Repeat until performance goal achieved

DRILL VARIATIONS/PROGRESSIONS
1. Move attack to middle with defense in base position single block

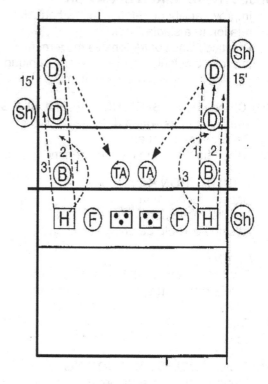

SYMBOLS
Coach C	Setter S
Hitter H	Shagger SH
Blocker B	Defense D
Tosser TO	Passer P/R
Target TA	Server Sr.
Feeder F	

Ball Cart

Coaches box

Path of player ⟶

Path of ball - - - ▶

DRILL: 3 / 6 FLOOR DEFENSE

TYPE OF DRILL: Player centered/training

INTENSITY LVL: High   **SKILL LVL:** 2-3

EQUIPMENT: 10+ Balls 1 cart

PERSONNEL: 12+

OBJECTIVE-DESIRED BEHAVIOR
1. Learn floor defense system/tactics
2. Improve individual floor defense skills
3. Practice defense to attack transition
4. Improve block technique - attack skills
5. Perform game like multiple repetitions

COACHING POINTS-TACTICAL EMPHASIS
1. Assume base position prior to attack
2. Middle blocker B communicates number-location of hitters
3. Read type/speed/location of set
4. Be stopped upon ball contact by hitter
5. Read position- angle of attack in relation to the location and position of block

CONCENTRATION KEYS
1. Read pass-setter-set-hitter
2. Read angle of attack
3. Evaluate block
4. Eyes focus on hitters arm and hand

ROTATION
1. Defense front to back 10 digs or blocks
2. Hitters move one position to right after each hit
3. Attack team to Defense upon each goal achievement

PERFORMANCE GOAL-SCORING
1. Game scoring to 25 points 1point for every dig or kill

SEQUENCE OF ACTION
1. Players divided into 2 teams of 6
2. Drill begins with **C** toss to **S** (**1**) who alternates approach to target from zones 1-4
3. **S**etter sets middle **H** (**2**) who hits quick set (**3**) in combination offense
4. Setter alternates attack on a random bases
5. Defensive team attempts to control the attack with block or dig
6. After dig defensive team plays ball to conclusion
7. Drill repeated until performance goal achieved

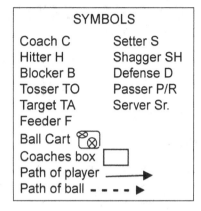

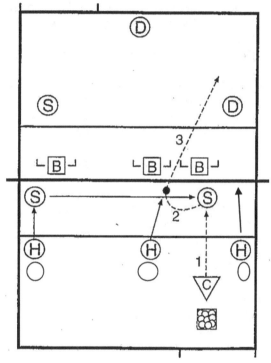

DRILL: DOUBLE BLOCK TEAM DEFENSE: Pr. #6

TYPE OF DRILL: Player centered/tactics

INTENSITY LVL: High   **SKILL LVL:** 3

EQUIPMENT: 20 Balls and cart

PERSONNEL: 10+

OBJECTIVE-DESIRED BEHAVIOR
1. Practice blocking/floor defense technique tactics against attack
2. Practice defensive transition and positioning
3. Reinforce the ability of defense to read block/ live attack
4. Provide multiple repetitions

COACHING POINTS-TECHNICAL EMPHASIS
1. Players move from base to point of attack
2. Right side base defender responsible for tip
3. Read attackers arm/hand position/ movement
4. Mini crossover step to outside by left side blocker

CONCENTRATION KEYS
1. Parallel movement
2. Base to recognition
3. On help
4. Read block/attack

ROTATION
1. Offense to defense on goal achievement
2. Defense front to back every 4 points
3. Attack team rotates position every 4 points

PERFORMANCE GOAL-SCORING
1. Game rally scoring to 15 points

SEQUENCE OF ACTION
1. Drill begins with **T** toss to **S** (**1**) **S** sets predetermined attacker or play action (**2**) **H** attacks set (**3**)
2. Floor **D**efensive players start in base position rotate after read of set
3. **B**lockers attempts to contact ball at net
4. **D**efense react to ball and point of contact after reading attack.
5. **D**efense pursues ball dug out of court area
6. Drill repeated until performance goal achieved

DRILL VARIATION/PROGRESSIONS
1. Alternate perimeter with rotation defense —Add back court attack

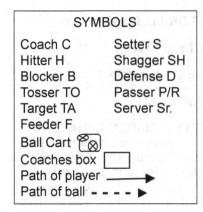

SYMBOLS

Coach C	Setter S
Hitter H	Shagger SH
Blocker B	Defense D
Tosser TO	Passer P/R
Target TA	Server Sr.
Feeder F	

Ball Cart
Coaches box
Path of player
Path of ball

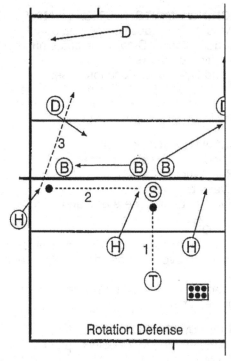

Rotation Defense

DRILL: 3 POSITION ATTACK vs. DEF

TYPE OF DRILL: Coach centered/training

INTENSITY LVL: High   **SKILL LVL:** 3

EQUIPMENT: 10+ Balls

PERSONNEL: 12+

OBJECTIVE-DESIRED BEHAVIOR
1. Learn to read block/floor defense
2. Reinforce attack/block technique/accuracy
3. Execute play action offense/tactics
4. Provide multiple attack/block/floor defense repetitions

COACHING POINTS-TACTICAL EMPHASIS
1. Read block and set appropriate attack
2. Read block/floor defense- attack open areas.
3. Vary speed, location and type of attack
4. Setters communicate play to be run -if play cannot be run hitter communicates set

CONCENTRATION KEYS
1. Read defense weakness
2. Vary approach angle
3. Attack perimeter

ROTATION
1. Offense to defense upon goal achievement
2. Defense team front to back every 5 points
3. Offense rotates left H/TO/F/H/H after each attempt

PERFORMANCE GOAL-SCORING
1. 15 successful attack executions of play called
2. Game situation scoring to 15 points

SEQUENCE OF ACTION
1. Players divided into 2 teams of 6
2. Offensive team provides F/TO
3. Setter calls play or set to be executed
4. Drill begins with **TO** toss to **S (1)**
5. **S**etter sets play option called **(2)**
6. **H**itter varies attack to randomly selected areas of the court **(3)**
7. Balls drugged by **D** are played to termination
8. Drill repeated until performance goal achieved:

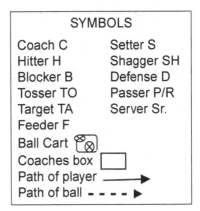

SYMBOLS

Coach C	Setter S
Hitter H	Shagger SH
Blocker B	Defense D
Tosser TO	Passer P/R
Target TA	Server Sr.
Feeder F	
Ball Cart	
Coaches box	
Path of player	
Path of ball	

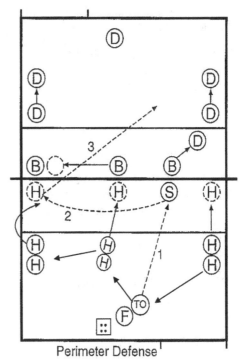

Perimeter Defense

DRILL: DOUBLE D QUICK

TYPE OF DRILL: Player centered/training

INTENSITY LVL: Medium   **SKILL LVL:** 3

EQUIPMENT
1. 15 balls
2. Ball cart and coaches boxes

PERSONNEL: 8+

OBJECTIVE
1. Improve dig technique
2. Practice reading attackers arm motion
3. Provide multiple dig repetitions

COACHING POINTS-TECHNICAL EMPHASIS
1. Maintain a low body position
2. Assume proper body position in relation to ball
3. Focus on attacker shoulder-arm-hand motion
4. Jump step prior to ball contact

CONCENTRATION KEYS-QUEUES
1. Place arms between ball and floor
2. Cushion ball to reduce force of attack

ROTATION
1. SH/D/TA/F

PERFORMANCE GOAL-SCORING
1. Number of repetitions 10
2. Number of passes to target 5 in a row

SEQUENCE OF ACTION
1. Two Defensive players- two targets- two attackers on box- two-feeders
2. **H**itter box **A** hits ball crosscourt to **D** (**1**) who passes ball to **TA** (**2**)
3. **H**itter box **B** hits ball cross court to **D** (**3**) (who passes ball to **TA** (**4**)
4. **H**itter box **A** hits ball down line to **D** (**5**) who passes ball to **TA**
5. **H**itter box **B** hits ball down line to **D** (**6**) who passes ball to **TA**
6. **TA** return ball to **F** ball cart
7. Repeat sequence until performance goal achieved

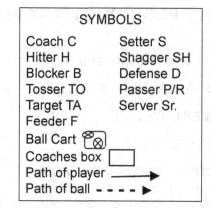

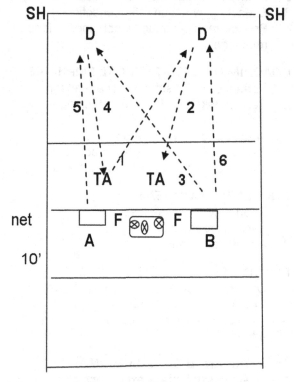

DRILL: PASS/DIG AND MOVE

TYPE OF DRILL: Player centered/training

INTENSITY LVL: Medium-high **SKILL LVL:** 2-3

EQUIPMENT
1. 15 balls
2. 15 Balls -1 cart- 1 Coaches boxes

PERSONNEL: 10+

OBJECTIVE
1. Improve dig technique
2. Practice defensive movement
3. Physical conditioning
4. Provide multiple repetitions

COACHING POINTS-TECHNICAL EMPHASIS
1. Maintain a low body position
2. Linear and non-linear passing technique
3. Go to floor only as last resort
4. Run through balls difficult to reach

CONCENTRATION KEYS
1. Read attackers body position-arm swing
2. Beat ball to spot
3. Split step prior to ball contact
4. Get arms between ball and floor

ROTATION
1. D/D-D/D-TA/F-SH/F /SH performance goal achievement

PERFORMANCE GOAL-SCORING
1. Number of repetitions 5 in each direction

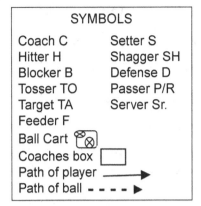

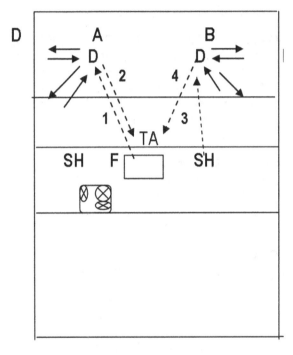

SEQUENCE OF ACTION
1. Hitter on box slaps then hits ball to **D A** (**1**) **D A** passes ball to **TA** (**2**) and slides or runs to pre-determined court position and back to original position
2. Hitter hits ball to **D B** (**3**) who passes ball to **TA** (**4**) and slides or runs to pre-determines court position and back to original position
3. Sequence of attack-action repeated with **D** running backward a predetermined distance after passing ball to target
4. Repeat until performance goal achieved

DRILL VARIATION/PROGRESSION

DRILL: READ AND ROTATE

TYPE OF DRILL: Player centered/training

INTENSITY LVL: Medium   **SKILL LVL:** 2-3

EQUIPMENT: 10+ Balls

PERSONNEL: 8+

OBJECTIVE-DESIRED BEHAVIOR
1. Train floor defenders to read set/attack location and rotate to proper court position
2. Practice floor defense techniques
3. Provide multiple dig repetitions

COACHING POINTS-TECHNICAL EMPHASIS
1. Read set location and transition one position in direction of set
2. Quick read of angle of attack, body position and arm swing in relation to ball and block
3. Be stopped on ball contact by Hitter
4. Defense stays in base position on middle hit

CONCENTRATION KEYS
1. Middle blocker plays hole in block
2. Right side D plays tip
3. Left side D Transitions to mid court
4. Left side B transition to 10' line

ROTATION
1. Defense rotates on goal achievement of 5 points
2. Hitters rotate after every attack
3. Offense to defense on attainment of goal

PERFORMANCE GOAL-SCORING
1. Game scoring to 15 points
2. 1 point for each dig to target and successful attack

SEQUENCE OF ACTION
1. Players divided into 2 teams of 6
2. Defense assumes base position
3. Drill begins with **TO** toss to **S** (**1**)
4. **S**etter sets outside, middle or play action set (**2**)
5. **H**itter attacks line-cross court or tips ball to open area of court (**3**)
6. **D**efense must read set direction and location of attack and rotate to correct defensive position
7. Repeat drill until performance goal achieved

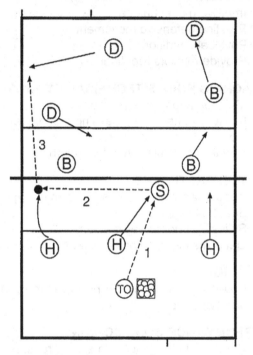

rotational movement

DRILL: NO BLOCK DIG THE BOX

TYPE OF DRILL: Player centered/training

INTENSITY LVL: High   **SKILL LVL:** 2-3

EQUIPMENT: 10+ balls and cart

PERSONNEL: 8+

OBJECTIVE-DESIRED BEHAVIOR
1. Improve defensive positioning
2. Practice floor defensive technique
3. Develop player-ball-court spatial-temporal orientation
4. Improve the ability to read attack angle
5. Provide multiple repetitions

COACHING POINTS-TECHNICAL EMPHASIS
1. Assume assigned court positions
2. Offside blocker responsible for middle tip
3. Use parallel movement on balls hit between defenders
4. Read attackers arm and hand position

CONCENTRATION KEYS
1. Read attacker
2. Stay deep
3. Forward body position
4. Run through
5. Parallel movement

ROTATION: SH/SH/D/D/D/D/SH/F after goal achievement

PERFORMANCE GOAL-SCORING
1. 10 balls dug to target
2. Timed intervals:

SEQUENCE OF ACTION
1. Drill begins by alternating hit to defensive players or open spaces forcing parallel movement
2. Repeat drill until performance goal achieved
3. Defensive players start in base position and reacts to point of contact with split step

DRILL VARIATIONS/PROGRESSIONS
1. Move attack to middle/right side

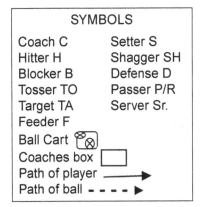

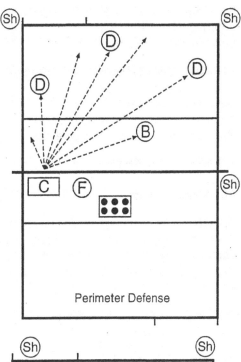

Perimeter Defense

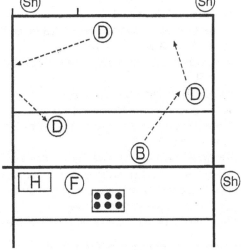

DRILL: QUEENS OF THE COURT

TYPE OF DRILL: Player centered/training

INTENSITY LVL: High   **SKILL LVL:** 2-3

EQUIPMENT: 10 balls

PERSONNEL: 9-12+

OBJECTIVE-DESIRED BEHAVIOR
1. Practice skills under game conditions
2. Develop team work and intensity
3. Warm up
4. Have fun
5. Improve movement skills
6. Instill motivation/competition

COACHING POINTS-TECHNICAL EMPHASIS
1. Pass high to target area
2. Serve weak passer
3. Assume balanced defensive position
4. Read approach/set and anticipate attack angle

CONCENTRATION KEYS
1. Read the hitter
2. Attack open areas

ROTATION
1. Winning team must rotate one position on each win
2. Server replaced when ball served out or into net

PERFORMANCE GOAL-SCORING
1. Loser out next team in

SEQUENCE OF ACTION
1. Players on court divided into 2 teams of 3
2. Team in Ct. **A** Serves—Team Ct. **B** receives
3. Drill begins with Serve by team in court **A** (**1**) to **R**
4. **R** in Ct. **B** passes ball to S (**2**)
5. **Setter** court **B** sets to either **R** (**3-4**)
6. Team winning rally stays in court **B** or moves from **A** to **B**
7. Additional players positioned along base line **A**
8. Team losing rally goes to end line court **A**
9. Next 3 players in line assume position in court **A** and prepare to Serve
10. Repeat drill until performance goal achieved

DRILL VARIATION/PROGRESSION:
Receiving team may pass with 3 players receiving serve player not receiving serve rotates to net and set hitters

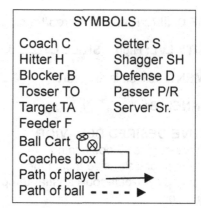

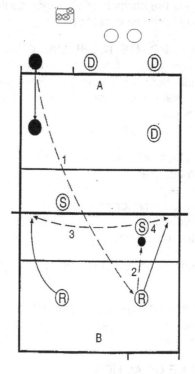

DRILL: FREEBALL TRANSITION

TYPE OF DRILL: Player Centered/tactics

INTENSITY LVL: High   **SKILL LVL:** 3

EQUIPMENT: 10+ Balls and Cart

PERSONNEL: 9-12

OBJECTIVE-DESIRED BEHAVIOR
1. Improve team work and communication
2. Reinforce the concept of team court transition
3. Instill game like situation and stress
4. Provide multiple game like repetitions

COACHING POINTS-TACTICAL EMPHASIS
1. Communicate and transition to defense before 3rd contact by attacking team
2. Ball should be pass on a low trajectory with two hand overhead pass if possible
3. Setter transition to target area as soon as it is determined ball cannot be attacked into area 1

CONCENTRATION KEYS
1. Quick retreat
2. Loud call for ball before it crosses net
3. Quick court transition

ROTATION - Teams rotation every 2 mini points

PERFORMANCE GOAL-SCORING
1. Wash scoring: game to 15 points
2. Game to 25
3. Situation scoring: Vary starting score

SEQUENCE OF ACTION
1. Players divided into 2 teams of 6
2. Drill begins with **S**erve from team in court **B** (**1**)
3. Ball passed to **S** (**2**) who sets attacker (**3**) ball is attacked in Ct. **B**
4. Play continues until terminated-terminating team gets a mini-point
5. A second ball is tossed by **C** to either the terminating or non-terminating team (**5**) **D** passes all to **S**etter (**4**) play continues until terminated
6. A team must get two mini-points in a row to score a point
7. Team getting a Big Point (two mini points in a row) starts next series with a serve
8. If score is 1-1, a wash occurs and scoring starts over
9. Play continues until performance goal achieved

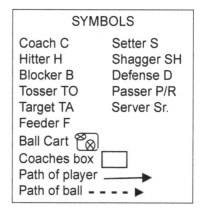

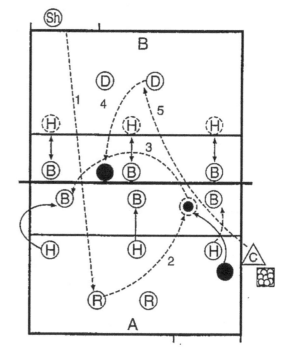

About the Author

When, Coach Spooner first started playing volleyball, there were very few coaches or books written on how to play and coach the game. Most players learned how to play the game by playing two-man volleyball on the beach and gradually added two-man indoor volleyball. As these players began to compete in tournaments, they were introduced to competitive 6 man volleyball run by the YMCA. During his early years Coach learned to play the game by watching and modeling these great players. As with many skills and games, "trial and error" learning often becomes the basic learning device. However, "trial and error" learning is very time consuming and sometimes not very efficient. Regardless of the lack of availability of knowledgeable coaching, he somehow was able to become a fairly proficient volleyball player. Coach achieved a #2 ranking (the highest on the beach at that time) as a beach player winning numerous tournaments on the sand and indoors. The highlight of Coaches development as volleyball player was receiving USVB All American honors as a setter in 1972 and 1976. This success was due to an excellent coaching by Jack Henn who was head men volleyball coach at San Diego State University.

When his playing days were over and he began a part time coaching career as a high school coach and of course he thought he knew all there was to know about how to coach the game. Boy!! Was that a mistake? All though his early coaching career was relatively successful, Coach began to realize that in order advance to higher levels as a volleyball coach; it would necessary to increase his knowledge about Volleyball, Sports Psychology, Motor learning and Biomechanics. So, he began to attend every seminar, clinic and read every book available.

While working on his Master's degree in History at Sonoma State University, he was fortunate to enough to coach at a topnotch private high school in northern California. At Branson, his men and women teams finished 2nd in the conference. This experience made it possible to moved up and become a very successful coach for 3 years at Solana College in Northern California. In 1988 Coach was lucky enough to get the opportunity to be become an assistant coach at Wichita State University. When he got this first opportunity to coach at the Division I, Coach was fortunate enough to have a head coach (**Phil Shoemaker**) who allowed him to organize and run practice under his supervision. Whatever we were doing together seemed to work as the teams began to get better and we achieved a high level of success. During these three years at Wichita State, the team progress to 2nd place in the Missouri Valley Conference. While coaching at Wichita State, Coach also established a club program that won the Mid-American championships with only 7 players all of whom received college scholarships at some level from Jr. College to Division I. In addition, he operated coach's clinics throughout the State of Kansas.

While working on by MA in Physical Education at Wichita State, Coach decided to do his thesis on Readiness to Learn Sports Skills. As part of this research project, was a questionnaire sent to 500 of the most successful Club, High School, Community College and Division I/II college volleyball coaches in America. What I discovered was startling, less than 20% of these coaches had any formal training in Sports Psychology, Motor Learning, Kinesiology, or Physical Education. Most gained their expertise as players, attending various camps, clinics, from text books or trial and error learning. However, Coach believes that today we would see a higher percentage of coaches with some background in Sports Science and Sports Psychology.

After his stint at Wichita State ended with graduation, Coach moved on the Memphis State for a year and then to Galveston College for 3 yrs. While coaching at Galveston the team became very successful ranking 2nd among the Community Colleges in Texas. After 3 yrs. at Galveston College, Coach accepted the head coaching position at Big Bend College in Washington State. At Big Bend he taught history, speech, lifetime wellness and was Department Chair and volleyball coach for 11 years. Although Big Bend was the smallest community college in the conference, with 1500 students, he was able to develop a very successful volleyball program. The team finished no lower than 4th and as high as 2nd in a conference of over 34 colleges from Idaho, Oregon and Washington. The team's success brought Coach of the Year honors.

Coach started this project regarding the science of practice and drill development strictly for his own benefit while coaching at Wichita State College. Through this extensive study and review of the latest research in the field of motor learning and sports psychology, he gained more experience, knowledge and understanding of how to teach volleyball skills and control human behavior. This knowledge had a tremendous effect on his approach, ability and success as a coach.

The investigation done for this manuscript is based mainly on information from the research conducted by such noted authors as Richard A. Schmidt's, a UCLA professor and experts in motor learning, a book on Motor Learning and Motor Behavior, by Douglas E Young's entitled Motor Learning a Practical Guide, and Carlene Kluka's book Motor Behavior from Learning to Performance. Most of the research in Sport Psychology was derived for Robert S. Weinberg's book Foundations of Sports Exercise and Psychology in addition to the other sources found the resources section of this book. Many of the principles on practice and drill development came from several books on Coaching Principles published by the American Sports Education Program and books and videos titled Successful Coaching by Rainer Martens. Publications and videos by The United States Tennis Association, Vic Braden and others also played an enormous role in his thinking on motor learning, practice and drill development. Tennis has tremendous programs in Sports Science and Sports Psychology that sponsor important research by such experts as Jack Groppel and James Loehr. In their books the Science of Coaching Tennis these authors provide some of the latest research is sports science and psychology.

The purpose or objective of this project is not to provide the reader with an in depth knowledge and understanding of the research in Motor Learning and Performance. Extensive research has all ready been conducted in these areas which provide varied conclusions. The objective was to take these very complex processes and simplify them for improving performance in the sport of volleyball. However, the information presented here can be revised to fit motor performance in almost any sport. The ideas and conclusions reached here are based solely on the results of research conducted by the researchers mentioned in the Reference section. Coach simply used their conclusions and his person perspective, experience and knowledge in an attempt to present the results to volleyball coaches in his own words. It is hoped that coaches at all levels and experience will review and apply these ideas to improve the performance of their volleyball teams He used the knowledge and research of these very talented authors to analyze, synthesize and draw conclusions based on reasoning and critical thinking to determine what would be most important and beneficial to what he was trying to accomplish. Therefore, the objectives of this work are to present well thoughtful out topics based his personal impressions/feelings after having logically analyzing each topic. Most of the startling theories, principles/conclusions presented did not originate with him. He only borrowed them.

References

Arnot, Robert Dr. and Charles, Gaines Sports Talent (1996) Viking Penguin Inc. New York.

Beilock, Sian, Dr. Department of Psychology, The University of Chicago Tennis Magazine June 2011

Braden, Vic Who Am I Who are You Vic Braden Sports Instruction Coto de Caza CA.

Braden, Vic Motor Learning Vic Braden Sports La Jolla CA.

Kozoll, Charles E PhD. Coaches Guide to Time Management (1985) Human Kinetics Publishers Champaign, Illinois

Kluka, Darlene A., Motor Behavior Form Learning to Performance (1999) Morton Publishing Englewood Colorado

Lane, A.M. Sport and Exercise Psychology (2008) Peak Performance Hodder-Stoughton, UK

Lane, A.M. Emotional Intelligence in Sports (2007) Nova Science Hauppauge, NY

Martins, R Coaches Guide to Sports Psychology (1986) Champaign IL

Martens R Successful Coaching (1990) Human Kinetics Champaign, IL

Niednagel, Jonathan P. Braden, Vic Brain Typing -Who Ami Who Are You Video Vic Braden Productions Coto de Caza, Ca 92679

National Coaching Certification Program (1988) Coaching theory Level I The Coaching Association of Canada Gloucester, Ontario

Neville William J, Coaching Volleyball Successfully ((1990) Leisure Press Champaign, IL.N-Doidge The Brain that Changes Itself, The Penguin Group New York

Schmidt, Richard A., Motor Learning & Performance From Principles to Practice, (1991) Human Kinetics Champaign IL.

Schmidt, Richard A., Motor Control and Learning Behavioral Emphasis, (1982) Human Kinetics Campaign IL

Silva, John M. III & Diane E. Stevens Psychological Foundation of Sports (2002) Allyn and Bacon

Spooner, Edward Factors Affecting Participant Readiness For Skill Acquisition in Volleyball (1992 Wichita State University Wichita Kansas

United State Tennis Association, Playing Better Tennis Under Pressure Human Kinetics Video

Vickers, J.N. Perception, Cognition and Decision Training: The Quiet Eye in Action (2007) Human Kinetics

Young, Douglas E. & William S., Husak Motor Learning A Practical Guide (1995) eddie bowers Dubuque, Iowa